JUST ADD
Sprinkles

A Colorful Collection of Fun, Easy Bakes
to Satisfy Your Sweet Cravings

TARYN CAMP
Creator of Life & Sprinkles

PAGE STREET
PUBLISHING CO.

Copyright © 2025 Taryn Camp

First published in 2025 by
Page Street Publishing Co.
27 Congress Street, Suite 1511
Salem, MA 01970
www.pagestreetpublishing.com

All rights reserved. No part of this book may be reproduced or used, in any form or by any means, electronic or mechanical, without prior permission in writing from the publisher.

Distributed by Macmillan, sales in Canada by The Canadian Manda Group.

29 28 27 26 25   1 2 3 4 5

ISBN-13: 979-8-89003-172-3

Library of Congress Control Number: 2024933709

Edited by Krystle Green
Cover and book design by Rosie Stewart for Page Street Publishing Co.
Photography by Taryn Camp

Printed and bound in the United States of America

Page Street Publishing protects our planet by donating to nonprofits like The Trustees, which focuses on local land conservation.

Dedication

This book is dedicated to my daughter, Hayley, aka Little Life and Sprinkles. She is the best taste tester, kitchen helper, advice-giver, cheerleader and, most of all, my ultimate inspiration.

Contents

6   Introduction

9   CLASSIC FLAVORS WITH A LITTLE FUN

11   Chocolate Peanut-Butterfinger® Cookie Sandwiches
13   Raspberry Cheesecake Cookie Bars
16   Brownie Sundae Dessert Pizza
19   Boston Cream Brownie Cups
21   Mint Chocolate Chip Mini Trifles
25   Cinnamon Sugar Marshmallow Treats
26   Dark Chocolate Cashew Pretzel Toffee
29   Red Velvet Cream Cheese Cookies
30   Marshmallow Peanut Butter Fudge
33   Banana Split Cupcakes
35   Sprinkle-Tastic Party Cake
39   Chocolate Chunk Sea Salt Cookie Cake

41   NO-BAKE DESSERTS

43   Irresistible Cookie Butter Pie
44   Ice Cream Sandwich Cake
47   Pistachio Marshmallow Milkshake
48   Graham Cracker Sandwiches
51   Cookie Truffles, Two Ways
54   Chocolatey Chip Pudding Cups
57   Brownie Blast Soft Serve
58   Loaded Edible Cookie Dough
61   Decadent Hot Fudge Sundae
62   Chocolate-Dipped Cookie Stacks
65   Movie Night Caramel Popcorn Bark
66   No-Churn Cookie Mashup Ice Cream

69   RECIPES FOR BAKE SALES, PARTIES AND MAKING MEMORIES

71   Giant Cookie Skillet
72   TGIF Dessert Board
77   Cookies 'n' Cream Cupcakes
78   Party Time Bundt Cake
81   Chocolate Cookie Banana Bread
82   Frosted Animal Cookie Blondies

85	M&M's® Chocolate Chunk Cookies
87	Triple-Layer Chocolate Bars
91	Jumbo Brookies
92	Peanut Butter Fudge Cookie Cups
95	Sweet and Chewy Granola Bars
96	Crunchy Cookie Bark Sticks

99 FRUITY AND FUN TREATS

101	Lemon Cream Pastry Cups
102	Banana Oatmeal Creme Pie Trifle
105	Sprinkled and Dipped Fruit Cones
106	Orange Amaretto Sheet Cake
109	Coconut Raspberry Cake Jars
112	Blueberry Pie Snack Mix
115	Strawberry Lime Poolside Slush
116	Glazed Fruit Tart
119	Lemon Strawberry Shortcakes
120	Berry Fluff Mini Parfaits
123	Strawberry Ice Cream Cake
124	Tropical Cake Bars

127 COMFORTING AND NOSTALGIC SWEETS

129	Cake on the Cover
130	Cinnamon Crunch Muffins
133	Snickerdoodle Latte Frosted Cookies
134	Cookie Butter Apple Pie Biscuits
137	Mint Chocolate Chip Brownies
138	Banana Nut Cinnamon Rolls
141	Frosted Flakes® French Toast
142	Vanilla Cinnamon Spice Cupcakes
145	Celebration Chocolate Chip Pancakes
146	Cookie Butter Mini Loaf Cakes
149	Chocolate Cherry Poke Cake
150	Maple Cinnamon Roll Casserole
153	Double-Coated Cinnamon Sugar Pretzels
154	Bonus Recipe: Homemade Sprinkles

156	*Acknowledgments*
157	*About the Author*
158	*Index*

Introduction

Hi everyone! I'm Taryn Camp, creator of the blog Life & Sprinkles—where food meets fun! I'm so happy to introduce you to *Just Add Sprinkles*, a book filled with exciting and approachable recipes that will become staples in your home.

I have lived in Orlando, Florida, for almost my entire life. I spent my younger years visiting theme parks, so I have a special love for the whimsical side of things. It's given me the motivation to make all celebrations magical, even the smallest ones. After I graduated high school, I attended the University of Central Florida and majored in hospitality management. I've been asked how I decided to pick my major, and, in all honesty, I was walking through the UCF bookstore and saw a textbook with Mickey Mouse on the cover. Right then and there, hospitality became my college plan.

After I graduated, I worked in food service for the university and managed everything from coffee shops to sporting events. From there, I went to work in sales for a chocolate factory for 13 years! I learned so much about chocolate, design and the ins and outs of desserts from the most amazing pastry chefs. In 2019, I left to work in marketing for a sprinkle company, which was extremely fitting for my personal blog and brand.

I decided to get into content creation a year before I started working with the sprinkle company. While I was still in college, I made a New Year's resolution. I had over a hundred cookbooks and never made a thing from them. I created a spreadsheet with recipes from each book that I wanted to try. Each Sunday, I'd randomly pick three or four and create those recipes. I learned so much, and after 15 years, I have still kept up with the resolution.

Which brings me to this book! I have found that the recipes I love the most are a combination of from-scratch and store-bought ingredients. I love to learn new things, so I try to incorporate a new skill or flavor into each recipe and pair it with a few time-savers. Plus, each recipe in this book has suggested toppings like crushed cookies, candy, sugar, spices or, of course, sprinkles! My goal with this cookbook was to make approachable and simple desserts that were just a bit more elevated and not too hard, but with elements that take the desserts to the next level! Some recipes are easier than others, but they're all beginner friendly with a few twists for long-time bakers.

I hope that, as you try these recipes, you remember to have FUN. Your creations don't have to look perfect, and you don't have to get them right every single time. Sprinkle a little laughter into your kitchen, and enjoy the sweet and simple magic of desserts.

Taryn camp

Classic Flavors
WITH A LITTLE FUN

When it comes to dessert, we all have our go-to favorite flavors that never fail to satisfy our sweet cravings. Some people are drawn to timeless classics like rich and creamy chocolate, traditional and comforting vanilla or nostalgic cookies 'n' cream. For those who crave a burst of fruity freshness, flavors like strawberry, raspberry or banana most definitely hit the spot. And let's not forget the irresistible goodness of flavors like caramel, peanut butter and cinnamon, which all add another layer of decadence to every treat.

I can tell you, no matter where I go, I will ALWAYS choose something with rainbow sprinkles. For me, vanilla anything plus rainbow sprinkles cannot be beat. My daughter couldn't agree less because she's a chocolate fan all the way. So, in this chapter, I'm going to spotlight a bunch of favorite flavor combos, adding a little twist that'll get everyone excited. Or, as I like to say, a little *sprinkle* of creativity. It's probably no surprise, but my favorite recipe in this chapter is the Sprinkle-Tastic Party Cake (page 35). It is a vanilla/rainbow sprinkle dream. But it's followed closely by the Chocolate Chunk Sea Salt Cookie Cake (page 39). I can't resist salty sweet. Let's get to baking and see which ones will become your favorites!

CHOCOLATE PEANUT-BUTTERFINGER® COOKIE SANDWICHES

This chocolate–peanut butter combo is made extra special by a little surprise: Butterfinger® candy! I always like to add a little bonus to classic combos, so I started with soft chocolate fudge cookies made from a cake mix and loaded with chocolate chips. In the middle, I sandwiched the most delicious salted peanut butter frosting with crushed Butterfinger pieces mixed right in. These cookie sandwiches are soft and chewy with little bits of crispy and flaky candy bar pieces. I truly cannot imagine a better addition to the ever-so-popular chocolate–peanut butter combo.

Preheat the oven to 350°F (177°C), and line two cookie sheets with parchment paper. (I love using pre-cut parchment paper; it is such a time-saver!)

To make the cookies, in a medium bowl, combine the fudge cake mix, vegetable oil and eggs and mix until you don't see any cake mix streaks. With a spatula, fold in the milk and semisweet chocolate chips until fully combined. I used regular and mini chocolate chips, so that there's a little bit of extra chocolate in each bite.

Using a 1¼-inch (3-cm) cookie scoop, add level scoops of dough onto the cookie sheets 2 inches (5 cm) apart. If you don't have a cookie scoop, measure out 1 tablespoon (14 g) of dough. I love using a cookie scoop because it helps keep them uniform in size. If desired, add a few chocolate sprinkles to the top for decoration. Repeat this process with the rest of the cookie dough. Bake for 9 to 11 minutes. You will know they are perfectly baked when the tops are no longer glossy and the edges are just set. Be careful to not overbake, as this type of cookie sandwich is better with a softer cookie. Let the cookies cool on the sheets for 5 to 10 minutes, and then move them to wire racks to cool completely. You can use a regular spatula but—fun fact—there are actually specific cookie spatulas made for this exact purpose!

(continued)

Makes: 12 cookie sandwiches

For the Cookies

1 (15.25-oz [432-g]) box fudge cake mix

½ cup (120 ml) vegetable oil

2 eggs

½ cup (84 g) milk chocolate chips

⅓ cup (55 g) mini semisweet chocolate chips

Chocolate sprinkles, for decorating (optional)

CLASSIC FAVORITES WITH A LITTLE FUN • 11

CHOCOLATE PEANUT-BUTTERFINGER COOKIE SANDWICHES (CONTINUED)

While the cookies are cooling, prepare the frosting by beating the butter until smooth. If you have a stand mixer, use the paddle attachment. If you don't have a mixer, a large mixing bowl and hand mixer will do the job. Mix on high until the butter is light and fluffy. Add 1 cup (120 g) of the powdered sugar and mix on low. Once it's combined, add the rest of the sugar, peanut butter, vanilla and 1 tablespoon (15 ml) of heavy cream. Continue to mix it until it's smooth. If the frosting is too thick to spread, add the remaining tablespoon (15 ml) of heavy cream. Gently fold in the crushed Butterfinger pieces until just combined. The frosting smells AMAZING at this point.

To assemble the cookies, lay them on a flat surface such as a cutting board. Make sure the flattest side of the cookie is facing up. Now, there are two ways to assemble these cookie sandwiches. First, you can use a spoon and add 2 rounded tablespoons (45–50 g) of frosting onto each cookie and flatten it with a knife. Top it with another cookie and you're done. The second option is to use a piping bag with an open or round tip to pipe the frosting onto one cookie. Top it with the other cookie, and voilà, a cookie sandwich! Regardless of which method you use, go nuts with the frosting, as it totally makes the dessert.

For the Frosting/Filling

½ cup (114 g) salted butter, softened

2 cups (240 g) powdered sugar, divided

¼ cup (65 g) smooth peanut butter

½ tsp vanilla extract

1–2 tbsp (15–30 ml) heavy cream

½ Butterfinger bar, crushed into small pieces (about 27 g)

RASPBERRY CHEESECAKE COOKIE BARS

Raspberries in desserts are my all-time favorite fruit/sweet-treat combo. I think it's a totally underrated flavor and a perfect fit for cheesecake. Although cheesecake is often made with a classic graham cracker crust, I had a sneaking suspicion that a chocolate chip cookie base would be next-level delicious, especially paired with the raspberries. I'm happy to report that it was! The combination of textures plus the mashup of contrasting flavors all come together for a treat that will blow your mind.

Preheat the oven to 350°F (177°C), and prepare a 9-inch (23-cm) square baking pan with baking spray. (I love the baking spray that has flour in it, but regular baking spray will also work.) Line the bottom of the pan with two strips of parchment paper in a crisscross pattern, with the edges hanging over. This makes it easier to pull the cookie bars out. Spray again with baking spray after the sheets are in place.

Remove the chocolate chip cookie dough from the package. The dough is so much easier to work with if it's at room temperature and not so cold. Place one piece of dough in the center of your palm and flatten it out. Press that piece of dough into the base of the baking pan and repeat with the rest. The dough should cover the entire bottom of the pan. If you're using a tube of dough, just press the whole thing into the pan.

Bake the chocolate chip cookie dough base for 15 minutes, and allow it to cool while you prepare the cheesecake filling. If it's still warm, that's okay because it's going back in the oven! You just don't want it to be so hot it burns your hands or causes the cheesecake to melt super fast.

(continued)

Makes: 9 rectangular bars

1 (16-oz [454-g]) package store-bought chocolate chip cookie dough*, room temperature

*Both the ready-to-bake pre-portioned dough and tube will work.

CLASSIC FAVORITES WITH A LITTLE FUN · 13

RASPBERRY CHEESECAKE COOKIE BARS (CONTINUED)

In a stand mixer or large mixing bowl with an electric mixer, beat the cream cheese and sugar on high speed until smooth. Add the eggs one at a time, and beat after each one until fully combined. Add the vanilla and mix until combined.

Pour the cheesecake mixture on the chocolate chip cookie base and smooth it with a spatula. Using a teaspoon, add scoops of the raspberry jam to the top of the cheesecake. Swirl the dollops lightly with a knife or toothpick until you get a marbled design. If you have larger dollops of jam, the cheesecake will crack in those areas. Don't sweat it though, it will taste just as amazing.

Bake the cheesecake for 35 minutes. The center will still be slightly jiggly when you remove it from the oven. Rest assured, it will continue to cook and set when you take it out of the oven.

Allow the cheesecake to cool completely in the pan, and then cover it with aluminum foil and chill it in the fridge for at least 4 hours, but preferably overnight. It keeps its shape and tastes much better cold. Cut it into nine rectangles and serve. If desired, for an extra chocolate touch, drizzle the bars with a little chocolate sauce and sprinkle mini chocolate chips on top.

2 (16-oz [454-g]) packages cream cheese, room temperature

½ cup (100 g) granulated sugar

2 eggs, room temperature

2 tsp (10 ml) vanilla extract

¼ cup (60 ml) raspberry preserves or jam, room temperature and stirred

Chocolate sauce and mini chocolate chips, for serving (optional)

BROWNIE SUNDAE DESSERT PIZZA

Get ready for some baking fun, because this is the most fun dessert to make and decorate with friends or family. Like a traditional pizza, you can top this with anything you love or even split the pizza so that it has a different combo on each side. Starting with a fudge brownie mix, it's baked in a rimmed pizza pan. We topped ours with a marshmallow creme–cream cheese mixture, but you can use almost anything for the "sauce," like peanut butter or Nutella®. I love adding fruit, so I added sliced strawberries and bananas. I finished it off with a few fun extras like marshmallows, chocolate chips and an extra drizzle of chocolate.

Preheat the oven to 350°F (177°C), and spray a 12-inch (30-cm) round pizza pan with baking spray. (I love the baking spray that has flour in it, but regular baking spray will also work.) I recommend cutting a piece of parchment paper to fit in the bottom of the pan and then spraying again.

Prepare the brownies according to the package instructions and pour the batter into the pan. Spread the batter evenly over the entire pan with a spatula. It'll be sticky, and the parchment paper will have a tendency to move, but put on some music and power through it. It'll wind up being so worth it in the end. Bake the brownie for 18 to 22 minutes, or until a toothpick comes out mostly clean. You'll want this to be completely set, so that you can hold it like a slice of pizza. Let it cool on a wire rack for 15 to 20 minutes, and then move it to the fridge to cool for at least 2 to 3 hours, preferably overnight.

In a mixing bowl, beat the marshmallow creme, cream cheese and vanilla until combined. Since it has marshmallow creme, it won't look like buttercream. It will be stickier, but as long as the ingredients are combined, it will frost the pizza perfectly. Spread the marshmallow mixture on top of the chilled brownie, leaving a little room at the edges like a pizza crust. Scatter the strawberry and banana slices on top of the pizza. Sprinkle the chocolate chips and rainbow sprinkles over the empty spaces on the brownie. Drizzle the entire brownie pizza with the melted chocolate. Let it set for 10 to 15 minutes before slicing and serving. If you use any creative toppings, send me the photos. I'd love to see them!

Makes: 1 (12-inch [30-cm]) brownie pizza (8 slices)

1 (16.3-oz [462-g]) box fudge brownie mix*

½ cup (52 g) marshmallow creme

4 oz (113 g) cream cheese, room temperature

2 tsp (10 ml) vanilla extract

2 whole strawberries, sliced

½ large ripe banana, sliced

1 tbsp (10 g) mini chocolate chips

2 tbsp (13 g) rainbow sprinkles, plus extra for sprinkling

2–4 tbsp (30–60 ml) melted semisweet chocolate, or to your taste

*Plus the ingredients listed on the package.

BOSTON CREAM BROWNIE CUPS

This recipe started as mini brownie bites, and while those are tasty, I wanted to take them to the next level. After a few experiments, I found the perfect addition (if I do say so myself). As a tribute to the classic Boston cream pie flavor combo, these are filled with sweet and creamy vanilla pudding and topped with chocolate chips, and an extra rich chocolate drizzle. They're truly everything you want in a brownie cup and then some.

Start off by making the vanilla pudding, since the Cook and Serve version takes a little longer to set. Prepare the pudding according to the package directions. Refrigerate until it's set. (The other pudding options totally work as well.) You won't need all the pudding, so you'll have some as a treat for later.

Preheat the oven to 350°F (177°C). Line a cupcake pan with liners and spray the insides with baking spray. (I love the baking spray that has flour in it, but regular baking spray will also work.) I tend to use parchment liners for these. If you haven't tried them, they are SO convenient when you need to remove the liner. They don't stick like the others, which is great when you're making brownies.

In a medium bowl, prepare the brownies according to the package directions. Divide the batter evenly among all 12 liners. Bake for 20 to 25 minutes, or until the brownies are set. A toothpick inserted should come out with wet crumbs but not batter. The brownies will still cook a bit after taking them out, so if you overbake them, they'll be crunchier on the outside. Let them sit for 5 to 10 minutes. You want them to be cooler so that when you do the next step, the brownies aren't scorching hot! Just don't leave them too long so that they set.

(continued)

Makes: 12 brownies

1 (3-oz [85-g]) box Vanilla Pudding Cook and Serve* (Jell-O® brand preferred)**

1 (18-oz [510-g]) box brownie mix* (such as Ghirardelli® Double Chocolate Brownie Mix)

½ cup (84 g) milk chocolate melting wafers (such as Ghirardelli)

2–3 tbsp (22–33 g) mini chocolate chips

*Plus the ingredients listed on the package.

**You can also use premade vanilla pudding cups or prepared instant vanilla pudding.

CLASSIC FAVORITES WITH A LITTLE FUN

BOSTON CREAM BROWNIE CUPS
(CONTINUED)

To make the brownies fillable, use the back of a tablespoon to create an indentation in the center. You may have to spray the tablespoon so that it doesn't stick to the brownie. The indent doesn't need to be terribly deep and shouldn't go all the way to the bottom; just enough to hold a scoop of the pudding. Move the pan to a wire rack to cool completely.

Once the pudding is set and the brownies are cool, heat the melting wafers in a microwave in 30-second intervals, stirring after each interval, for 90 seconds, or until fully melted.

To assemble, spoon the vanilla pudding filling into each brownie cup. With another spoon or drip bottle, drizzle the melted chocolate over each cup and top with a sprinkle of mini chocolate chips.

MINT CHOCOLATE CHIP MINI TRIFLES

I used to order a mint sundae at a local ice cream parlor, and it had a Thin Mint™ cookie on top and tons of hot fudge sauce. It's not my usual ice cream order, but I got it time and time again because it's seriously delicious! I used that sundae throwback to inspire these Mint Chocolate Chip Mini Trifles. If you don't have mini trifle dishes, use whatever you have on hand! You can even make it as one large trifle or layer it in a glass bowl. It starts with a base of fudgy chocolate mint cookie brownies. They're topped with a layer of minty whipped filling, mini chocolate chips and a ton of mini marshmallows. Add a swirl of fudge on top, and it's a mint chocolate chip lover's dream.

Preheat the oven and prepare a pan based on the brownie mix's directions. (Use any size pan specified on the package, since the brownies will be cut into smaller bites.) Make the brownie mix according to the package instructions, and then fold in the chopped mint cookie pieces and spread the batter evenly into the pan. Bake according to the package instructions and let them cool completely. Cut the brownies into bite-size pieces. They should be the size of large salad croutons.

(continued)

Makes: 6–8 mini trifles (depending on your dish size)

1 (18-oz [510-g]) box brownie mix*

8 mint cookies (I use either Oreo® Mint Flavor Creme or Thin Mints), chopped into small pieces (about 116 g)

*Plus the ingredients listed on the package. All brownie mixes will work, but I love the kind with chocolate chips in them!

CLASSIC FAVORITES WITH A LITTLE FUN · 21

MINT CHOCOLATE CHIP MINI TRIFLES (CONTINUED)

To prepare the mint layer, scoop the whipped topping into a medium mixing bowl. Stir in the mint and vanilla extracts and food coloring, until the streaks of color are completely gone and you reach your desired color. (You could always make homemade whipped cream if you'd like, but this is a bit of a time-saver.) Fold in the mini marshmallows and mini chocolate chips. Place the mint topping in the fridge for 3 to 4 hours, or until set. You want it to be nice and cold so it brings out the fresh mint flavor.

To assemble, layer a generous cup of brownie pieces into the bottom of each trifle dish, or simply divide the brownies among the six dishes. Top that with ¾ cup (180 ml) of the mint-marshmallow filling or divide it evenly. Finish each trifle with 2 tablespoons (30 ml) of warmed hot fudge topping and/or a drizzle of chocolate syrup and chocolate sprinkles.

Can you layer this in a dish and serve it at a party? Absolutely ☺!

1 (8-oz [226-g]) container whipped topping, thawed

¼ tsp mint extract

1 tsp vanilla extract

Mint or light green food coloring

1 cup (46 g) mini marshmallows

½ cup (84 g) mini chocolate chips

¾ cup (180 ml) store-bought jar hot fudge topping or chocolate syrup

Chocolate sprinkles, for topping

CINNAMON SUGAR MARSHMALLOW TREATS

When I was developing this recipe, I was so torn between making flavored Rice Krispies Treats™ versus Cinnamon Toast Crunch™ treats. Each is a classic cereal treat favorite, so I made a combo of both! Over time, while posting on social media, I've found that marshmallow treats are just so nostalgic, and I couldn't agree more. For these treats, I added a hint of extra sweetness by tossing in white chocolate chips. If you'd like to add your own "sprinkle of creativity," you can always swap the Rice Krispies for the frosted version or even use French Toast Crunch™ instead of regular. To theme them for a party or holiday, drizzle extra colored chocolate on top or add themed sprinkles. Psst! Have you seen the holiday limited edition Sugar Cookie Toast Crunch™ or Gingerbread Toast Crunch™? Way too good!

Spray an 8-inch (20-cm) square pan with baking spray and set it aside.

In a large bowl, combine the crushed Cinnamon Toast Crunch and Rice Krispies so that they're evenly mixed. The Cinnamon Toast Crunch pieces should be around the size of Cheerios™, small but not crumbs.

Using a large pot over medium heat, melt the butter and mini marshmallows together, stirring frequently. Once it's fully melted, remove the pot from the heat and stir in the vanilla bean paste. Why vanilla bean paste? It adds such a delicious kick of vanilla to recipes. It's deeper and sweeter than vanilla extract. They have it at my local grocery store, but it's also at specialty stores or online. Pour the cereal into the marshmallow mixture and stir until evenly coated. Fold in the white chocolate chips until everything is just combined. If you overmix, the chocolate might get a little melty. Transfer the mixture to the prepared pan.

Using a spoon or spatula sprayed with baking spray, lightly press the mixture into the pan so that it's flat. Fun fact: I always use a fondant smoother for this part! I spray it with baking spray, and it's become one of my favorite kitchen tools. Sprinkle on a little bit of extra cinnamon sugar for fun! You can either mix a bit of each in a bowl (about a teaspoon of each) or get cinnamon-sugar premixed in a spice jar. Let the mixture cool for at least 1 hour, and then cut it into bars and serve.

Makes: 6–12 bars

2 cups (82 g) Cinnamon Toast Crunch, crushed into small pieces

4 cups (112 g) Rice Krispies cereal

4 tbsp (56 g) salted butter

1 (10-oz [283-g]) bag mini marshmallows

1 tsp vanilla bean paste or vanilla extract

½ cup (84 g) white chocolate chips

Cinnamon sugar, for sprinkling

DARK CHOCOLATE CASHEW PRETZEL TOFFEE

If you've never had toffee bark before, I hope you give it a try because it is THAT good. I've never met a single person who didn't love it. This recipe can also be referred to as cracker candy, and it's super popular to make over the holidays. I decided to put a spin on it and create this cashew toffee flavor. It's sweet, salty, buttery AND crunchy. The base is a layer of pretzels covered in an easy homemade toffee sauce. It's topped with creamy dark chocolate, and then sprinkled generously with chopped salted cashews. This is one of those desserts that you'll bring to a party and get asked to make again and again.

Preheat the oven to 350°F (177°C). Line a 12 x 18-inch (30 x 45–cm) rimmed baking sheet with aluminum foil and spray it with baking spray.

Place the pretzels in a single layer on the sheet. Keep them as close as possible, and it's fine if they overlap a bit. The reason you need them close is because, traditionally, this is made with saltine crackers or even graham crackers. Since the pretzels have spaces, it'll just help the toffee cover the whole layer. If you don't cover the pretzels completely, it's fine! Even with a little bit of coating, they're absolutely delicious.

Melt the butter and brown sugar in a small pot over medium-low heat, stirring occasionally so that the sugar doesn't burn. Allow the mixture to come to a boil for 5 minutes. Remove the pot from the heat and carefully pour the mixture evenly all over the pretzels. It's hard to spread, so go slow so that you don't pour it all in the same place and run out! Bake for 5 to 7 minutes.

In the microwave, heat the melting wafers in 30-second intervals, stirring after each interval, for 90 seconds, or until fully melted. Remove the sheet from the oven and immediately pour the melted chocolate on top. With a knife or spatula, gently spread the chocolate over the entire surface of the toffee. Sprinkle the cashews over the melted chocolate.

Allow the toffee bark to fully cool and set at room temperature for 3 to 4 hours. Once fully cooled and set, break the toffee into pieces and serve.

Makes: 12 servings

10 oz (283 g) Snack Factory® Original Pretzel Crisps®*

1 cup (227 g) butter

1 cup (220 g) light brown sugar

15 oz (425 g) dark chocolate melting wafers (such as Ghirardelli)

1 cup (150 g) chopped salted cashews (small pieces)

*These are the thin, flat pretzels, and you can get 10 ounces (283 g) from one party-size bag or two smaller bags.

RED VELVET CREAM CHEESE COOKIES

One thing that posting online has taught me is that red velvet is an extremely polarizing flavor. Who knew?? I love a good cream cheese frosting, so I decided to stick with the classic pairing, but I bake the cream cheese right into the cookie. It starts with a boxed cake mix, and it's one of the easiest recipes you could ask for. I added white chocolate chips, but if you prefer more of a deep rich chocolate flavor, simply add dark or semisweet chocolate. The sanding sugar adds a delicious touch of crunch to these ooey-gooey cookies, and I bet a red-and-green combo would look gorgeous for the holidays!

Preheat the oven to 350°F (177°C), and line two baking sheets with parchment paper. (I love the pre-cut parchment paper. All you have to do is grab a sheet from the box and you're good to go!)

In a stand mixer or medium bowl with an electric hand mixer, beat the cake mix, cream cheese, butter, egg and vanilla until completely combined. (You won't see any streaks of cake mix, and it'll look like one cohesive mixture.) Gently fold in the white chocolate chips, until evenly distributed. Refrigerate the dough for at least 30 minutes so that it's easier to handle.

Using a small 2-inch (5-cm) cookie scoop, roll level scoops of dough into balls, and then place them on the prepared baking sheets 2 inches (5 cm) apart. Sprinkle each cookie with the sanding sugar so that it lightly covers the tops. (It adds a nice little crunch and a little extra color.) Bake the cookies for 10 to 11 minutes, or until the cookie edges are set but still appear slightly underbaked in the center. That's the magic that keeps the most delicious texture. Let them cool completely on the pans. This is crucial, so that they retain their shape and get that gooey cookie consistency! Once they're set, serve right away.

Makes: 16–18 cookies

1 (13.25-oz [375-g]) box red velvet cake mix

1 (8-oz [226-g]) package cream cheese, softened

½ cup (114 g) salted butter, room temperature

1 large egg

1 tsp vanilla extract

½ cup (84 g) white chocolate chips

¼ cup (50 g) white or red sanding sugar, for sprinkling

MARSHMALLOW PEANUT BUTTER FUDGE

I have a lot of favorite desserts (no surprise there), but fudge has an extra-special story for me. When my daughter was very young, I used to put her in her stroller and walk around the local mall. There was a fudge shop that had the most creative flavors, so I would treat myself to a piece while browsing the stores. Those days were so memorable since she's quite grown up now! I decided on a peanut butter marshmallow fudge, and it turned out to be even better than I expected. It is super chewy with a creamy peanut butter base, and packed full of chopped white chocolate peanut butter cups and fluffy marshmallows. With flavors like this, my daughter and I get to enjoy fudge together years later.

Prepare an 8-inch (20-cm) square pan with baking spray. Line the bottom of the pan with two strips of parchment paper in a crisscross pattern with the edges hanging over. This makes it easier to pull the fudge out. Spray again with baking spray after the sheets are in place. This fudge is sticky!

In a small pot over medium-low heat, melt the peanut butter chips, butter and condensed milk, stirring frequently so that the chips don't stick to the bottom of the pot. Once completely melted, remove from the heat and stir in the vanilla. The mixture will be very thick! You're on the right path! Fold in the chopped peanut butter cups. It might take a bit to make sure they're evenly distributed, but it'll be worth it to have the peanut butter cups in every bite.

Pour the fudge into the prepared pan. You'll have to press it in gently, so that you don't move the parchment paper too much. Once it's evenly spread, lightly press the mini marshmallows on top. Refrigerate for at least 6 hours, but I highly recommend overnight. It makes a really big difference in the texture and consistency of the fudge. Remove the fudge from the refrigerator and cut it into pieces. Serve cold or wait until it gets to room temperature.

Makes: 16 squares (or they can be cut smaller, if needed)

3 cups (504 g) peanut butter chips (you'll need 2 bags)

¼ cup (57 g) salted butter

1 (14-oz [300-ml]) can sweetened condensed milk

½ tsp vanilla extract

1 cup (145 g) chopped white chocolate peanut butter cups

1 cup (45 g) mini marshmallows, for topping

BANANA SPLIT CUPCAKES

Let me tell you, I spent a lot of time coming up with the right combo for these cupcakes. I wanted to include all the crucial elements that capture the full experience of the most nostalgic ice cream shop order. I decided to go with a sweet banana cake base, rich fudge filling and vanilla bean frosting. I just had to include lots of rainbow sprinkles (of course) and chopped peanuts. If you aren't a nut fan or cannot have them, just sub with chocolate chips! Either way, every bite is a banana split in cupcake form. The secret to these ice cream–inspired cupcakes is the vanilla bean paste in the frosting. It gives them a true vanilla ice cream flavor.

Preheat the oven to 350°F (177°C), and line two cupcake pans with 24 cupcake liners. (Or you can use a single 24-cavity cupcake pan. I have one, and it is my favorite!)

In a medium bowl, combine the cake mix, water, oil, eggs and banana pudding mix, and mix until you don't see any cake streaks and the batter is smooth. Fold in the bananas and mix until fully combined. (The bananas should be fully distributed throughout the batter.) Using a small cookie scoop or spoon, divide the batter among the 24 liners. Fill them two-thirds of the way full.

Bake for 19 to 21 minutes, or until lightly browned. Let the cupcakes cool for 5 minutes in the pans, and then remove them to a wire cooling rack to completely cool. Once cool, move them to the fridge for at least 2 hours. It's easier to fill the cupcakes if they're cold.

Once they're nice and cold, use a cupcake corer or apple corer to remove the inside of each cupcake. Press down into the cupcake and be sure not to hit the bottom because you don't want the filling to seep out. Set the inside parts aside. Fill the cupcake holes with the fudge topping. This can be done in a couple of different ways. You can use a spoon and hold it over the opening, and then use a second spoon to push the filling into it. Alternatively, place the fudge into a piping bag and cut the tip, then pipe the fudge into the cupcakes. Replace the cupcake parts that you removed. Set aside.

(continued)

Makes: 24 cupcakes

1 (13.25-oz [375-g]) yellow cake mix

1 cup (240 ml) water

½ cup + 1 tbsp (135 ml) vegetable oil

4 eggs

1 (3.4-oz [96-g]) box instant banana pudding mix

2 ripe bananas, mashed

1 (11.75-oz [333-g]) store-bought jar hot fudge topping

BANANA SPLIT CUPCAKES (CONTINUED)

In a large mixing bowl or stand mixer, beat the butter for 2 to 3 minutes, or until smooth. Add 2 cups (240 g) of the powdered sugar and mix for 2 minutes. Add the vanilla bean paste, heavy cream and remaining powdered sugar, and mix for 2 to 3 minutes, or until smooth. If it's too thick, add another tablespoon (15 ml) of heavy cream and mix again.

To frost the cupcakes, either spread a generous dollop of the prepared frosting on top of each one, or place the frosting into a piping bag with a 1M tip and pipe a swirl of frosting on the top of each cupcake. Top each cupcake with ½ teaspoon of sprinkles and ½ teaspoon of chopped peanuts. If you want more of each, do it! I personally load mine with the rainbow sprinkles, as expected. Serve and remember that the best part is they don't melt!

1 cup (227 g) butter, softened

4 cups (480 g) powdered sugar, divided

1 tbsp (15 ml) vanilla bean paste*

¼ cup (60 ml) heavy cream, plus more if needed

¼ cup (52 g) rainbow sprinkles

¼ cup (32 g) chopped peanuts

*Substitute with vanilla extract if desired, but the paste is really so amazing in this recipe!

SPRINKLE-TASTIC PARTY CAKE

To say that I love sprinkles is an understatement. I don't need anything fancy, just regular classic rainbow sprinkles. Point me to a bakery display case, and I will always choose a sprinkle cake, donut or cupcake. So, it's safe to say that this sprinkle-tastic cake is what I'd consider the ultimate dessert. This is the perfect upgrade from a classic birthday cake with its combination of sweet vanilla cake, creamy vanilla frosting and bright sprinkles inside and out. It's perfect for any celebration or a weekday surprise for your favorite sprinkle lover (hint, hint).

Preheat the oven to 350°F (177°C). Prepare a 9 x 13–inch (23 x 33–cm) pan with baking spray. (I love the baking spray that has flour in it, but regular baking spray will also work.) Line the bottom of the pan with two strips of parchment paper in a crisscross pattern with the edges hanging over. This makes it easier to pull the cake out (see note). Spray again with baking spray after the sheets are in place.

To make the cake, in a mixing bowl, combine the cake mix, pudding mix, buttermilk, oil and eggs. The mixture will be thick, so I'd suggest using a spoon instead of a whisk. Fold in the sprinkles, and then pour the batter into the pan. Use a spatula or the back of a spoon to make sure it's evenly distributed throughout the whole baking pan.

Bake for 25 to 27 minutes, or until lightly golden brown. Let the cake cool completely. If you're going to remove it from the pan, lift it out of the dish after 30 minutes, or until mostly cooled, and place it onto a wire rack.

(continued)

Makes: 15 small slices, 12 large slices or 9 "I love cake!" slices

For the Cake

1 (15.25-oz [432-g]) box yellow cake mix

1 (3.4-oz [96-g]) box instant vanilla pudding mix

1 cup (240 ml) buttermilk

⅓ cup (80 ml) vegetable oil

3 eggs

⅓ cup (64 g) rainbow sprinkles, plus more for decorating

SPRINKLE-TASTIC PARTY CAKE (CONTINUED)

To make the frosting, in a large mixing bowl, beat the butter until smooth. Add half of the powdered sugar and mix on low. You'll want it to be mostly dissolved. Then, add the remaining sugar, vanilla and heavy cream. The consistency I prefer for sheet cakes is on the softer side and easier to spread. I use 5 tablespoons (75 ml) of heavy cream, but if you want it thicker, use less. If you feel like it's still too thick, add 1 tablespoon (15 ml) at a time until it's your desired consistency. Why would it be too thick, you ask? If the starting temperature of the butter was cooler than the starting temperature of my butter, it would make yours thicker. It's completely fine; all you have to do is add more cream! If you like less frosting on the cake, you can cut the frosting recipe in half or save any extra that you don't use for another dessert.

Spread the frosting onto the cake and top with rainbow sprinkles. I use a *generous* amount of sprinkles, but add as many as you like. Alternatively, you can just add sprinkles to the border. Slice the cake into rectangles or squares and serve!

Note: You don't have to remove the cake from the pan. If you're going to be eating it at home or serving it directly from the pan, that is 100 percent fine!

For the Frosting

1 cup (227 g) salted butter, softened

4 cups (480 g) powdered sugar, divided

2 tsp (10 ml) vanilla extract

4–5 tbsp (60–75 ml) heavy cream, or more as needed

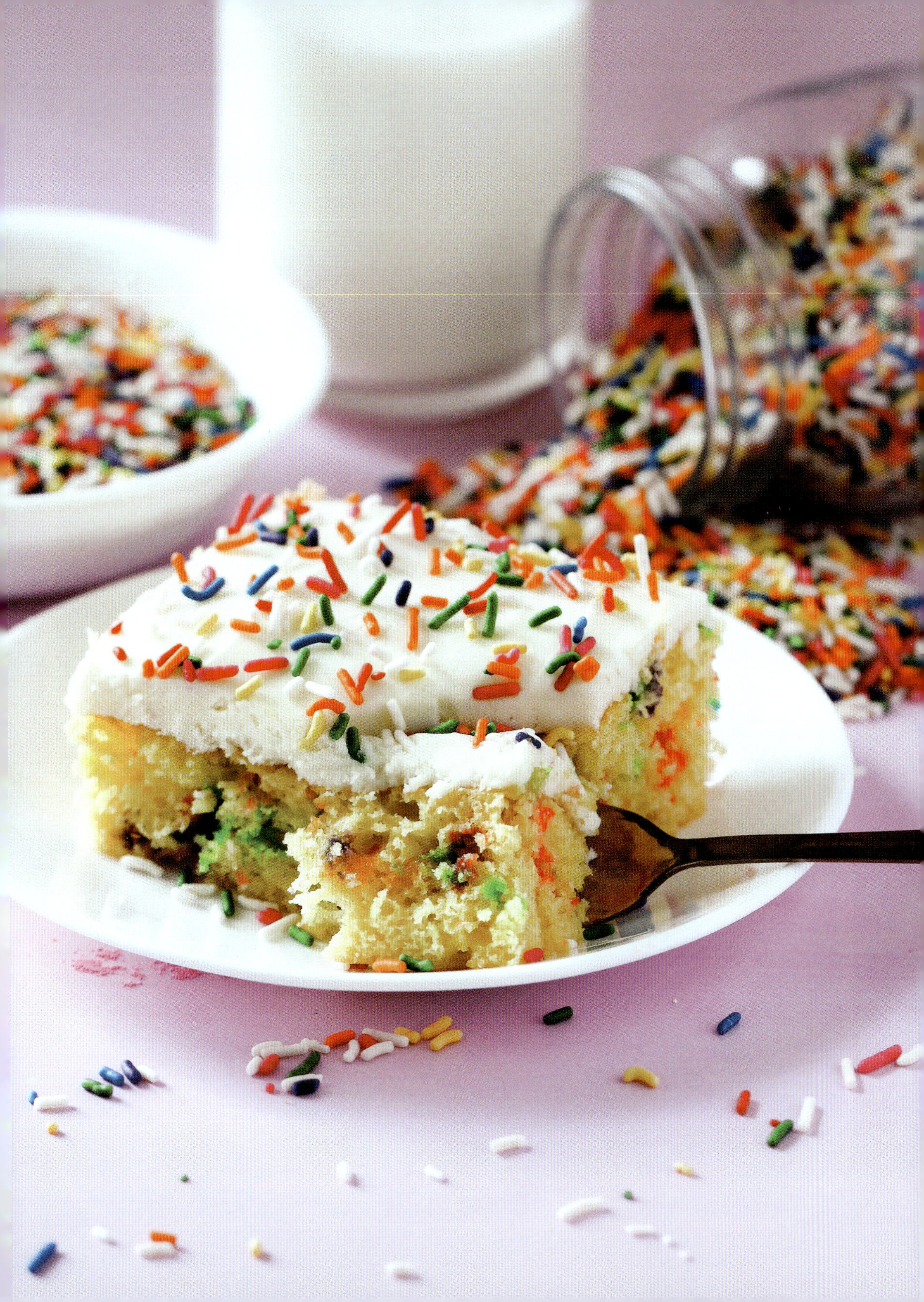

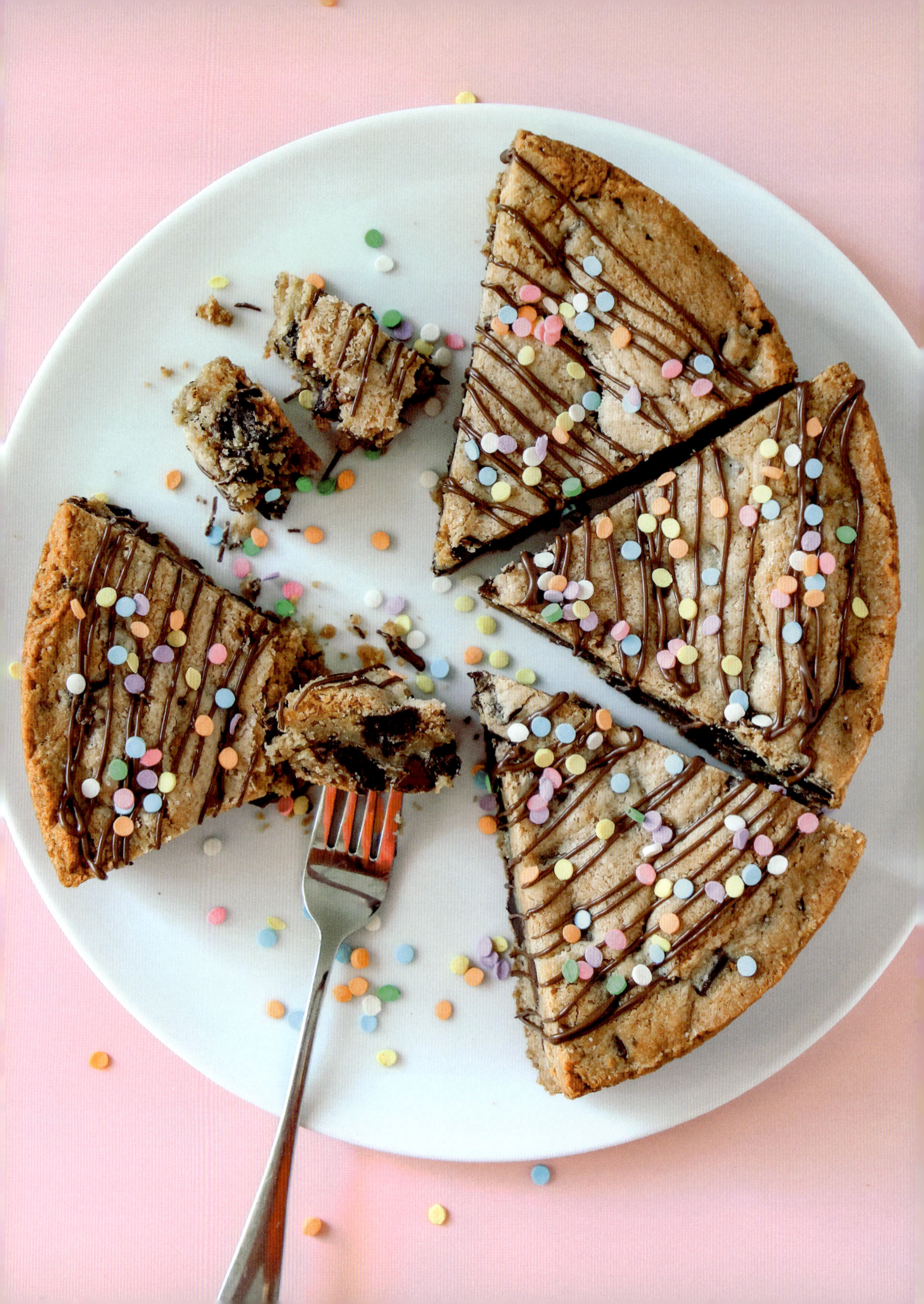

CHOCOLATE CHUNK SEA SALT COOKIE CAKE

There's just something special about a cookie cake that sets it apart from a regular cookie. Maybe it's the thick, chewy texture or the fact that it feels like a celebration treat. Whatever it is . . . nothing beats a good slice of cookie cake. This particular cookie cake has both chocolate chunks and chocolate chips in it with a hint of sea salt sprinkled on top. It's the perfect combination of sweet and salty, and it'll be your new go-to recipe!

Makes: 12 small or 8 large slices

1¼ cups (156 g) all-purpose flour

½ tsp baking soda

½ tsp salt

½ cup (114 g) unsalted butter, softened

¼ cup (50 g) granulated sugar

¾ cup (165 g) brown sugar

½ tsp vanilla extract

1 egg

½ cup (84 g) dark or milk chocolate chunks

½ cup (84 g) semisweet chocolate chips

Pinch of fine sea salt

Melted dark or milk chocolate, for drizzling (optional)

Confetti sprinkles (optional)

Preheat the oven to 350°F (177°C). Line the bottom of an 8-inch (20-cm) round cake pan with parchment paper and spray it with baking spray. You can place the cake pan on top of a sheet of parchment paper, trace a circle and then cut it, OR they make pre-cut parchment paper, which I highly recommend if you do a lot of baking!

In a small mixing bowl, combine the flour, baking soda and salt. In a medium mixing bowl, using a hand mixer or stand mixer with the paddle attachment, beat the butter, granulated sugar, brown sugar and vanilla together until smooth and creamy. Add the egg and mix until fully combined. Add the flour mixture into the bowl and beat until combined. Make sure that it's fully mixed through and you don't see any of the flour mixture, but do not overmix. That's the cookie recipe sweet spot! With a spoon, gently mix in the chocolate chunks and chocolate chips.

Spread the batter evenly into the prepared pan and press it down into a smooth layer. Cookie batter is sticky, so it gets a bit tricky to move it around the parchment paper. Just take your time, and spray the back of a spoon with baking spray to press the dough into the pan and help you out, if needed. Bake for 20 to 25 minutes, or until the edges are a light golden brown and the center is set. You want it to be soft but baked in the middle, so that when it cools, it'll have a soft, chewy texture (not dry).

Let it fully cool in the pan on a wire rack. Once cooled, remove the cookie cake from the pan and place it on a serving dish or plate. Drizzle it with melted chocolate and add confetti sprinkles, if desired. If you don't want to add the drizzle and sprinkles, I can assure you it's amazing as is!

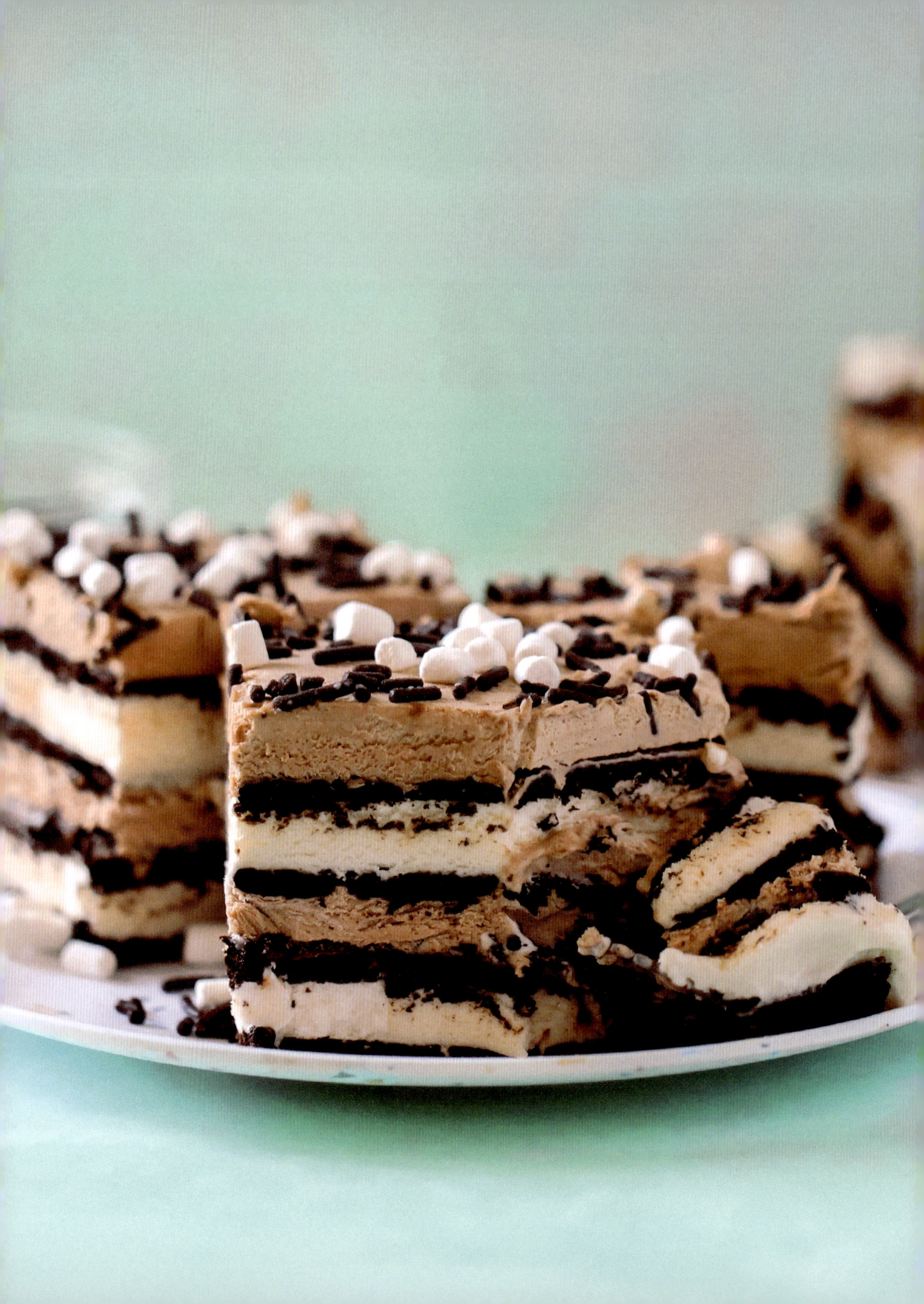

No-Bake Desserts

No-bake desserts seem to shine during the warmer months, but the recipes in this chapter are sensational year-round! For starters, the Irresistible Cookie Butter Pie (page 43) is my most requested dessert of all time. It can easily pass for both a summer or fall pie. My personal favorite is the Loaded Edible Cookie Dough (page 58). We used to have an edible cookie dough shop near me, which was dangerous! Now, I make my own, and I must admit, mine is so much better. (Mostly because I get to customize the flavors and theme the mix-ins for the holidays.) My favorite part about no-bake desserts is that they're very kid-friendly. It's easy to get them involved in the process, and there are a bunch of these I can guarantee they'll love. (Specifically, the Ice Cream Sandwich Cake [page 44])! So take a break from the oven, because there's no baking required in this chapter!

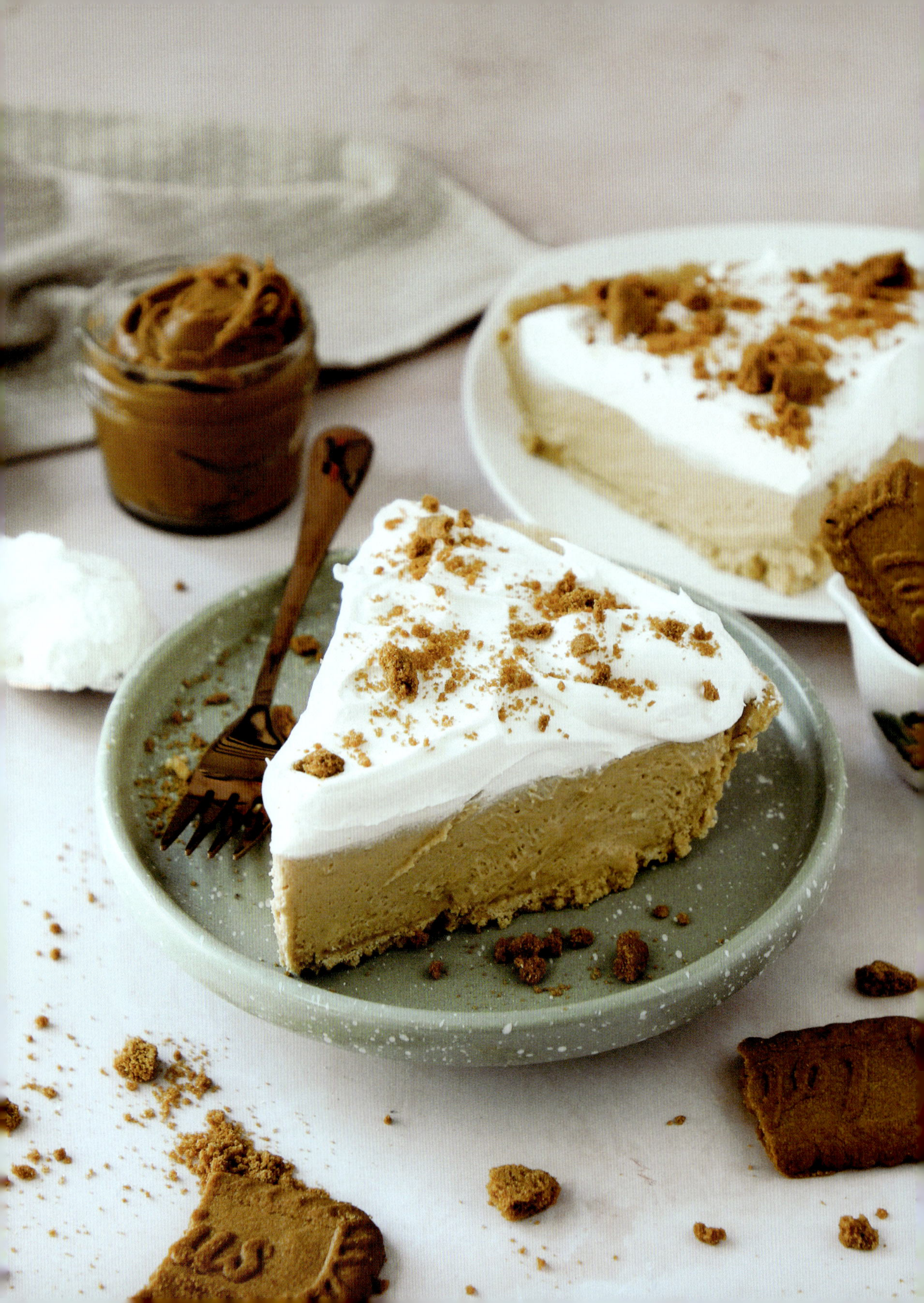

IRRESISTIBLE COOKIE BUTTER PIE

You know that recipe you have, the one that everyone always asks you to make? For me, that's this Irresistible Cookie Butter Pie. It starts with an easy store-bought graham cracker crust, and it's filled with a cream cheese and cookie butter combo. I get asked about cookie butter a lot, and it's basically smooth and spreadable crushed cookies. Usually, the base is made from speculoos cookies, which are spiced cookies sort of like gingerbread. The flavor goes perfectly with cream cheese, and this pie is finished with whipped topping and a generous sprinkle of even more cookies. The pie is comforting and simple to make, but I guarantee it'll blow your mind.

Makes: 10 slices

1½ cups (360 ml) heavy cream

1 (8-oz [226-g]) package cream cheese, room temperature

¼ cup (55 g) lightly packed brown sugar

¼ tsp salt

1 tsp vanilla extract

1 cup (480 g) creamy cookie butter (such as Biscoff® Cookie Butter)

1 (10-inch [25-cm]) graham cracker crust

1 (8-oz [226-g]) container whipped topping

4–5 Biscoff cookies, crushed, for sprinkling

Using a stand mixer with a whisk attachment (or just a bowl and hand mixer if you don't have one available), beat the heavy cream on high for 4 to 5 minutes, or until stiff peaks form. When you pull the whisk attachment from the bowl, the cream should stick to it and not run down back into the bowl. To me, it looks like thick shaving cream. Remove the whisk from the mixer and transfer the whipped cream to a separate bowl.

Add the cream cheese to the (now empty) mixing bowl and beat with the paddle attachment until it's smooth. Add the brown sugar, salt and vanilla, and mix. Beat in the cookie butter until it's completely smooth and well blended. Gently fold in the whipped cream you just made little by little until it's fully incorporated. This takes a little bit, but on the plus side, you'll get your arm workout for the day!

Spoon the filling into the pie crust. Use a spoon or spatula to flatten the top. Cover and refrigerate for 4 to 6 hours, or until it is fully set. It should appear smooth, and the center will not jiggle when gently moved. When you're ready to serve this amazing pie you just created, top it with the whipped topping and sprinkle with the crushed cookies. You don't have to use the whole container of whipped topping, but make sure it has a really nice, thick layer because it is so good paired with the cookie butter filling. For the cookies, I crush mine into the size of pebbles because I like a little crunch but not actual huge chunks, and then sprinkle on top. Also, it'll be way easier to slice the pie when they're in smaller pieces.

ICE CREAM SANDWICH CAKE

Sometimes the easiest recipes are the biggest hits, and this is one of them! It's a classic ice cream sandwich cake that kids and adults flip over. During the hot summer months, it's a cold and tasty treat that can also double as a crowd-favorite party cake! It's made up of delicious layers of ice cream sandwiches, fudge topping and fluffy chocolate whipped cream. Forget the ice cream truck; this cake will satisfy all of your ice cream cravings.

Remove the ice cream sandwiches from the wrappers, and place them into a storage container so that they're ready to use. Put them back into the freezer while you make the whipped cream.

In a mixing bowl, beat the heavy cream until bubbles form. It should only take 10 seconds. Add the powdered sugar, cocoa powder and vanilla. Continue beating until stiff peaks form. You'll know it's done when you remove the beater blades or attachment and it sticks. It should look like shaving cream.

Set out a 9 x 13–inch (23 x 33–cm) pan and remove half of the ice cream sandwiches from the freezer. Place them at the bottom of the pan, three across and four down. Be sure to press them together so that there aren't any gaps. If using regular-size ice cream sandwiches, you'll need to cut them to fit the gaps. Spread the fudge topping over the sandwiches, covering the top in an even layer. Add half of the chocolate whipped cream over the fudge and spread it out evenly. Remove the rest of the ice cream sandwiches from the freezer, and lay them directly on top of the whipped cream in the same three-by-four pattern. Add the rest of the whipped cream on top in an even layer. Sprinkle mini marshmallows and chocolate sprinkles on top. Use as many as you'd like! Freeze for at least 6 hours or overnight, and when serving, drizzle with chocolate sauce, if desired.

Makes: 32 slices

24 mini ice cream sandwiches* (about 924 g)

1½ cups (360 ml) heavy cream

1 cup (120 g) powdered sugar

2 tbsp (11 g) cocoa powder

1 tsp vanilla extract

½ cup (120 ml) store-bought jar hot fudge topping, room temperature

Mini marshmallows, for topping

Chocolate sprinkles, for topping

Chocolate sauce (optional)

*You can use regular size as well.

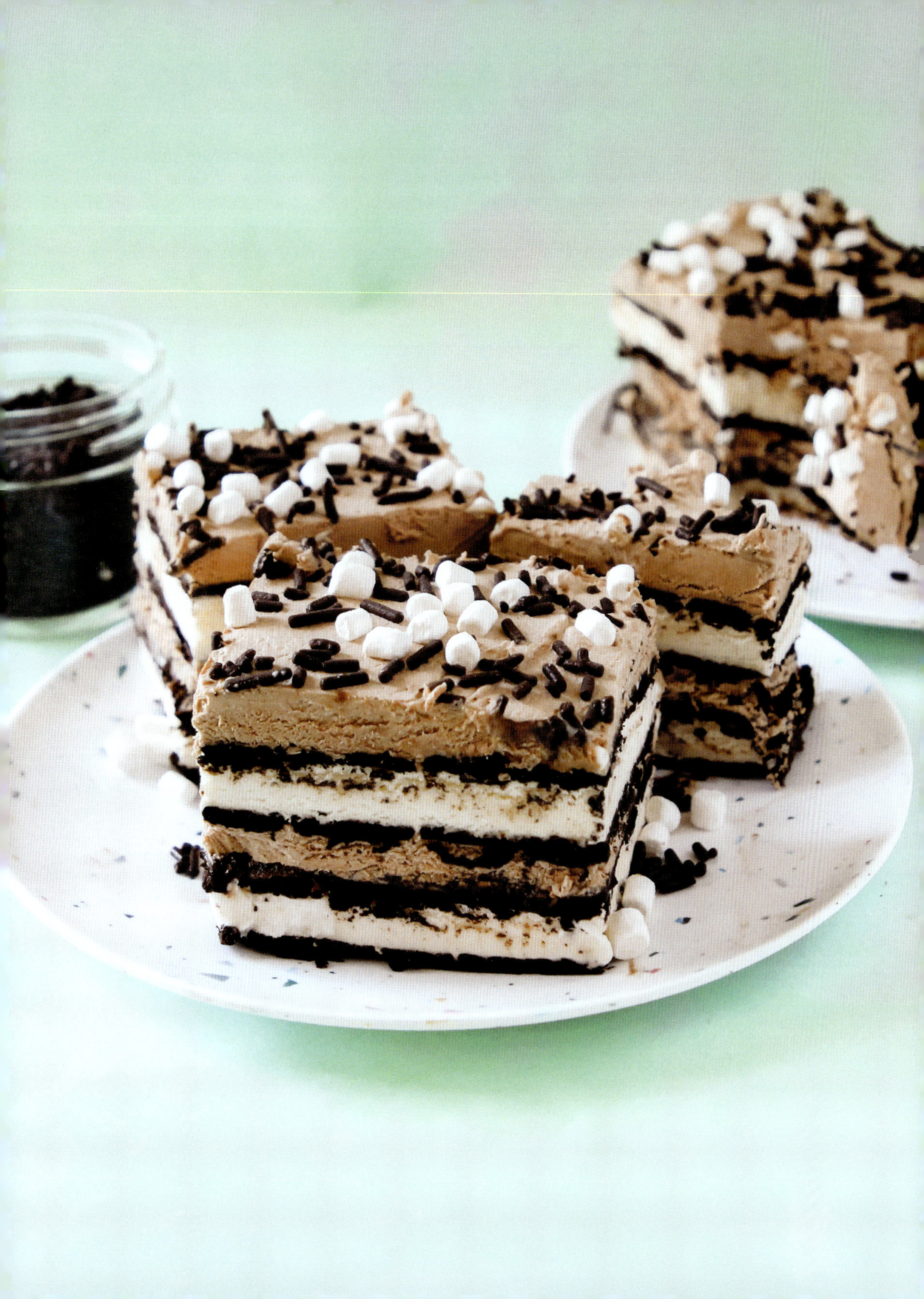

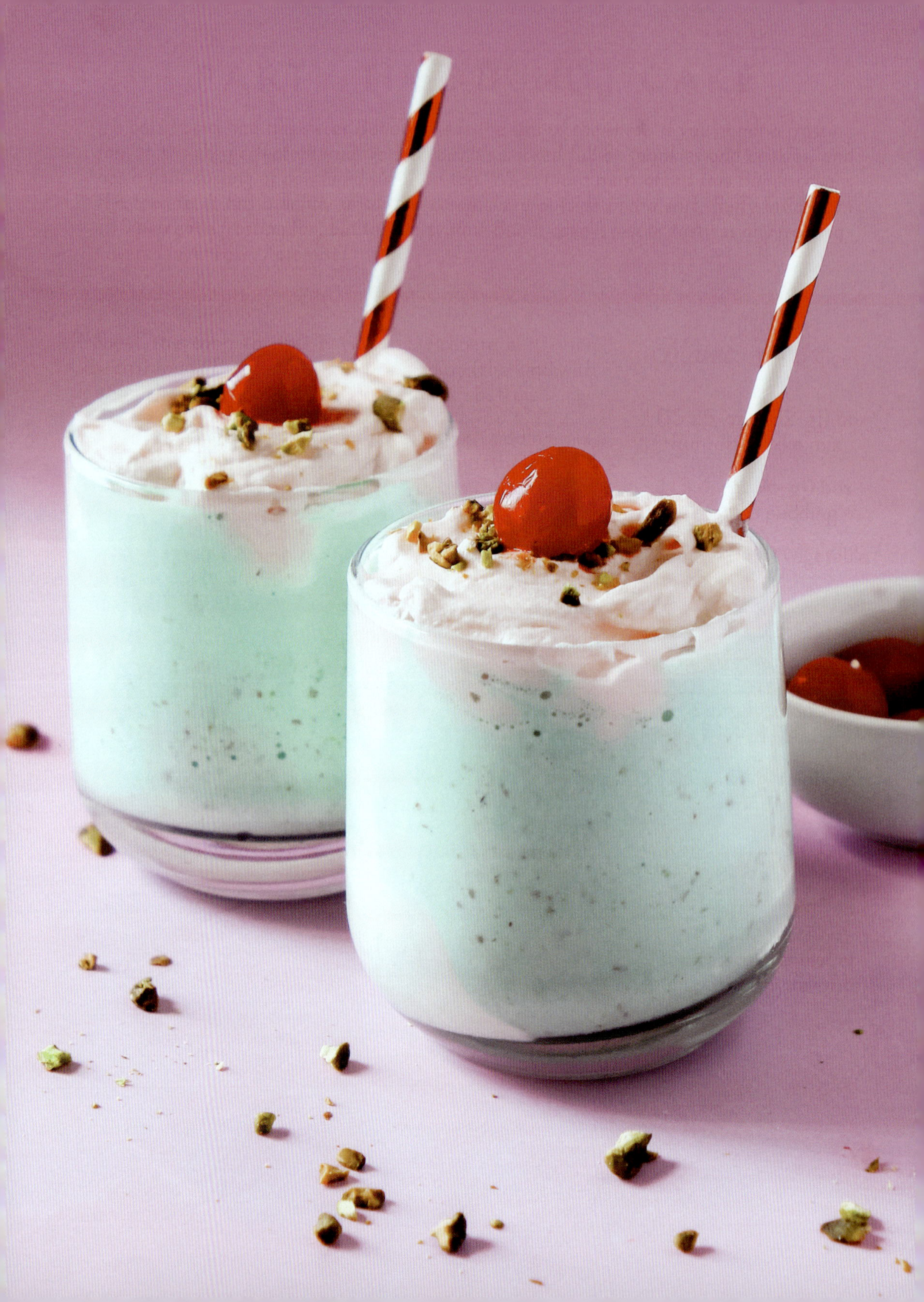

PISTACHIO MARSHMALLOW MILKSHAKE

I never knew how good pistachio was until I got older. I was too stubborn to try it, but I was totally missing out! I am now obsessed with the nutty and creamy flavor and use it in so many more recipes—like this milkshake! I wanted to add a fun surprise to go with the pistachio, so to ramp up the sweetness, I swirled it with marshmallow creme. Head's up: I used the kind that goes on ice cream, not marshmallow fluff. The finishing touch is a maraschino cherry whipped cream with extra pistachios and a bright red cherry on top.

Makes: 2 shakes

½ cup (120 ml) heavy whipping cream

4–5 tsp (20–25 ml) maraschino cherry juice

½ cup (60 g) powdered sugar

3 cups (360 g) pistachio ice cream

½ cup (120 ml) cold milk

2 tsp (10 ml) pistachio syrup (optional, but highly recommended; I use LorAnn® Gourmet Pistachio Nut)

2 tbsp (30 ml) marshmallow creme

1 tsp chopped pistachios, for sprinkling

2 maraschino cherries, for topping

In a medium bowl, beat the whipping cream until bubbles form. It should take less than 1 minute. Add the cherry juice and powdered sugar, and whip the mixture until it thickens. It should be the consistency of whipped topping from the grocery store, so instead of stiff peaks, you're looking for more of a thickened whipped topping consistency. Set in the refrigerator until ready to use.

Add the ice cream, milk and pistachio syrup (if using) to a blender. Mix on medium to high speed until it's completely smooth. Pour the milkshake into two glasses. Add 1 tablespoon (15 ml) of marshmallow creme to the top of each and lightly swirl it through the shake. Top with a generous amount of the cherry whipped cream. Sprinkle pistachios on top of each milkshake and garnish with a cherry. Feeling fancy? Get a whimsical straw for an extra touch!

GRAHAM CRACKER SANDWICHES

S'mores have a special place in my heart. I've made a TON of them on social media, and they've become one of my favorite desserts to create. There are so many ways to experiment with the flavor combinations; the possibilities are endless! The biggest difference is that I make s'mores in a chocolate mold and serve them at room temperature. These are similar but hand-dipped, so I updated the name to "graham cracker sandwiches." I used different spreads on mine, so feel free to get creative!

Place the graham crackers on a flat surface. Using a knife, spread 1 teaspoon of Nutella on the back of each of the 4 graham cracker squares. Spread 1 teaspoon of cookie butter on the back of each of the other 4 graham cracker squares. Refrigerate for 10 minutes. This will make the crackers easier to work with when you're dipping them into the chocolate.

Place 1 tablespoon (8 g) of marshmallow creme on the cookie butter side of each of the graham crackers. Top with the other crackers, Nutella spread side down, and very gently press together. Try not to let the creme squish to the edges. If the topping seeps into the chocolate, it will sometimes cause cracks when it sets. Even if it does, they'll still be extremely tasty, don't worry! Refrigerate them for 10 minutes.

Line a baking sheet with parchment paper and set it aside.

(continued)

Makes: 4 sandwiches

4 graham cracker sheets (8 squares)

4 tsp (21 g) Nutella®

4 tsp (21 g) cookie butter or peanut butter*

¼ cup (32 g) marshmallow creme

*Or you could simply double the Nutella.

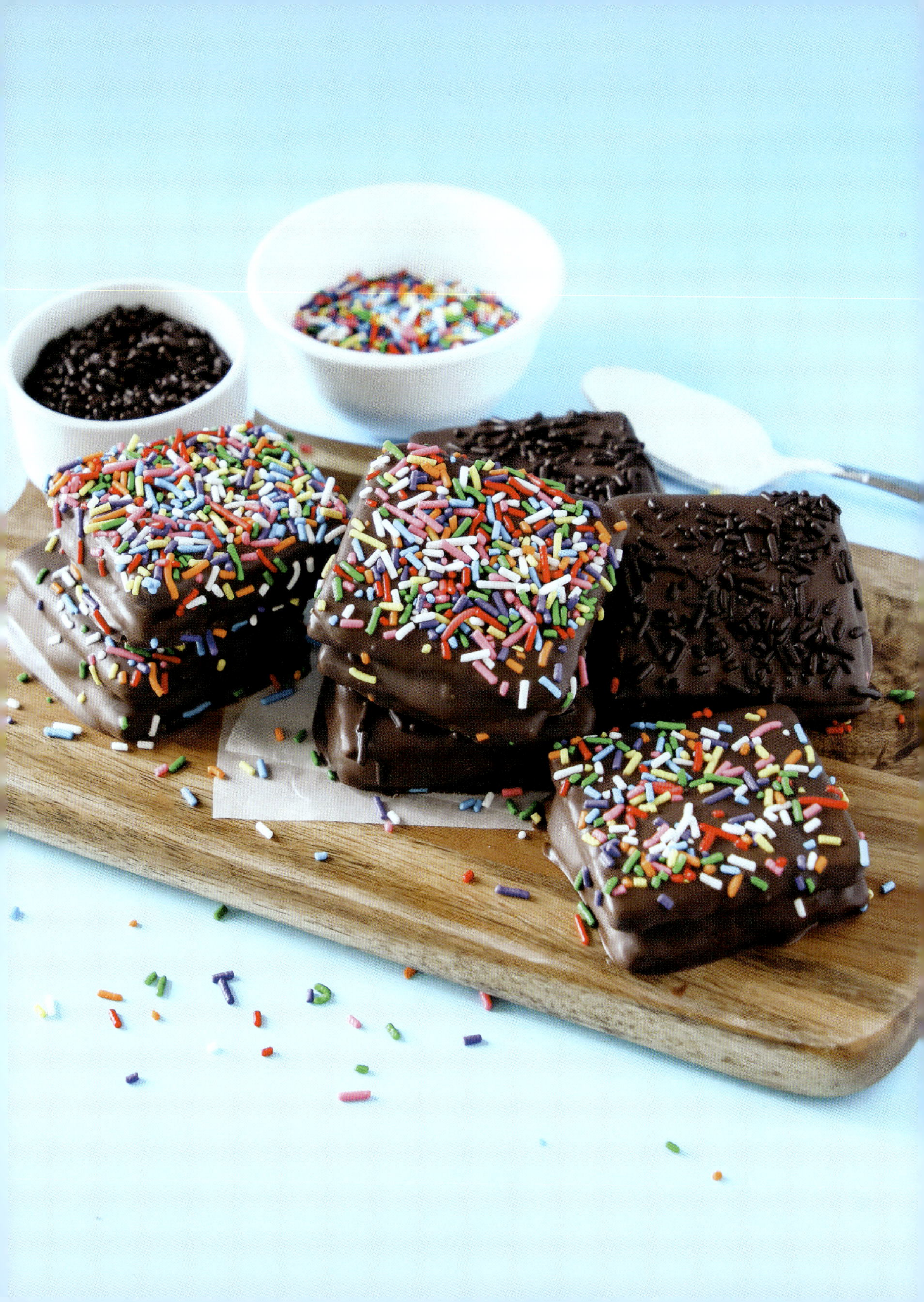

GRAHAM CRACKER SANDWICHES (CONTINUED)

In the microwave, heat the melting wafers in 30-second intervals, stirring after each interval, for 90 seconds, or until fully melted. Use a deep bowl to make the dipping process easier. It should be one that you can easily work with but that is tall enough to dip each sandwich in. Remove the graham cracker sandwiches from the refrigerator. By this time, they should be set and ready to dip! One by one, submerge each sandwich into the chocolate using a fork at the bottom to hold the sandwich steady. Be sure to cover it completely. Lift the sandwich out with the fork. Lightly shake it, and gently tap it on the outside of the bowl to remove the excess chocolate. Scrape the base of the sandwich on the bowl's rim, and then place it onto the prepared baking sheet.

Before the chocolate sets, add the sprinkles to the top of each sandwich. Place them in the fridge for 10 to 15 minutes to set. The length of time really depends on the outside temperature and humidity. You'll want them to harden completely, so that when you take them out of the fridge, they don't immediately melt. After you remove them from the fridge, let them get to room temperature and then serve. If by chance marshmallow seeps out the sides, the creme got a little too close to the edges. No worries. Just eat those first, or stick them back into the fridge to harden and then "seal" them with a little melted chocolate.

1 (10-oz [284-g]) bag milk chocolate melting wafers (such as Ghirardelli)

Assorted sprinkles, for topping

COOKIE TRUFFLES, TWO WAYS

If given the choice, my daughter would gladly eat cookie truffles every single day until the end of time. I have created two different truffle versions: The strawberry shortcake truffle is made with dried strawberries, which gives it the perfect hint of pure strawberry flavor. I used whipped cream cheese, which is key for the perfect texture! If you can't find the strawberry cream cheese, feel free to use regular whipped cream cheese. The second flavor, chocolate Oreo, gets a boost of extra flavor from the addition of Nutella. After they are dipped, they're the supreme double dose of chocolate. I truly can't decide which one I like more, so you'll have to be the judge!

Makes: 22–24 truffles

For the Strawberry Shortcake

In a food processor or blender, pulse the full bag of Golden Oreo cookies for 1 minute, or until you have fine crumbs. Pour the crumbs into a mixing bowl, and add the cream cheese and dried strawberries. With an electric handheld mixer or stand mixer, mix for 2 minutes, or until fully incorporated. Alternatively, you can mix by hand with a spoon. Place the mixture into the fridge for at least 1 hour.

Line a cookie sheet with parchment paper and set it aside. When the dough has chilled, use a 1¼-inch (3-cm) cookie scoop to scoop out a slightly rounded portion of the dough. If you don't have a scoop, measure 1 tablespoon (15 g) of dough. Using your hands, roll the dough into a ball, and place it onto the prepared cookie sheet. Repeat with the remaining cookie dough and place the cookie sheet into the fridge for 1 to 2 hours.

Once chilled, melt the white chocolate in 30-second intervals, stirring between each interval. Place a cookie dough ball into the chocolate. Using a fork, lift the ball out of the white chocolate and shake it lightly to remove any excess chocolate. Place it back onto the cookie sheet to set. Once you've coated all the balls, place the tray back into the fridge for 30 minutes. When the chocolate has set, remove it from the fridge and drizzle each ball with melted pink chocolate, if desired. Let them set at room temperature, and then eat right away! If you're saving them for later, place them in an airtight container and return them to the fridge.

(continued)

For the Strawberry Shortcake

1 (9.5-oz [270-g]) package Golden Oreo cookies

1 (7.5-oz [227-g]) container whipped strawberry cream cheese, softened

1 tbsp (10 g) finely ground dried strawberries

1 (10-oz [284-g]) bag white chocolate melting wafers (such as Ghirardelli)

Pink candy melting wafers, melted, for decorating (optional)

Note: Psst, add rainbow sprinkles to a Golden Oreo/white chocolate combo and you'll have birthday cake!

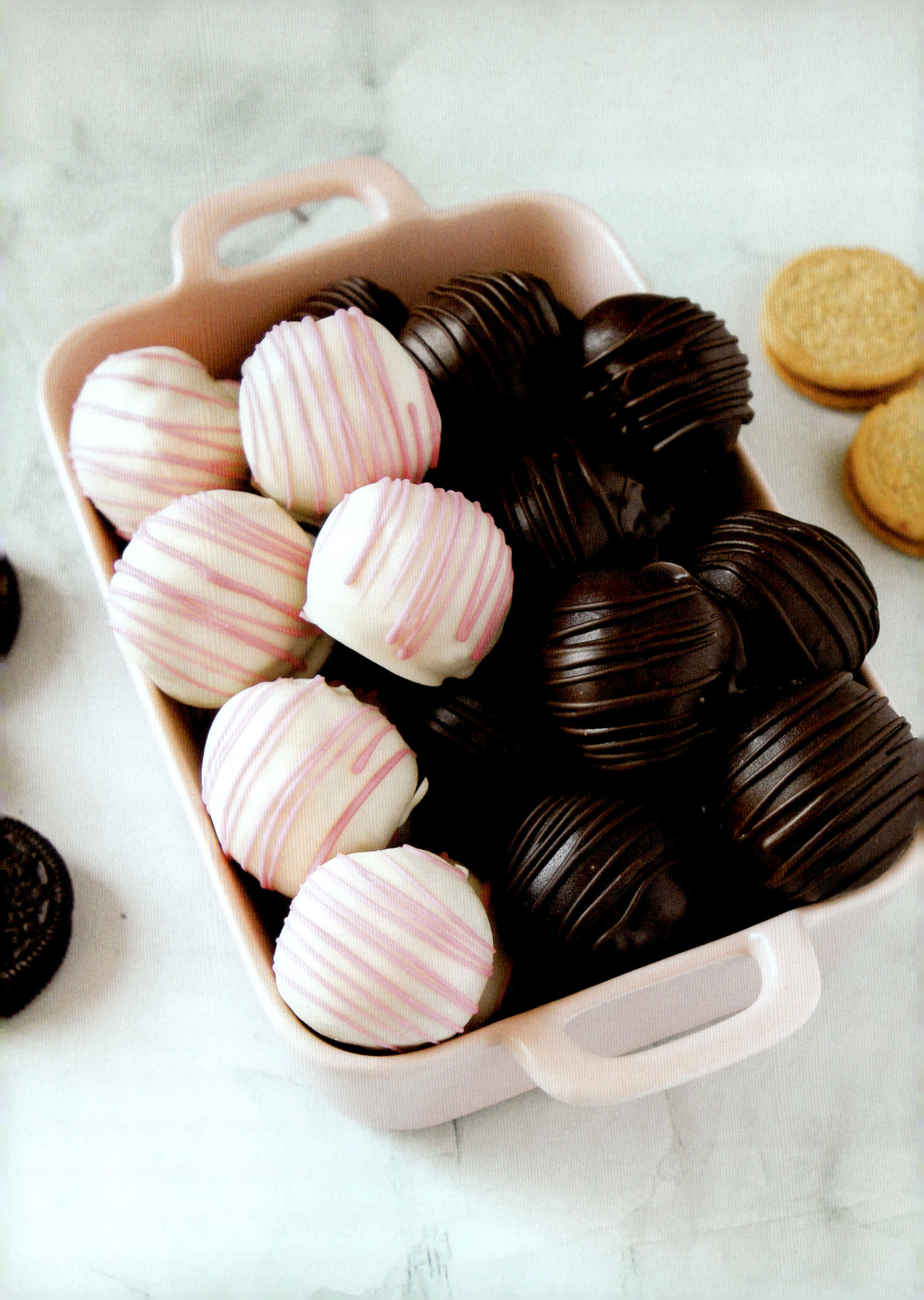

COOKIE TRUFFLES, TWO WAYS (CONTINUED)

For the Chocolate Oreo

In a food processor or blender, pulse the full bag of cookies for 1 minute, or until you have fine crumbs. Reserve some for decorating later, if desired. Pour the crumbs into a mixing bowl and add the cream cheese and Nutella. With an electric handheld mixer or stand mixer, mix for 1 to 2 minutes, or until fully incorporated. Alternatively, you can mix by hand with a spoon. Place the mixture in the fridge for at least 1 hour. Reminder, it makes them much easier to work with!

Line a cookie sheet with parchment paper and set it aside.

When the dough has chilled, use a 1¼-inch (3-cm) cookie scoop to scoop out a slightly rounded portion of the dough. If you don't have a scoop, measure 1 tablespoon (15 g) of dough. Using your hands, roll the dough into a ball, and place it onto the prepared cookie sheet. Repeat with the remaining cookie dough and place the cookie sheet into the fridge for 1 to 2 hours.

Once chilled, melt the dark chocolate in 30-second intervals, stirring between each interval. Place a cookie dough ball into the dark chocolate. Using a fork, lift the ball out of the chocolate and shake it lightly to remove any excess chocolate. Place it back onto the cookie sheet and sprinkle the top with cookie crumbs, if desired. (You may want to use an extra cookie sheet so that they aren't too close together.) Place the tray back into the fridge for 30 minutes. If you're saving them for later, place them in an airtight container and return them to the fridge.

For the Chocolate Oreo

1 (9.5-oz [270-g]) package Oreo cookies

1 (7.5-oz [227-g]) container whipped cream cheese, softened

½ cup (130 g) Nutella

1 (10-oz [284-g]) bag dark chocolate melting wafers (such as Ghirardelli)

CHOCOLATEY CHIP PUDDING CUPS

One of the most kid-friendly desserts that I know of is a pudding cup. So I decided to take them to the next level with even more elements that kids (and adults) love! These easy chocolatey chip pudding cups start with a chocolate pudding mixture filled with crushed chocolate wafer crumbs. I used regular chocolate cookies minus the cream in the center to bring out the full chocolate flavor. Each cup is layered with crushed, crunchy chocolate chip cookies, rich chocolate syrup and loads of sprinkles for the tastiest upgraded pudding treat.

In a medium bowl, combine the chocolate pudding and milk, and make the pudding as directed on the package. Let it set for 5 minutes, and then gently fold in the cookie crumbs. Then fold in the whipped topping until there are no white streaks. Refrigerate for at least 2 to 3 hours. You'll want the pudding to be set and not runny or too thin.

Set eight to ten serving glasses (5 ounces [142 g] in size, ideally) on a flat surface. At the bottom of each glass, crush 1 chocolate chip cookie into small to medium pieces. Top that with ¼ cup (60 ml) of the pudding mixture, then 1 tablespoon (15 ml) of chocolate sauce, another ¼ cup (60 ml) of pudding and then chocolate sprinkles. Use as many sprinkles as you'd like to give it a nice crunch. If you're using different cups, just be sure to layer the pudding, sauce and sprinkles, and you won't have to stick with the amounts! Serve immediately.

Makes: 8–10 cups

1 (3.4-oz [96-g]) box instant chocolate pudding mix

2 cups (480 ml) cold milk

½ cup (45 g) chocolate wafer cookie crumbs*

1 (8-oz [226-g]) container whipped topping, thawed

8–10 chocolate chip cookies (such as non-chewy Chips Ahoy®)

Chocolate sauce**

Chocolate sprinkles, for topping

*These are the cookies that are just chocolate wafers, not chocolate sandwich cookies like Oreo cookies. If you do use Oreo cookies, just take out the cream center.

**Ideally not chocolate syrup, but more like the Ghirardelli brand.

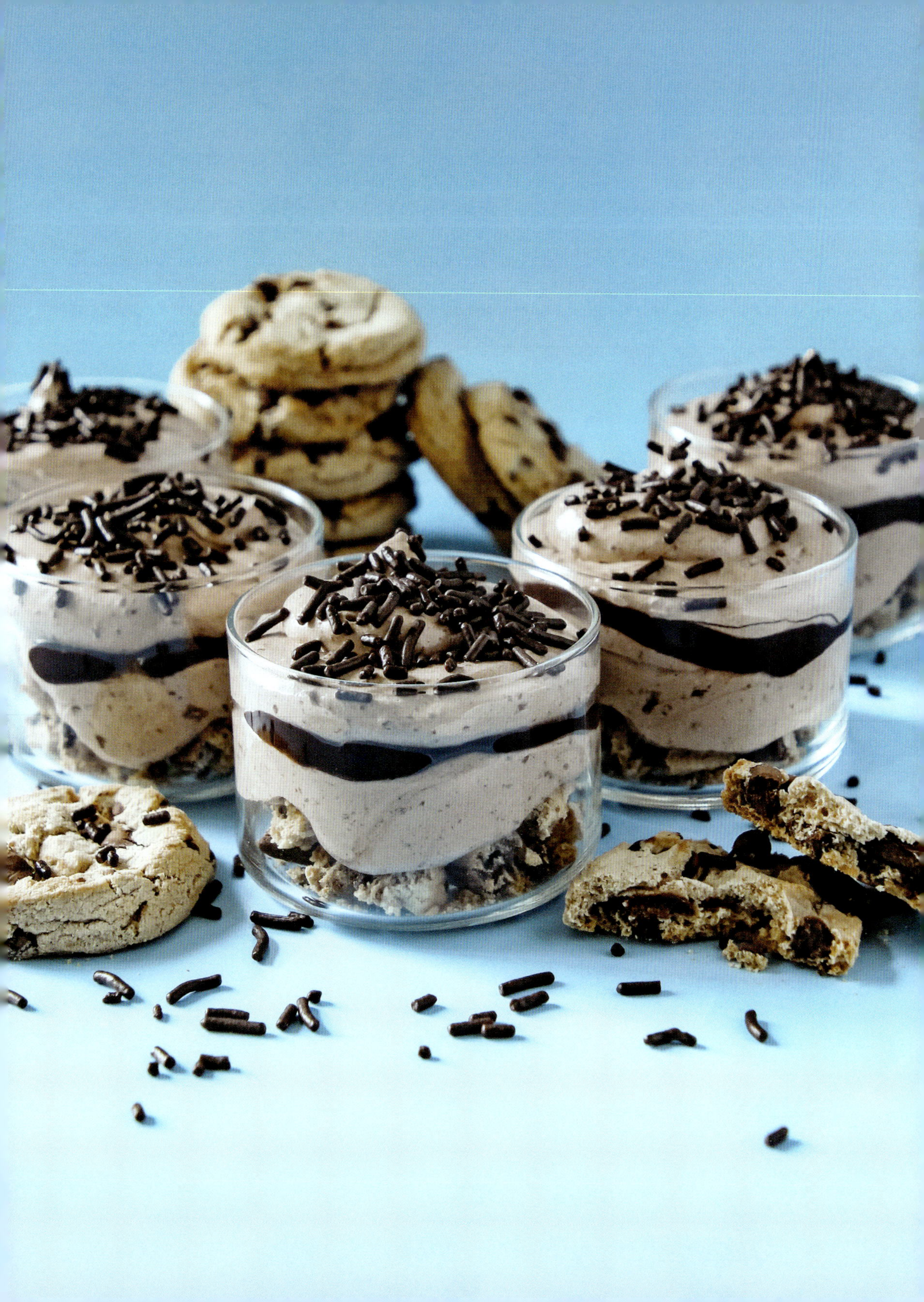

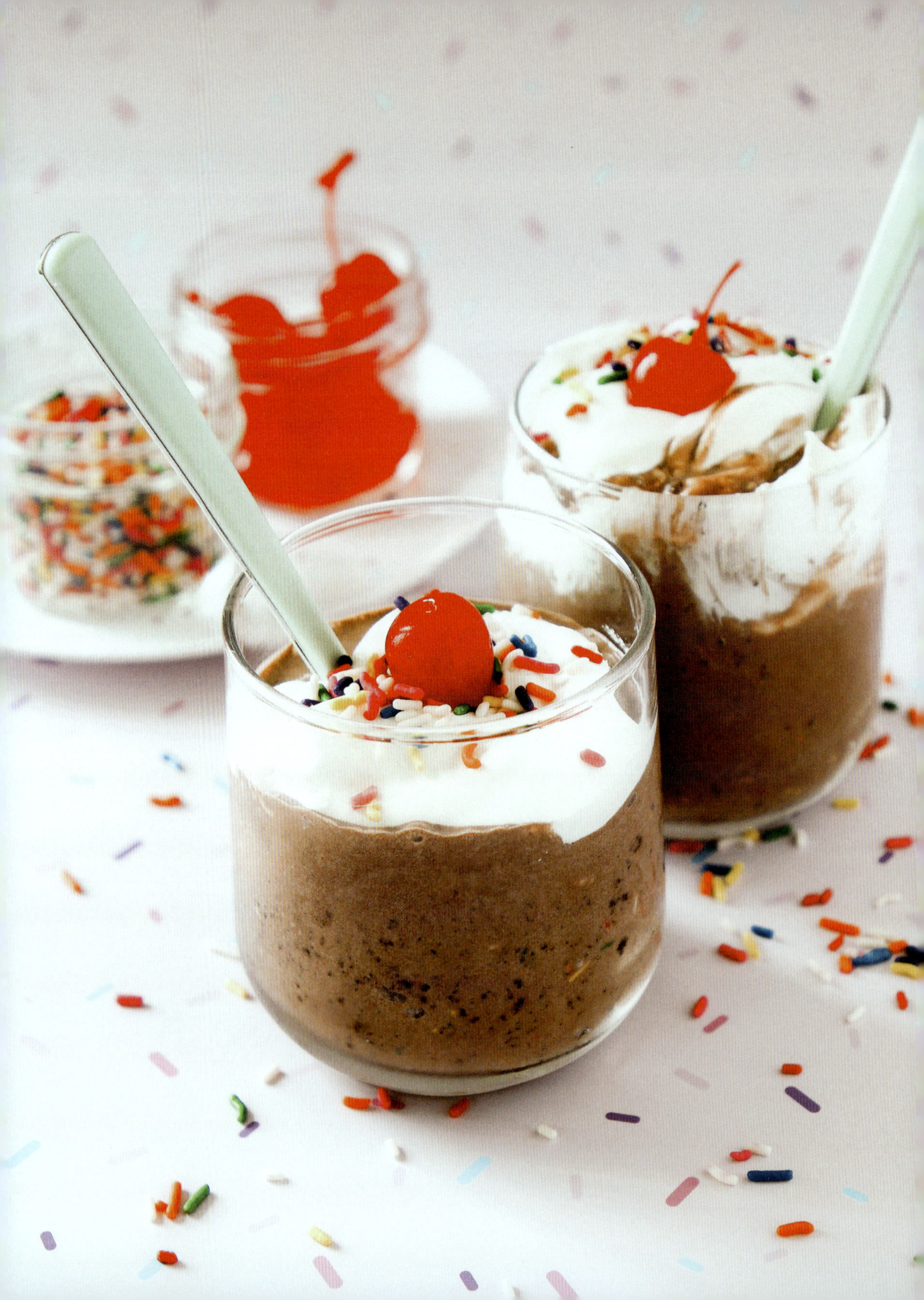

BROWNIE BLAST SOFT SERVE

I have to admit, I love ice cream when it gets a little bit melty, so I am a gigantic fan of soft serve ice cream. To me, it has the perfect texture! This dessert is a mashup of soft serve ice cream mixed to a Dairy Queen® Blizzard®–like consistency. My homemade version starts with chocolate ice cream, which is then swirled with fudge, brownie bits, rainbow sprinkles, whipped topping and, of course . . . a cherry on top. Now that you can make your own at home, have fun experimenting with your favorite flavor combos!

In the bowl of a stand mixer with the paddle attachment or a large mixing bowl with a handheld electric mixer, beat the ice cream for 1 minute on low. You want a smooth and creamy texture.

Add the fudge, chopped brownies and sprinkles, and mix until just incorporated. You can use the mixer or just fold the toppings in with a spatula or spoon. Pour the mixture into a glass or bowl and top with a dollop of whipped topping, extra rainbow sprinkles and a cherry. It really is that easy!

Makes: 2 blasts

4 cups (480 g) chocolate ice cream*

2 tbsp (38 g) cold chocolate fudge

⅔ cup (76 g) chopped brownies (not frosted)

2 tbsp (26 g) rainbow sprinkles, plus more for serving

Whipped topping

Maraschino cherry, for topping

*Keep the ice cream very cold, and don't take it out until you're starting.

LOADED EDIBLE COOKIE DOUGH

My greatest dessert weakness is edible cookie dough. I simply cannot say no, and I don't ever foresee myself getting sick of it. The combination of different add-ins is absolutely irresistible. If I ever opened a storefront or pop-up shop, I would specialize in cookie dough creations year-round. This loaded dough has a base similar to a chocolate chip cookie and is packed with semisweet chocolate chips, chocolate-covered pretzels and toffee. Feel free to swap out the fillings for your favorites. You can add sea salt, crushed candy bars, sprinkles, nuts or any of your favorites!

One of the top questions I get asked when making edible cookie dough is, "Why do we need to heat treat the flour?" Well, it's to kill any bacteria that may be in the flour, and I promise you it's super simple. Here's how: Spread the flour evenly in a microwave-safe bowl or plate. Use a wide, shallow dish for more even heating. Heat the flour in the microwave on high for 30-second intervals. Stir the flour well after each interval to ensure even heating and to break up any clumps. Use a food thermometer to check the flour's temperature. It needs to reach 165°F (74°C) to be safe. Let it cool completely. Alternatively (if you don't mind using the oven for this step), you can bake the flour in the oven for 5 to 10 minutes at 350°F (177°C). Let cool completely. Pick the option easiest and available to you!

In a stand mixer or medium mixing bowl with an electric mixer, beat the butter and sugar on high for 3 minutes. It should look smooth and fluffy. Add the vanilla and salt, and mix again until fully incorporated. Add the heat-treated and fully cooled flour to the bowl, and mix until a dough forms. Pour in the milk, and mix one last time until it's smooth and completely combined. Gently fold in the chocolate chips, toffee bits and pretzels with a spatula. You can most definitely eat it right away, but I prefer it cold. I let mine sit in the fridge for at least 2 to 3 hours, but ideally overnight. Store leftover edible cookie dough in an airtight container in the fridge for up to 5 days.

Makes: 6 servings

1 cup (125 g) heat-treated all-purpose flour*

½ cup (114 g) salted butter, room temperature

¾ cup (165 g) packed dark or light brown sugar

1 tsp vanilla

½ tsp salt

2 tbsp (30 ml) milk

¼ cup (42 g) semisweet chocolate chips

2 tbsp (30 g) crushed toffee pieces

6 milk chocolate-covered pretzels, roughly chopped

*You can heat treat regular all-purpose flour in the oven beforehand if you'd prefer.

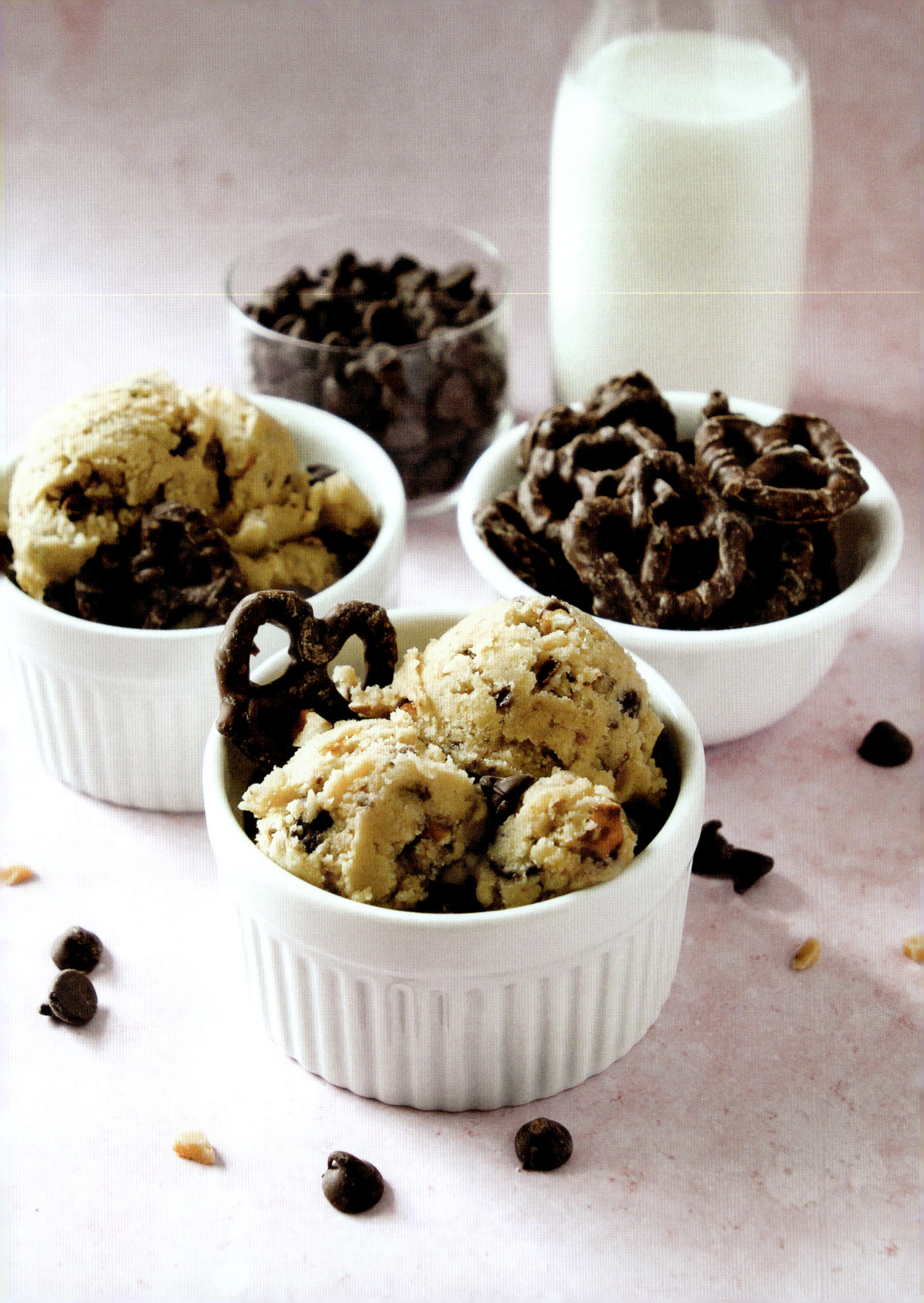

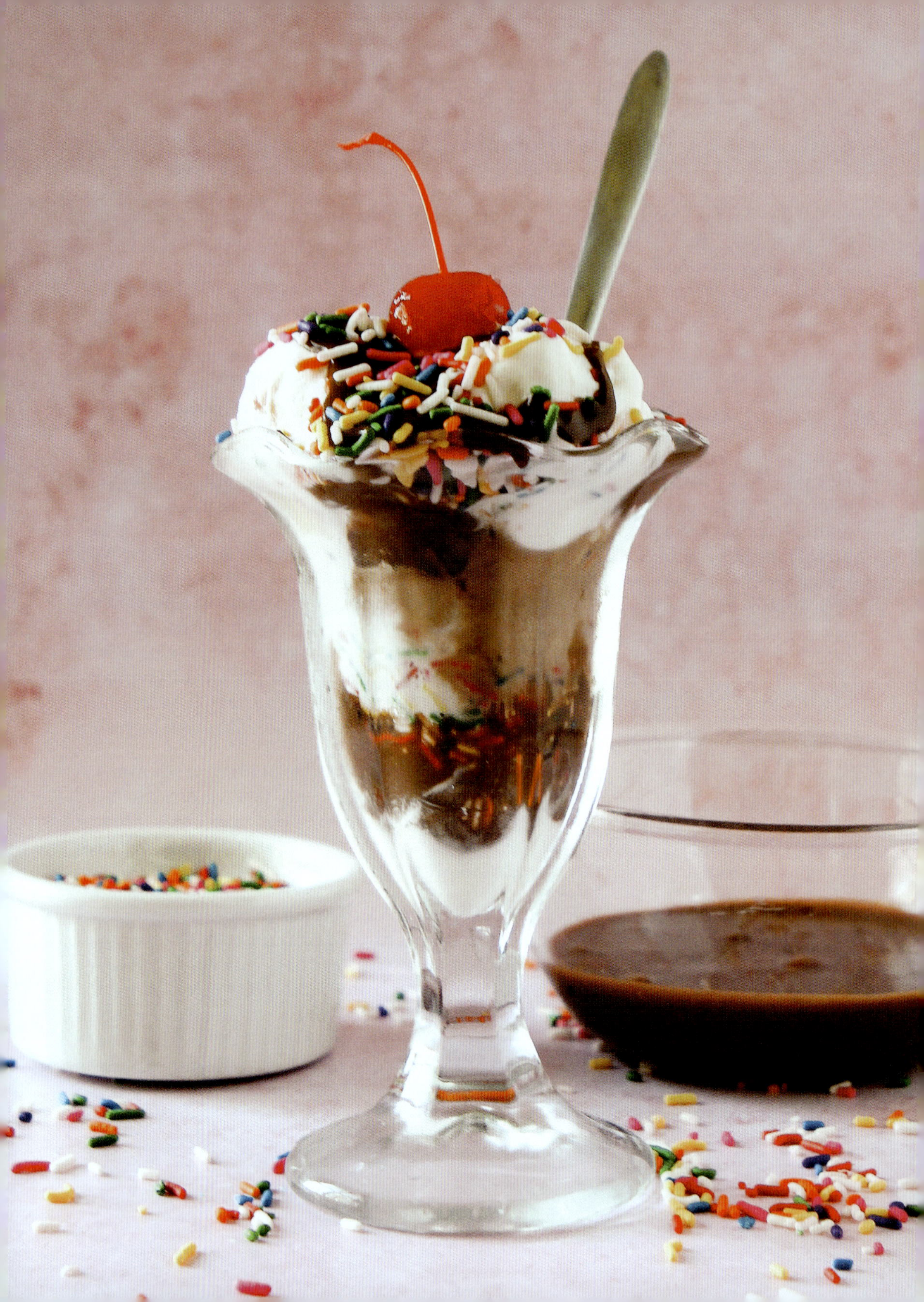

DECADENT HOT FUDGE SUNDAE

This homemade hot fudge is the perfect classic sundae topping. It's rich and creamy, and absolutely decadent. I used milk chocolate chips, which are my preferred choice of chocolate, but you can easily swap them for semisweet or dark chocolate. Fill sundae glasses with your favorite ice cream, and add dollops of fudge and all the extras. I chose to make a Neapolitan ice cream treat, but it's also amazing on brownie sundaes and chocolate cake! Whatever hot fudge you don't use can be refrigerated, so get excited for a full week of scoop-tacular sundaes.

In a small pot, combine the condensed milk and chocolate chips over medium heat, and stir until the chocolate chips are fully melted. Be sure to keep stirring so that the chocolate doesn't stick to the bottom of the pot.

Remove the pot from the heat and stir in the butter and vanilla. Keep stirring until the butter is completely melted and incorporated.

In sundae glasses, layer the ice cream and fudge, and top with sprinkles and a cherry. I like a double layer of everything instead of only having it at the top!

Makes: 1 sundae

1 (14-oz [300-ml]) can sweetened condensed milk

1 cup (168 g) milk chocolate chips

2 tbsp (28 g) unsalted butter, room temperature

1 tsp vanilla extract or vanilla bean paste

Neapolitan ice cream, or your favorite flavor

Rainbow sprinkles, for topping

Maraschino cherry, for topping

CHOCOLATE-DIPPED COOKIE STACKS

On a visit to Gatlinburg, Tennessee, I saw a version of these epic cookie stacks and had to recreate them as soon as I got home. I've experimented with a few different combos, but this is most definitely my personal favorite. I used Double Stuf® Oreo cookies and Reese's Thins® for the perfect flavor combination in each bite. These are made with half white chocolate and half milk chocolate peanut butter cups, but you can always swap them out for dark chocolate or flavored standard size cups.

Twist the tops off 24 cookies. We are only going to be using the cream side. You can use the plain side to crush and sprinkle on top for a different snack. Somehow, mine seem to get stolen along the way. Hmm . . .

Line a baking sheet with parchment paper and set it aside.

Add one Reese's Thin on top of one Oreo half, cream side up. Place another Oreo half, cream side down, on top of the Reese's Thin and very gently press together. Melt the milk chocolate according to the package directions. Start with 30 seconds and be sure to stir after each 30-second interval. Mine usually takes 90 seconds.

Place a cookie stack on a fork and gently dip it into the melted chocolate. Be sure to fully submerge the cookie without knocking it over. I usually use the fork to make sure that it's completely covered in chocolate, but if needed, use a spoon. Lift the cookie up with the fork and lightly shake off any excess chocolate.

Place the cookie stack onto the baking sheet and immediately top it with sprinkles. Repeat with the remaining cookie stacks, and then refrigerate them for 30 minutes. Pull them from the fridge once set, and then let them get to room temperature before enjoying.

Makes: 10–12 cookie sandwiches

1 (9.2-oz [261-g]) package Double Stuf Oreo cookies

12 Reese's Thins, flavor of your choice

1 (10-oz [284-g]) bag milk chocolate melting wafers (such as Ghirardelli®)

Rainbow sprinkles, for topping

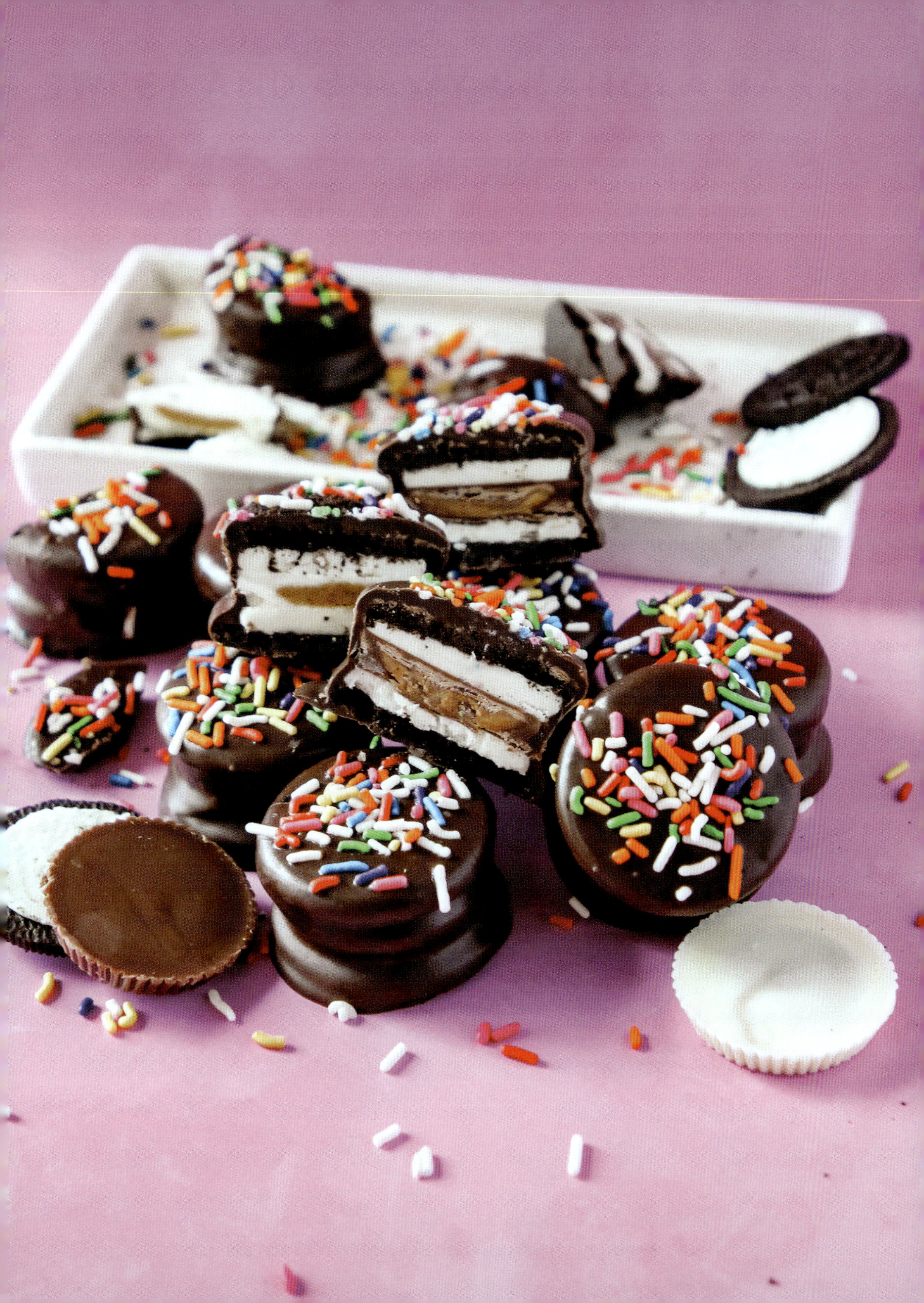

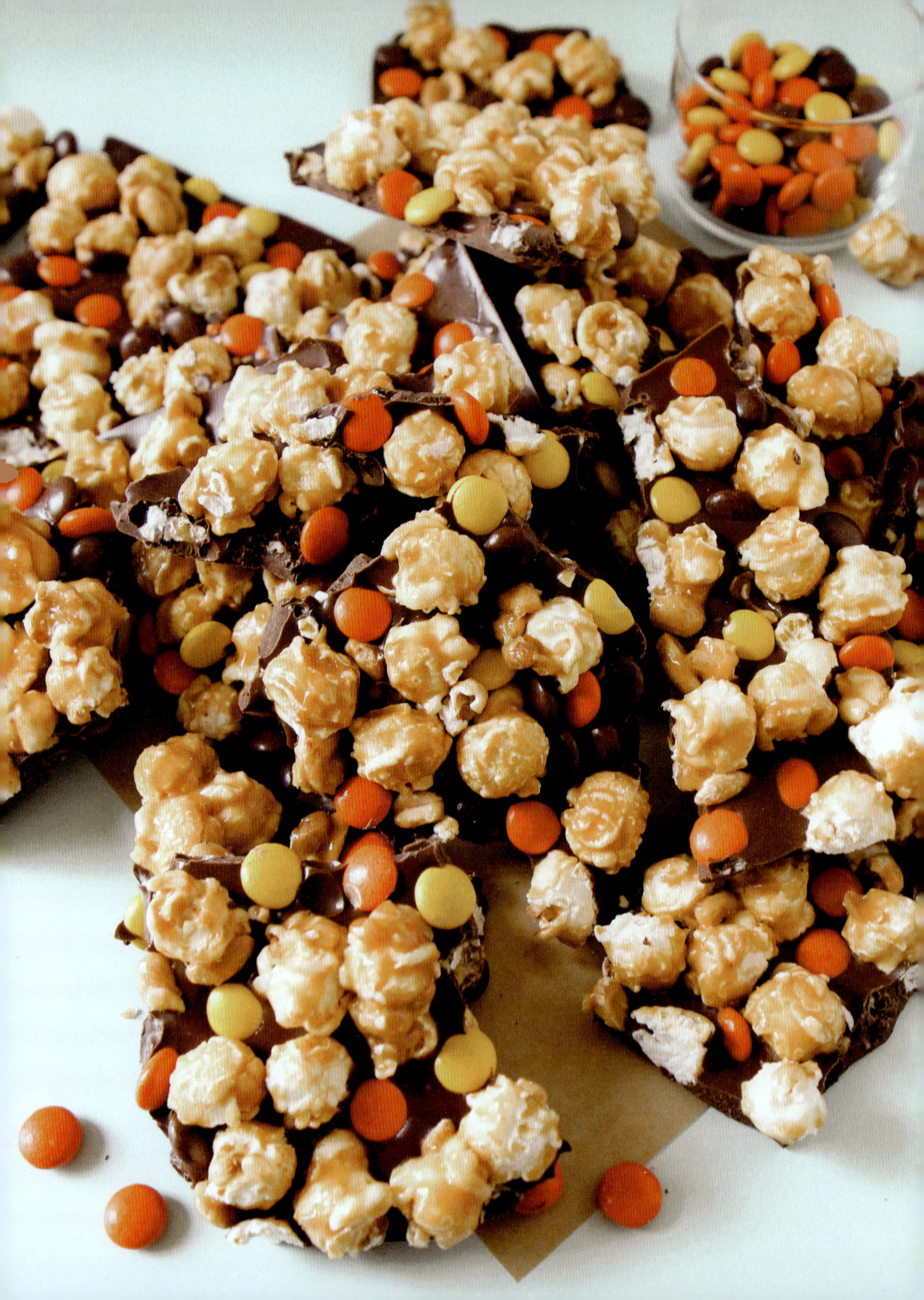

MOVIE NIGHT CARAMEL POPCORN BARK

Movie night snacks are the best of both worlds: salty and sweet. It's so hard to choose between popcorn, nachos, gummies, sour candy and chocolate! Seeing as how I always get BOTH popcorn and chocolate, it only made sense to combine the two. I used a mix of both dark and milk chocolate and then topped it with a classic movie theater candy: Reese's Pieces®. For the popcorn addition, I went with caramel popcorn and nuts. This bark has the best balance of salty and sweet with a tasty touch of peanut butter crunch. Cashews, M&M's® or even crushed pretzels would all be equally delicious, so mix it up for the next movie night!

Makes: 12 pieces

1 (10-oz [284-g]) bag milk chocolate melting wafers (such as Ghirardelli)*

1 (10-oz [284-g]) dark chocolate melting wafers (such as Ghirardelli)*

8–10 oz (226–284 g) caramel popcorn with nuts

½ cup (84 g) Reese's Pieces

*Or any combo of the two.

Line a 10 x 15–inch (25 x 38–cm) baking pan with parchment paper. Let a little bit hang over the sides so that you can pull the bark out easily.

In the microwave, heat one bag of melting wafers at a time in 30-second intervals, stirring after each interval, for 90 seconds, or until fully melted. Pour both bowls of melted chocolate onto the parchment-lined baking pan, and spread the chocolate into an even layer using an offset spatula. It should look a bit marbled if you are using two different kinds of chocolate.

Scatter the popcorn evenly on top of the chocolate, lightly pressing it down. The bark will be quite full of popcorn! Add the Reese's Pieces in the open spots and press them down into the chocolate. Let the bark set at room temperature. If you need to put it into the fridge, be sure not to leave it too long as the popcorn will get stale. Once the bark is completely set, break it into pieces and serve.

NO-CHURN COOKIE MASHUP ICE CREAM

A recipe that I make year-round is no-churn ice cream. It's so easy and a great way to use up leftover cookies, candy or nuts. I loaded this version with both Oreo cookies and cookie dough bites. I am a texture person, so the mix-ins are crucial. I love the crunch and chewy contrast, but the best part about this recipe is how versatile it is. Change out the cookie and cookie dough flavors to suit whatever mood you're in, and don't forget about the sprinkles ☺!

In a large mixing bowl, beat the heavy cream until stiff peaks form. When you remove the beater, the whipping cream peaks should be stiff and not run or droop. To me, it looks like shaving cream. In a medium mixing bowl, gently fold together the whipped cream and sweetened condensed milk until fully combined and smooth. Fold in the evaporated milk and vanilla. Add the finely crushed cookie crumbs and gently mix until it's fully combined.

Add both the coarsely chopped cookies and cookie dough bites to the bowl and gently fold them in. I prefer a really heavy topping-to–ice cream ratio, but if you prefer more ice cream than mix-ins, cut the mix-in measurements in half.

Transfer the ice cream mixture to a 9 x 5–inch (23 x 13–cm) loaf pan and freeze overnight. When you're ready to serve, use an ice cream scoop and fill your bowls to the top! This ice cream is soft and creamy, so enjoy right away —and don't forget to top it with some rainbow sprinkles!

Makes: 8 servings

2 cups (480 ml) heavy whipping cream

1 (14-oz [300-ml]) can sweetened condensed milk

¼ cup (60 ml) evaporated milk

1 tsp vanilla bean paste or vanilla extract

½ cup (38 g) finely crushed Oreo cookies, plus 6 cookies coarsely chopped

1 cup (224 g) chocolate chip cookie dough bites (such as Ben & Jerry's®)

Colorful sprinkles, for topping

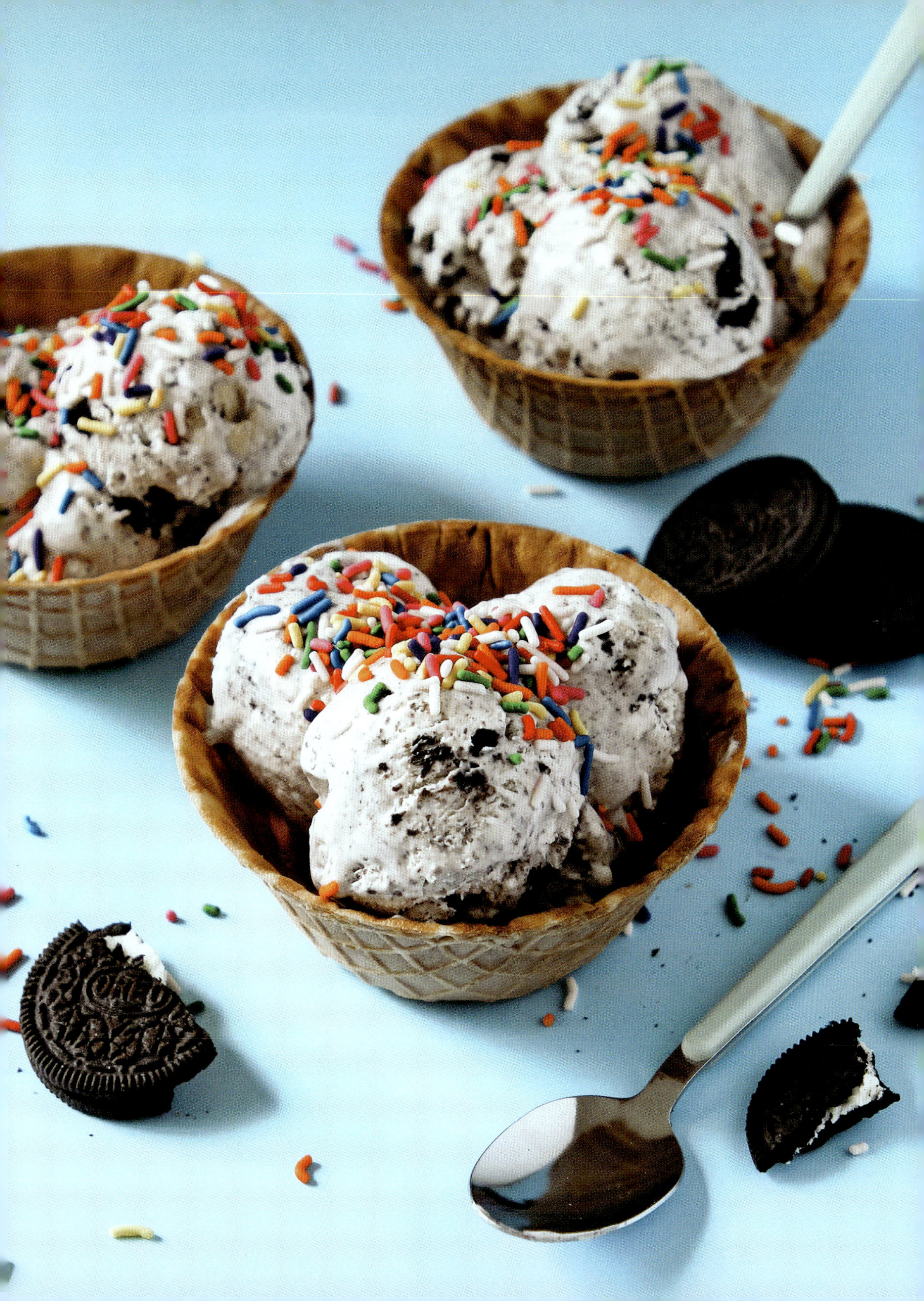

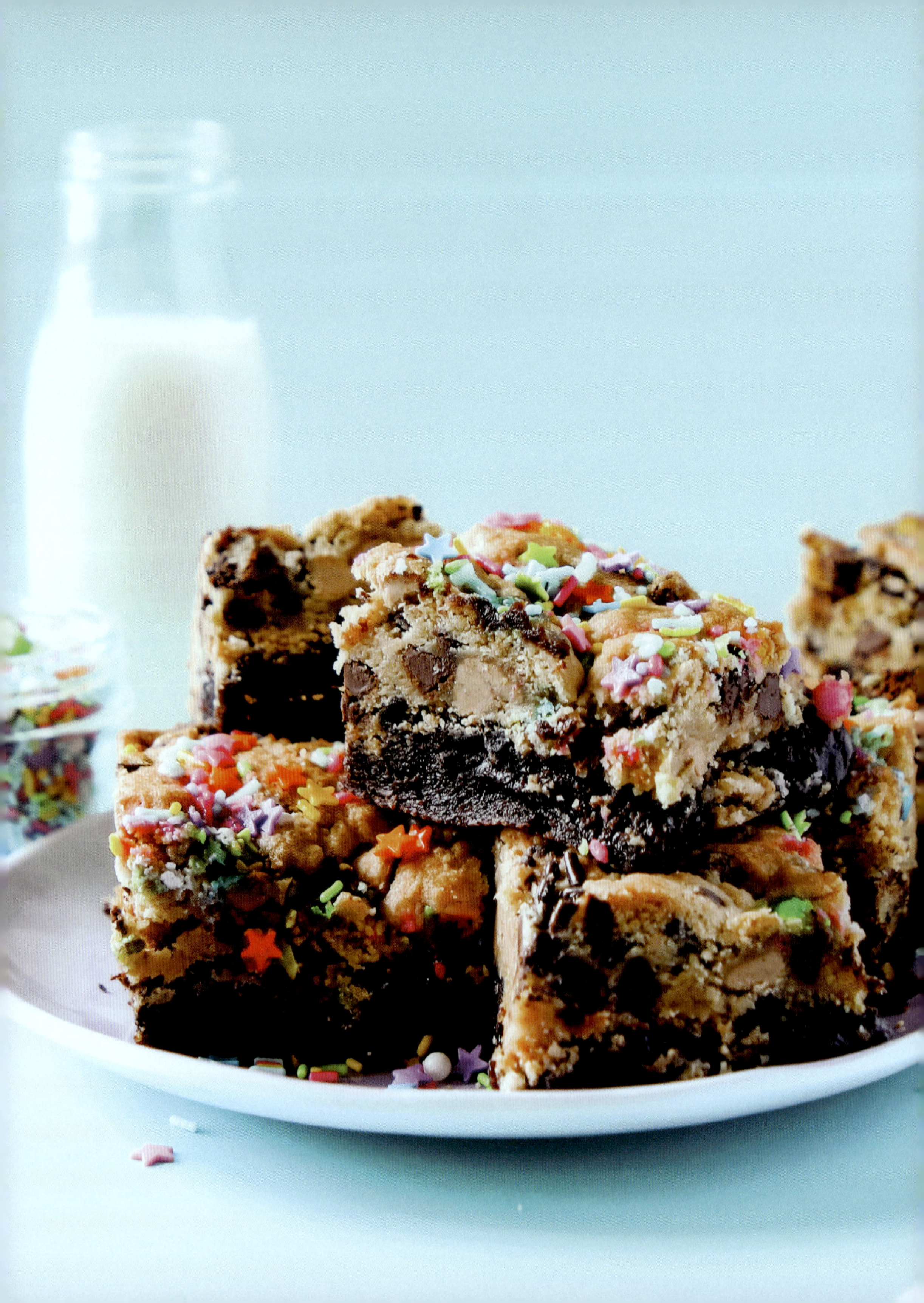

RECIPES FOR BAKE SALES, PARTIES AND

Making Memories

This chapter is centered around recipes that are perfect for parties with friends, school bake sales or celebrations with family. My favorite part about making desserts is getting to share it with people. I love to stay up late with my family watching movies and sharing a dessert board full of treats. Bringing cupcakes to my daughter's classes always brings tears to my eyes. I love how excited she gets when we bring in homemade treats. Baking desserts like the Frosted Animal Cookie Blondies (page 82) or Jumbo Brookies (page 91) for local bake sales puts me in touch with old friends, and their reactions always make my day! I can't wait for you to sprinkle some fun into your kitchen and start making memories!

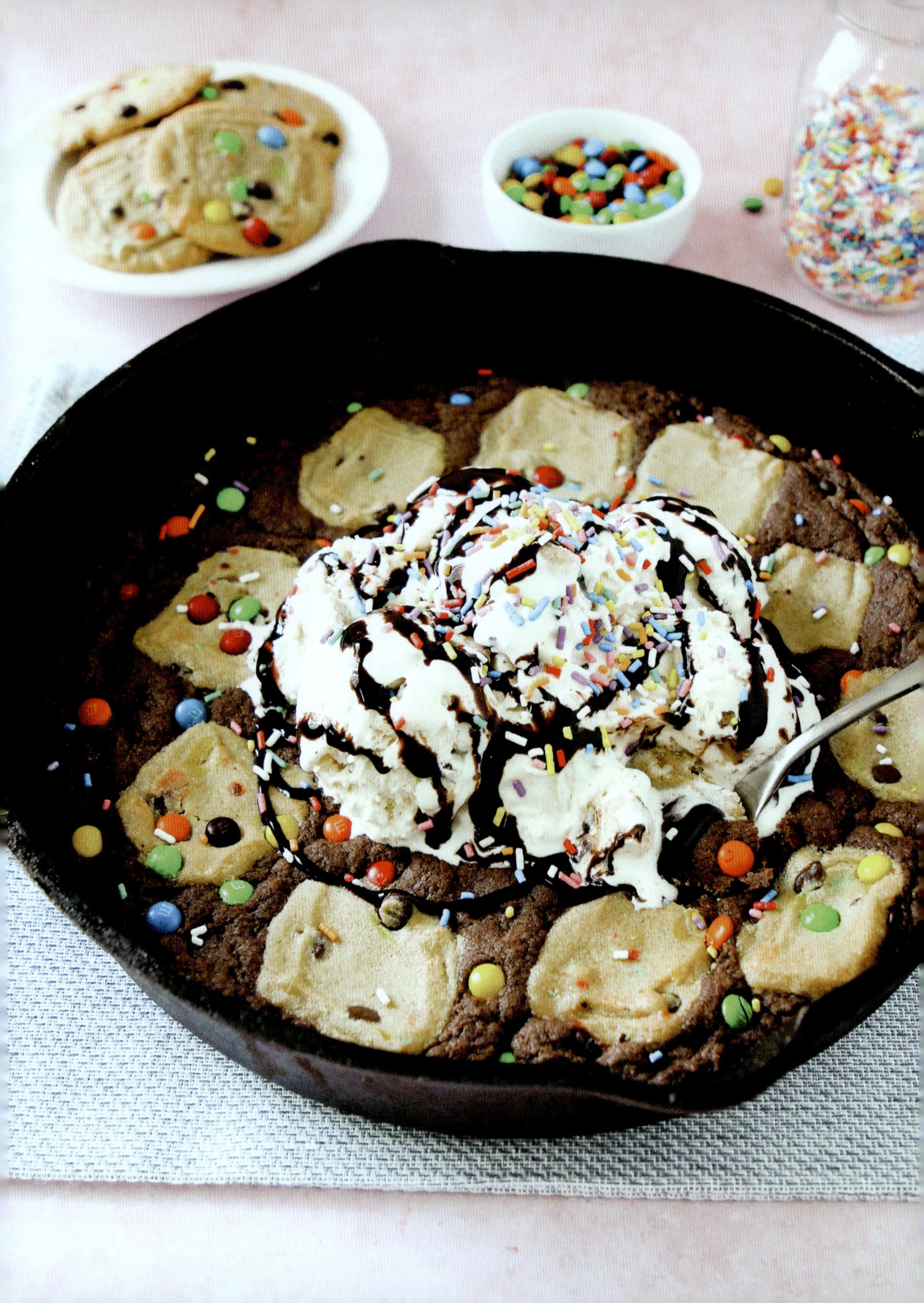

GIANT COOKIE SKILLET

I've been making these cookie skillets for a while now, and they have yet to disappoint. You just can't beat a warm cookie with ice cream and toppings. These are super easy to make (meaning they're very hard to mess up)! All you need is a cookie dough mix or premade dough, a large skillet and your favorite ice cream. The key to getting the best consistency is to eat the cookie while it's still warm and gooey! The cookie will be baked all the way, but the skillet lets it stay warm enough so that it doesn't totally set right away. Watch scoops of ice cream start to melt as soon as they hit this giant cookie! For more fun, sprinkle your favorite toppings and dig in!

Preheat the oven to 350°F (177°C), and spray a 12-inch (30-cm) round skillet with baking spray. If you do not have a skillet this large, you can most definitely use a smaller one. Just be sure to check the cookie as it bakes, and remove it from the oven when it starts to turn golden brown. Reminder, cookie skillets are best when they're cooked through but still a little gooey.

Make the cookie mix according to the package directions. Fold in the crushed M&M's. Spread the dough evenly on the entire bottom of the skillet. It may look like it's not enough to fit the entire pan, but keep spreading it with your fingertips. The dough will also fill the skillet as it bakes. Place the ready-to-bake M&M's cookies on top of the dough, leaving a little bit of room between the cookies. Add extra mini M&M's on top in between the cookies.

Bake for 20 to 25 minutes, or until lightly golden brown. Remove the skillet from the oven and allow it to cool for 5 minutes. Move the skillet to a hot pad or table protector on a surface where you'll be serving it. Top the cookie with the ice cream, chocolate syrup and rainbow sprinkles. Serve immediately.

Note: If you don't intend to serve this all at once, scoop the cookie into a bowl, and then add the ice cream and toppings. Alternatively, you can just put the ice cream on half, and then save the other half for later. Just reheat it in the oven or microwave!

Makes: 5–6 servings

1 (17.5-oz [496-g]) package double chocolate chunk cookie mix

⅓ cup (105 g) crushed mini or regular M&M's, plus more as needed

1 (14-oz [396-g]) package Nestlé® Toll House® M&M's Minis Chocolate Chip Cookie Dough*

2 cups (240 g) chocolate chip cookie dough ice cream, plus more as desired

Chocolate sundae syrup or chocolate fudge, for drizzling

Rainbow sprinkles, for topping

*Use regular ready-to-bake chocolate chip cookie dough, if desired.

TGIF DESSERT BOARD

It's the end of the week and time to get ready for the weekend! Ideally, this involves dessert. (Wink, wink.) There's nothing better than sharing a sweet snack party board with friends and family. Since creating these treats is half the fun, make the assembly part of the plan. Get everyone ready to dip, sprinkle and drizzle because it's Friday! You'll need a large serving board AND extra candy if desired, like Twizzlers®, Sour Patch Kids®, Junior Mints® and Skittles®. Switch up the candy each week or use it for other events. They're so much fun to serve at sleepovers, birthday parties and late-night streaming.

Line a baking sheet or large cutting board with parchment paper.

In the microwave, heat the melting wafers in 30-second intervals, stirring after each interval, for 90 seconds, or until fully melted. Let the chocolate cool for 2 minutes. This makes it easier to work with—just make sure that the chocolate is still warm but not burning hot. Pour the melted chocolate into a deep cup that will be used to dip/coat the marshmallows. It should be similar to a drinking glass.

Dip half of each marshmallow into the melted chocolate. Shake off any excess chocolate. Hold the marshmallow over an empty bowl and add the sprinkles and nuts, making sure to cover all the chocolate. Be sure not to sprinkle it over the bowls of toppings, so that chocolate doesn't drip down into it. It can create huge clumps! Let the marshmallows set at room temperature, or move them to the refrigerator for 5 to 10 minutes to set faster.

(continued)

Makes: 1 large dessert board

Dipped Marshmallows

1 (10-oz [284-g]) bag dark chocolate melting wafers (such as Ghirardelli)*

16 large marshmallows (about 113 g)

Rainbow sprinkles

Crushed nuts of your choice

*You can use chocolate chips instead, but first add ½ teaspoon of coconut oil when heating.

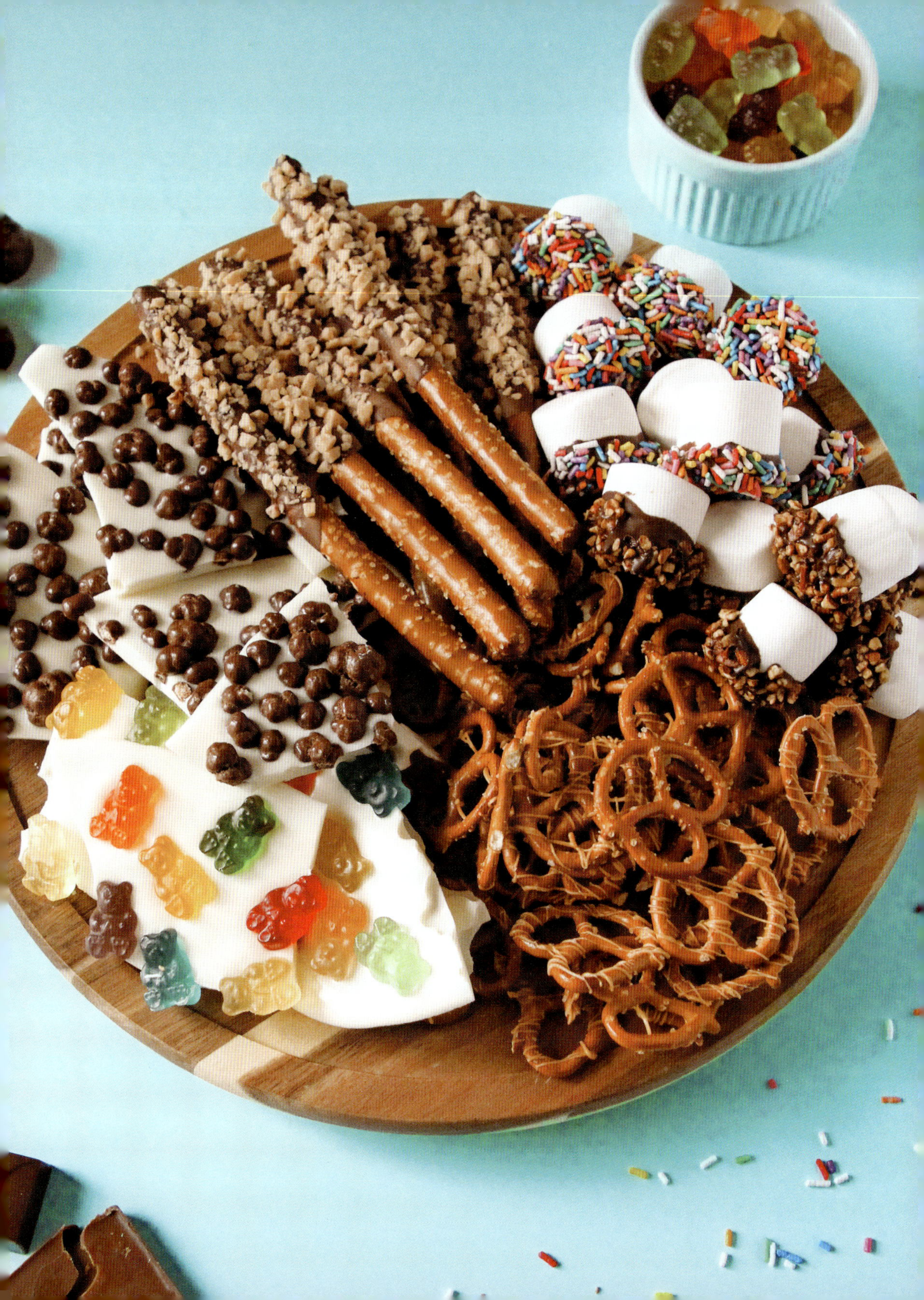

TGIF DESSERT BOARD (CONTINUED)

Pretzel Rods

1 (10-oz [284-g]) bag dark chocolate melting wafers (such as Ghirardelli)*

10–12 pretzel rods

1 (7-oz [200-g]) bag crushed toffee pieces

*You can use chocolate chips instead, but first add ½ teaspoon of coconut oil when heating.

Line a baking sheet or large cutting board with parchment paper.

In the microwave, heat the melting wafers in 30-second intervals, stirring after each interval, for 90 seconds, or until fully melted. Let the chocolate cool for 2 minutes. This makes it easier to work with—just make sure that the chocolate is still warm but not burning hot. Pour the melted chocolate into a deep cup that will be used to dip/coat the pretzel rods. It should be similar to a drinking glass.

Dip each pretzel into the melted chocolate and gently shake off any excess chocolate. Hold the pretzel over an empty bowl and sprinkle toffee pieces over the pretzel, covering it on all sides. Place it onto the prepared baking sheet. Repeat with the remaining pretzel rods. Let the pretzels set at room temperature or move them to the refrigerator for 5 to 10 minutes to set faster.

Easy Candy Bark

1 (10-oz [284-g]) bag white chocolate melting wafers (such as Ghirardelli)

½ cup (60 g) Nestlé Buncha Crunch® or chopped Kit Kat® bars

½ cup (100 g) gummy bears

Line a half sheet pan or small rimmed baking sheet with parchment paper.

In the microwave, heat the melting wafers in 30-second intervals, stirring after each interval, for 90 seconds, or until fully melted. Pour the chocolate onto the baking sheet in an even layer. On one half of the chocolate, sprinkle the Buncha Crunch. Sprinkle the gummy bears on the other side. Place the chocolate in the refrigerator for 10 to 15 minutes to set. Bring it back to room temperature and break it into bark-sized pieces.

Drizzled Pretzels

2 cups (80 g) Rold Gold® Tiny Twists pretzels

½ cup (84 g) butterscotch chips

½ tsp coconut oil

Sparkling sugar, for sprinkling (optional)

Line a baking sheet with parchment paper, and set the pretzels on the sheet in an even layer. In the microwave, heat the butterscotch chips and oil in 30-second intervals, stirring after each interval, until fully melted. To drizzle the pretzels, use a spoon and lightly add the butterscotch, moving slowly so that you don't get a huge puddle in one place. Alternatively, fill a piping bag or bottle with the melted butterscotch and drizzle it on. Sprinkle on the sparkling sugar, if desired, and let them set at room temperature.

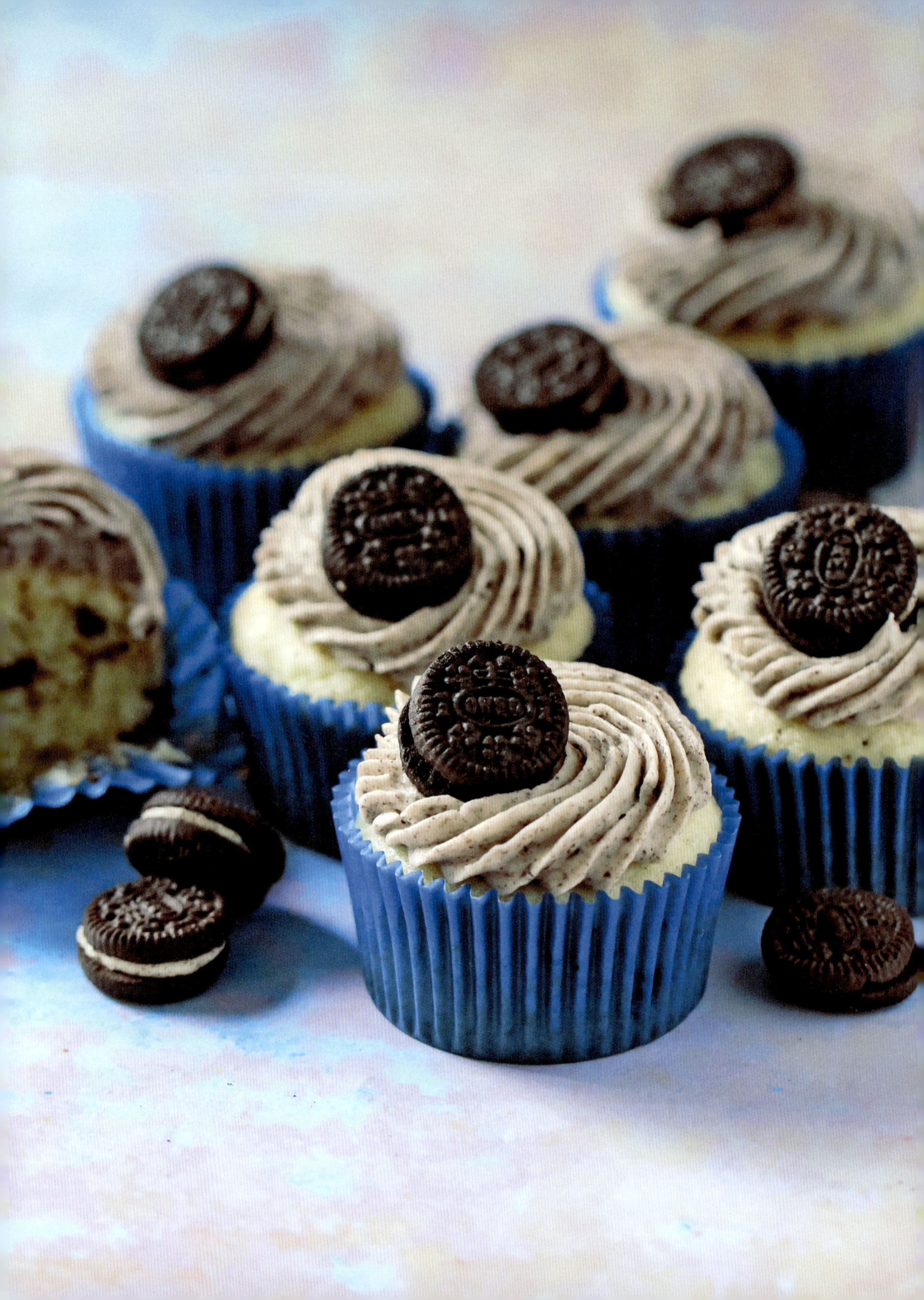

COOKIES 'N' CREAM CUPCAKES

These cupcakes are extra special because not only do they have Oreo cookies in the buttercream, but they also have them in the cake batter. To keep it fun and interesting, I change these cupcakes with the seasons. In fall, it's all about the Pumpkin Spice Flavor Creme Oreo cookies and a spiced cake base. Winter brings out chocolate cupcakes filled with Peppermint Creme Oreo cookies and minty cookies 'n' cream frosting. It's such a simple way to switch up a classic treat or to even match a party theme!

Preheat the oven to 350°F (177°C). Line a cupcake pan with cupcake liners. If you don't have a 24-cavity cupcake pan, simply use two 12-cavity pans or bake in batches.

To make the cupcakes, in a medium bowl, combine the cake mix, oil, buttermilk and eggs and mix until smooth. Fold in the Oreo cookie pieces. Fill each cupcake liner two-thirds of the way full. Bake according to the package directions, and let the cupcakes cool completely.

To make the frosting, in a stand mixer or in a large mixing bowl with a hand mixer, beat the butter for 2 minutes, or until smooth. Add 2 cups (240 g) of the powdered sugar and mix until combined. Add the remaining powdered sugar, heavy cream, vanilla and Oreo cookie crumbs. Mix until completely combined.

To frost the cupcakes, either use a butter knife or pipe swirls of frosting onto the top of each with a 6B piping tip and piping bag. Top each one with a mini Oreo cookie. Be sure to add the mini cookie right before serving, or else it will soften.

Makes: 24 cupcakes

For the Cupcakes

1 (15.25-oz [432-g]) box white cake mix

½ cup (120 ml) vegetable oil

1 cup (240 ml) buttermilk

3 eggs

½ cup (57 g) finely chopped Oreo cookies

For the Frosting

1 cup (227 g) salted butter, softened

4 cups (480 g) powdered sugar, divided

5 tbsp (75 ml) heavy cream

2 tsp (10 ml) vanilla extract

½ cup (57 g) ground Oreo cookies (very fine crumbs)

24 mini Oreo cookies, for decoration

PARTY TIME BUNDT CAKE

It's party time, and this sweet Bundt cake is the star of the show. If you're not a frosting fan, this is the perfect alternative for you. It's packed full of sprinkles and cookies, and has a light dusting of powdered sugar on top. What I love most about this Bundt cake is the texture. It has a lightly crisp and caramelized outside and a soft, fluffy inside. I'm 100 percent a frosting fan, but this party time Bundt cake is just as tasty as any frosting-covered layer cake. I promise!

Preheat the oven to 350°F (177°C). Prepare a 10-inch (25-cm) round Bundt pan with baking spray (the kind with flour in it) or generously grease the pan with butter.

In a large mixing bowl, combine the cake mix, pudding mix, oil, egg whites and milk, and mix until smooth and well combined. With a spatula, gently fold in the Oreo cookies and sprinkles.

Spread the cake batter into the pan and bake for 40 minutes. Take a look, and if the top of the cake is getting dark, tent it with aluminum foil to prevent over-browning. You don't have to wrap the pan tightly with the foil, just cover it lightly. Put the pan back in the oven and allow it to bake for another 5 to 10 minutes, or until a toothpick comes out clean.

Remove it from the oven and let it cool in the Bundt pan on a wire rack for 1 hour. Then flip the cake onto a plate, remove the pan and let it cool completely. Dust the top with powdered sugar and serve. My favorite way to dust powdered sugar is to use a mini dusting wand, sieve or sifter.

Makes: 12–16 slices

1 (15.25-oz [432-g]) box Funfetti® cake mix

1 (3.4-oz [96-g]) box instant vanilla pudding mix

1 cup (240 ml) vegetable oil

4 egg whites

½ cup (120 ml) milk

18 coarsely chopped Oreo cookies*

⅓ cup (64 g) rainbow sprinkles

Powdered sugar, for dusting

*You can use regular or Double Stuf (my favorite)!

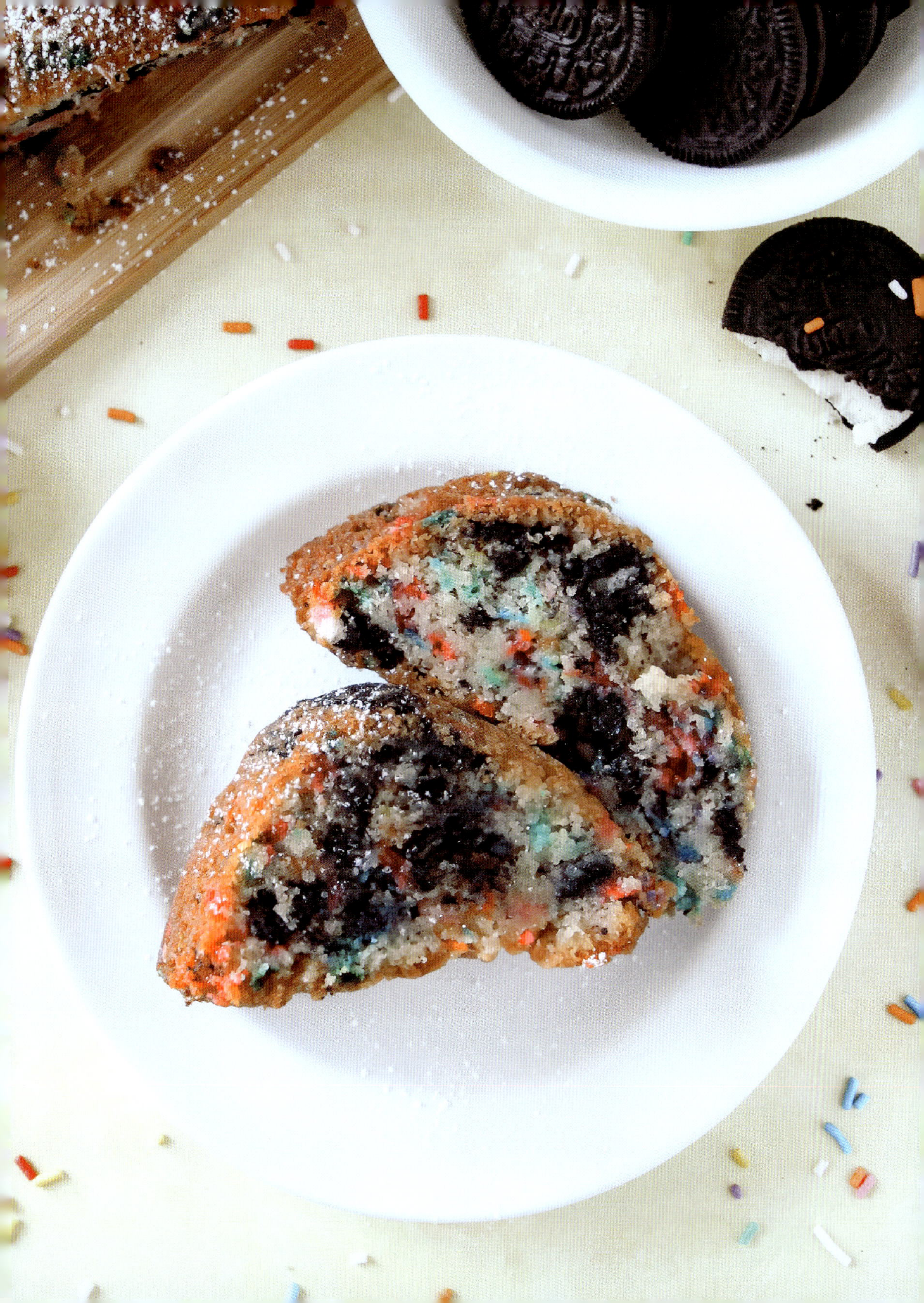

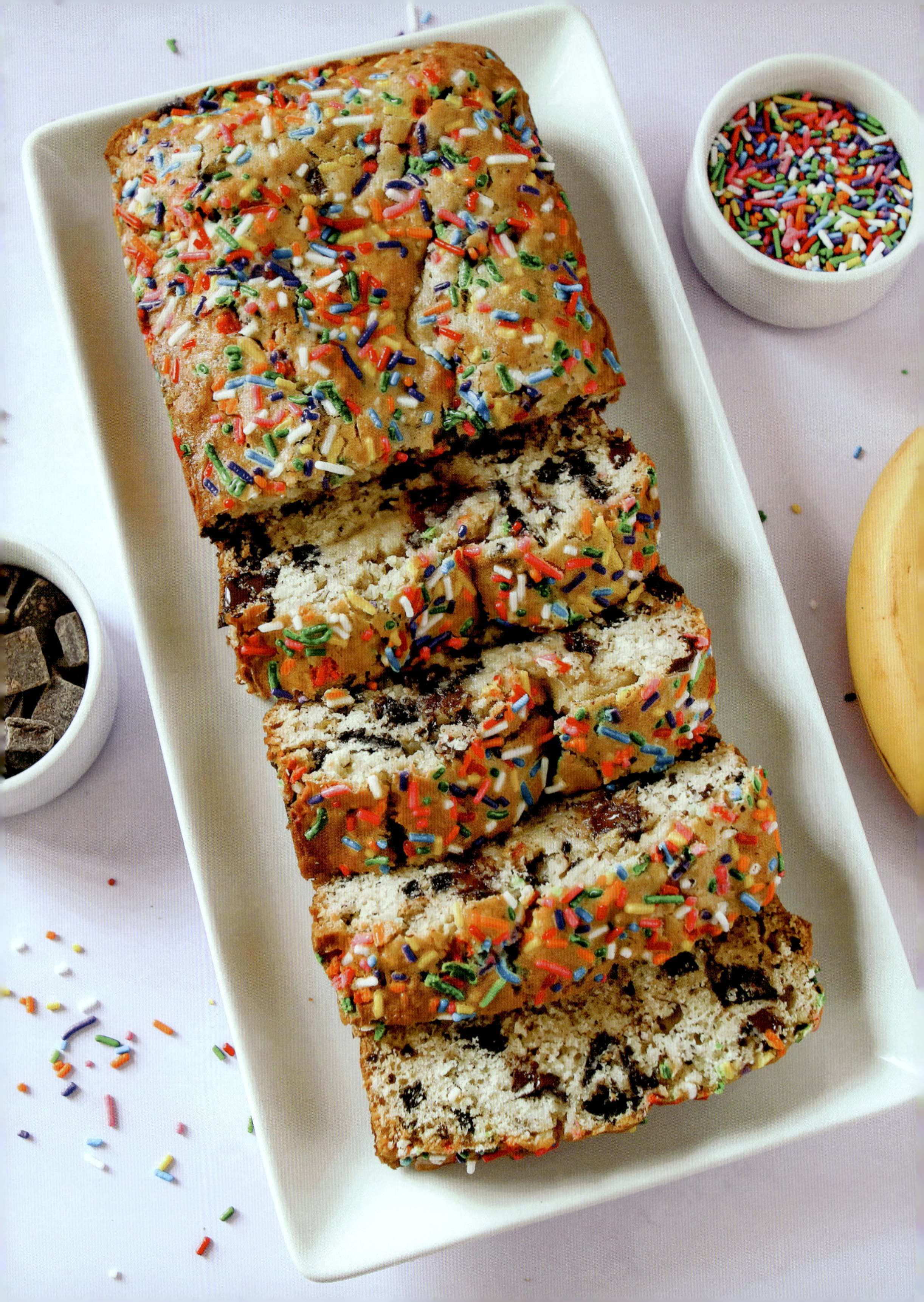

CHOCOLATE COOKIE BANANA BREAD

Years ago, a friend from work gave me a banana bread recipe, and over time, I experimented with all sorts of flavors. This is by far my favorite, and it's absolutely delicious. It has the traditional sweet and comforting banana bread base, but it's loaded with chocolate chunks and sandwich cookies. I describe it as a dessert-style banana bread. Dress it up with a chocolate drizzle, a scoop of ice cream or both!

Preheat the oven to 350°F (177°C). Prepare a 9 x 5–inch (23 x 13–cm) loaf pan with baking spray, then line the bottom with two strips of parchment paper in a crisscross pattern with the edges hanging over. This makes it easier to pull the bread out. Spray again with baking spray after the sheets are in place.

In a large mixing bowl, mash the bananas until they are mostly smooth. It's okay to have small chunks. Stir in the melted butter. Add the sugar, egg, vanilla, baking soda and salt, and mix until combined. Slowly add the flour and mix until just combined. Be careful not to overmix the batter at this point. Gently fold in the chopped Oreo cookies and chocolate chunks. Pour the batter into the prepared loaf pan and top with rainbow sprinkles.

Bake for 25 to 28 minutes, or until a toothpick comes out clean. The top of the banana bread should be a light golden brown.

Allow the bread to cool for 10 minutes in the pan before removing it to a wire rack to fully cool. Slice, serve and enjoy! Store leftover banana bread in an airtight container at room temperature for up to 5 days.

Makes: 12 slices

2 large overripe bananas

⅓ cup (80 ml) melted butter, slightly cooled

¾ cup (150 g) granulated sugar

1 egg, beaten

1 tsp vanilla extract

½ tsp baking soda

⅛ tsp salt

1½ cups + 1 tbsp (188 g) pastry flour or cake flour*

6 Oreo cookies, chopped into small pieces

½ cup (84 g) dark or milk chocolate chunks

Rainbow sprinkles, for topping

*If you use all-purpose flour, use 1½ cups (188 g).

FROSTED ANIMAL COOKIE BLONDIES

I never thought I could love a blondie as much as I love brownies, but these completely changed my mind. A lot of people refer to blondies as vanilla brownies, so I decided to give these a birthday cake vibe. They're filled with chopped frosted animal cookies, and if you haven't tried them, they're so tasty. I threw in extra white chocolate chips and sprinkled nonpareils on top. Now these are definitely a sweet treat, so if you're missing the chocolate addition, sub milk or dark chocolate chips for the white chocolate. Either way, you'll now be a fan of both brownies and blondies!

Preheat the oven to 350°F (177°C). Prepare a 9 x 13–inch (23 x 33–cm) pan with baking spray (the kind with flour in it).

In a medium bowl, whisk together the flour, baking powder, cornstarch and salt. In a stand mixer or using a mixing bowl and hand mixer, beat the butter and sugars until light and fluffy. Add the vanilla and then the eggs, one at a time, and beat until incorporated.

Slowly mix in the dry ingredients and beat until just combined. Fold in the white chocolate chips and ½ cup (64 g) of the animal cookies. The cookies should be chopped small, about the size of a chocolate chip. Press the batter into the prepared pan. It is very, very sticky, so if needed, spray a spatula with baking spray to smooth out the batter. Sprinkle the nonpareils on top and then lightly press in the remaining cookies.

Bake for 22 to 25 minutes, or until golden brown. Let them cool completely in the pan, cut them into squares and serve.

Makes: 32 squares

2 cups (240 g) all-purpose flour

¾ tsp baking powder

1 tsp cornstarch

½ tsp kosher salt

¾ cup (170 g) salted butter, softened

1 cup (200 g) granulated sugar

½ cup (100 g) packed brown sugar

2 tsp (10 ml) vanilla extract

2 large eggs

½ cup (84 g) white chocolate chips

1 cup (127 g) finely chopped frosted animal cookies, divided

Rainbow nonpareils, for sprinkling

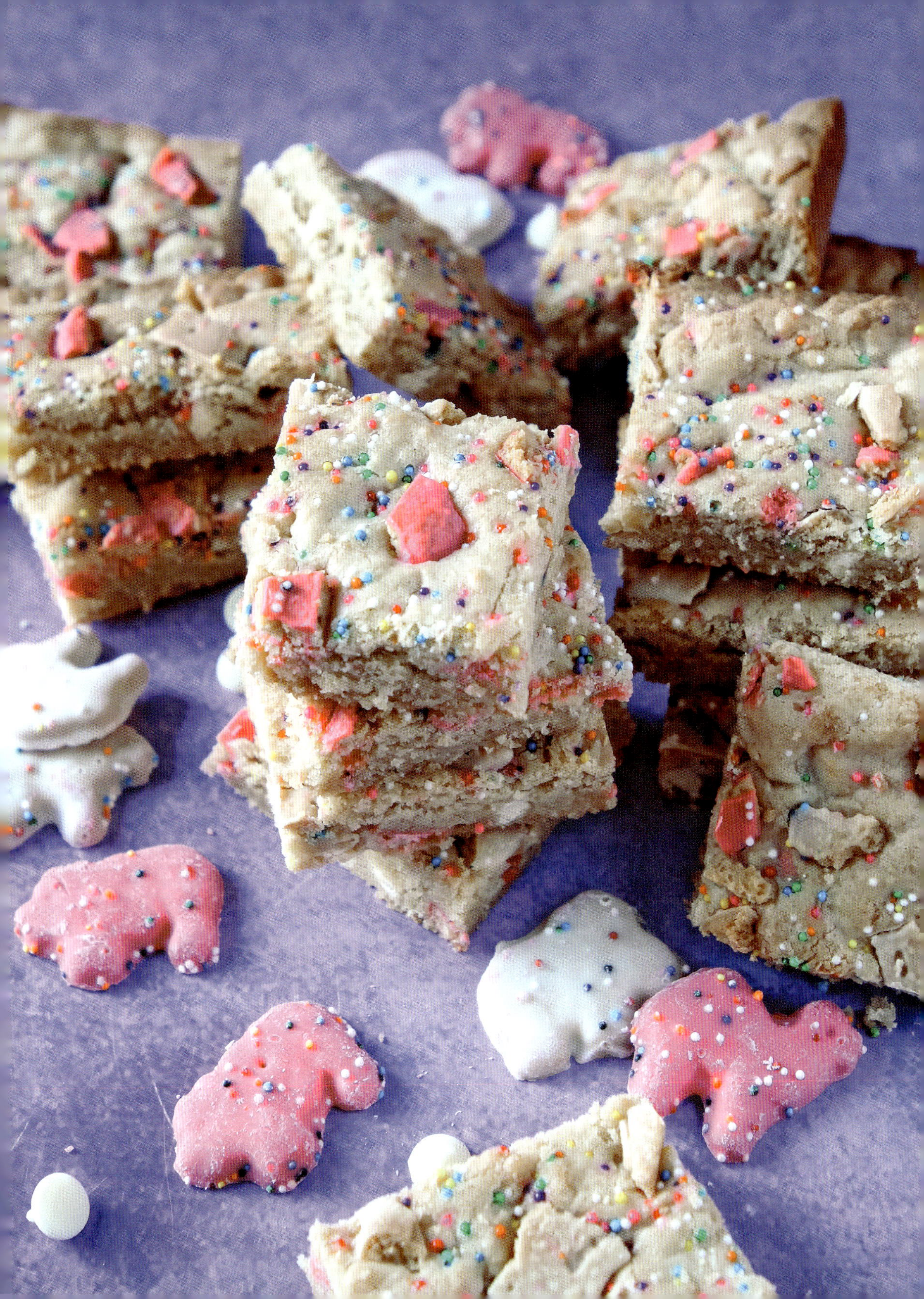

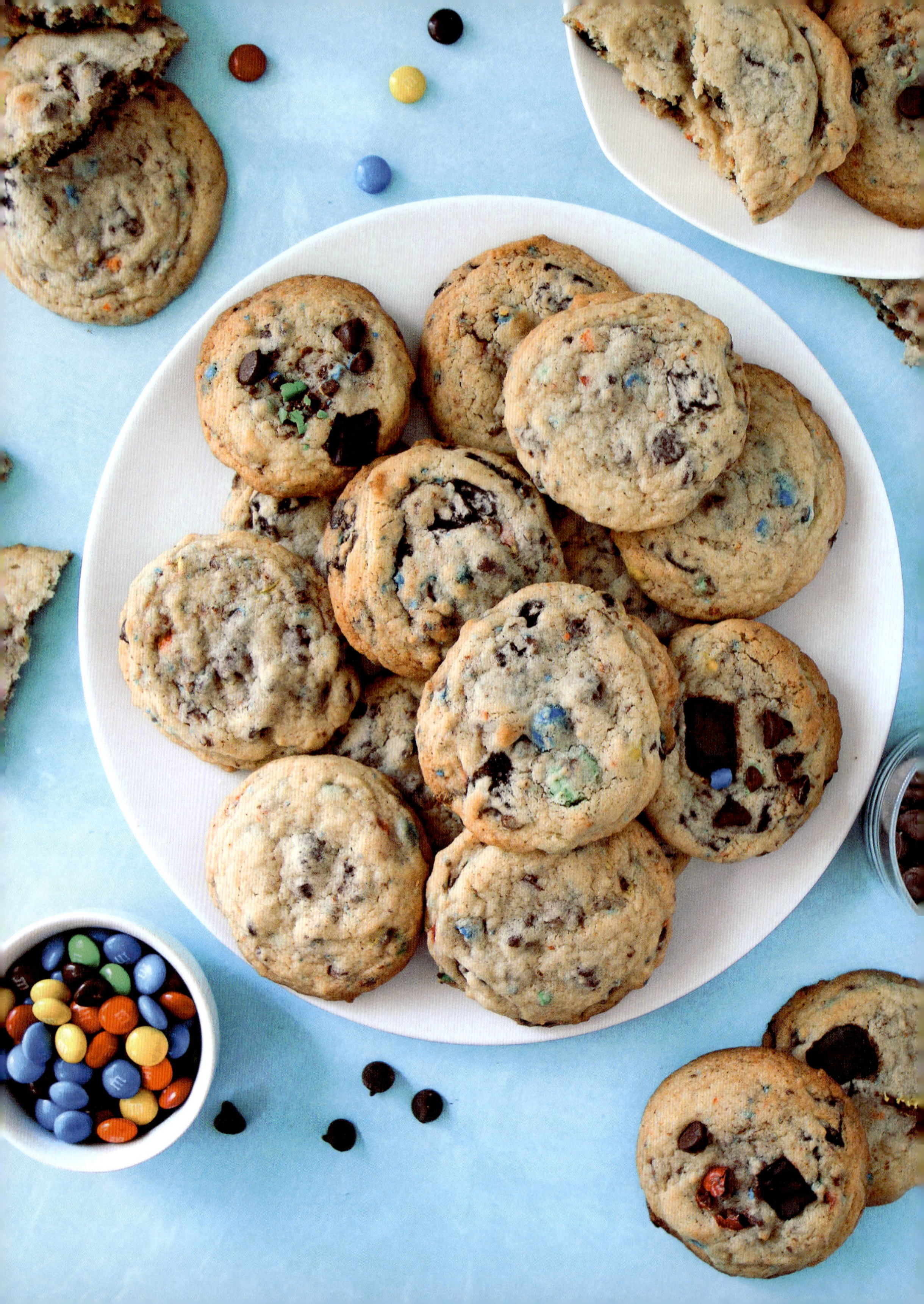

M&M'S CHOCOLATE CHUNK COOKIES

This is my go-to cookie recipe for all of my daughter's special events. They're super simple, super chocolatey and super satisfying. They're a hit with kids and adults alike, so all of my bases are covered! My favorite part is the amount of chocolate in each cookie. They're filled with both semisweet chips and chocolate chunks, which gives you the perfect amount of chocolate in every bite. Want to put a spin on them? Switch out the regular M&M's for peanut butter or a seasonal flavor!

Preheat the oven to 375°F (191°C). Line two baking sheets with parchment paper.

Place the butter and both sugars in a bowl. You can either use a stand mixer or a medium-sized bowl and a hand mixer. Cream the butter and sugars together on high speed for 2 to 3 minutes, or until light and fluffy. Add the eggs in, one at a time, mixing after each egg. Add the vanilla and mix until fully combined and smooth.

(continued)

Makes: 26–28 cookies

1 cup (227 g) salted butter, softened

1 cup (220 g) light brown sugar

½ cup (100 g) granulated sugar

2 eggs

1 tsp vanilla extract

RECIPES FOR BAKE SALES, PARTIES AND MAKING MEMORIES

M&M'S CHOCOLATE CHUNK COOKIES (CONTINUED)

In a separate bowl, whisk together the flour, baking soda and salt. Add this dry mixture to the wet mixture, little by little, until fully mixed. You can either pour it into your stand mixer on low speed, or add it to your bowl in three or four intervals and mix it with the hand mixer after each addition. Continue mixing until a dough forms. Gently fold in the chocolate chips, chocolate chunks and M&M's.

Using a 2-inch (5-cm) cookie scoop, add scoops of dough onto the prepared sheets 2 inches (5 cm) apart. Make sure that they are level scoops, but not overly packed. They should resemble ice cream scoops.

Bake the cookies for 10 minutes, or until the edges are lightly golden brown. Let them cool on the pan for 3 to 5 minutes, and then move them to wire racks to finish cooling completely.

2⅔ cups (333 g) all-purpose flour

1 tsp baking soda

1 tsp salt

4 oz (113 g) semisweet chocolate chips

4 oz (113 g) dark chocolate chunks

⅔ cup (111 g) coarsely crushed M&M's*

*To coarsely crush the M&M's, I place them in a resealable bag and use a kitchen mallet to crush them. Alternatively, you can add them to a food processor and pulse for a couple of seconds.

TRIPLE-LAYER CHOCOLATE BARS

I would love to write an entire cookbook on layered dessert bars. There's simply no end to the fun combinations of different flavors and textures. Sweet, salty, smooth and crunchy—the perfect layered bar has every single element. These triple-layer chocolate bars are based on a favorite treat of my friend Katie. I made her recipe a few years ago and decided to put a decadent dark chocolate spin on it! It starts with a crunchy chocolate, almond and coconut base. Next, it's topped with a smooth layer of chocolate frosting and finished with a creamy dark chocolate ganache. These have the perfect balance of sweetness, and any Mounds® bar fans will flip over them. (PS: My friend recipe-tested these, and they're Katie approved!)

Makes: 16 squares

Line the bottom of an 8-inch (20-cm) square pan with two strips of parchment paper in a crisscross pattern with the edges hanging over. This makes it easier to pull the bars out. Spray with baking spray after the sheets are in place.

To make the base, in a medium saucepan, melt the butter, sugar and cocoa powder over medium-low heat. Add the egg, and stir it right away so that the heat doesn't cook the egg. Mix for 1 to 2 minutes, or until it thickens. Remove the pot from the heat, then add the graham cracker crumbs, coconut and almonds, and stir until combined. Pour the mixture into the prepared pan and press it into an even layer. Place it into the fridge while you make the frosting.

(continued)

For the Base

½ cup (114 g) salted butter

¼ cup (50 g) granulated sugar

5 tbsp (25 g) dark cocoa powder

1 egg, beaten

1¾ cups (210 g) graham cracker crumbs

1 cup (93 g) sweetened shredded coconut

½ cup (72 g) chopped almonds

TRIPLE-LAYER CHOCOLATE BARS (CONTINUED)

To make the frosting, in a mixing bowl, beat the butter for 5 minutes, or until smooth. Add 1 cup (120 g) of the powdered sugar and mix for 1 minute. Add the remaining powdered sugar, cocoa powder, heavy cream and vanilla, and beat for 5 minutes, or until smooth. Spread the frosting evenly over the base layer and return it to the refrigerator.

To make the topping, in a small microwave-safe bowl, heat the heavy cream for 45 seconds, or until it starts to bubble. Remove it from the microwave and add the chocolate chips. Let this sit for 60 seconds, and then stir with a whisk until smooth. Spread the chocolate ganache on top of the frosting layer.

Refrigerate for at least 1 hour, or until the chocolate layer is set, ideally overnight. The longer you leave this, the nicer it will cut! Remove from the fridge, top with chocolate sprinkles, slice into bars and serve.

For the Frosting

½ cup (114 g) salted butter, softened

2 cups (240 g) powdered sugar, divided

2 tbsp (11 g) dark cocoa powder

3–4 tbsp (45–60 ml) heavy cream

1 tsp vanilla extract

For the Topping

¼ cup (60 ml) heavy cream

4 oz (113 g) dark chocolate chips

Chocolate sprinkles, for topping

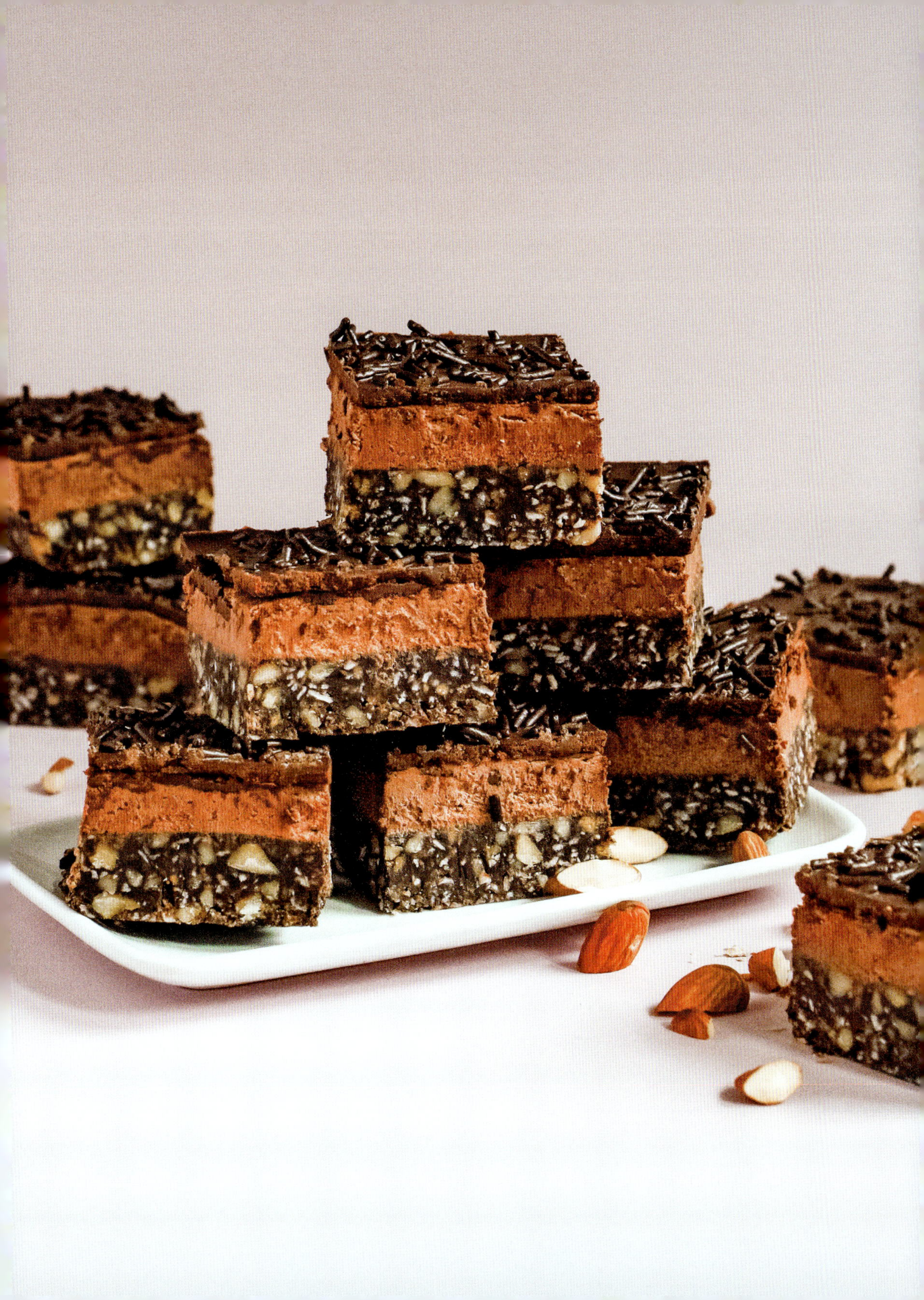

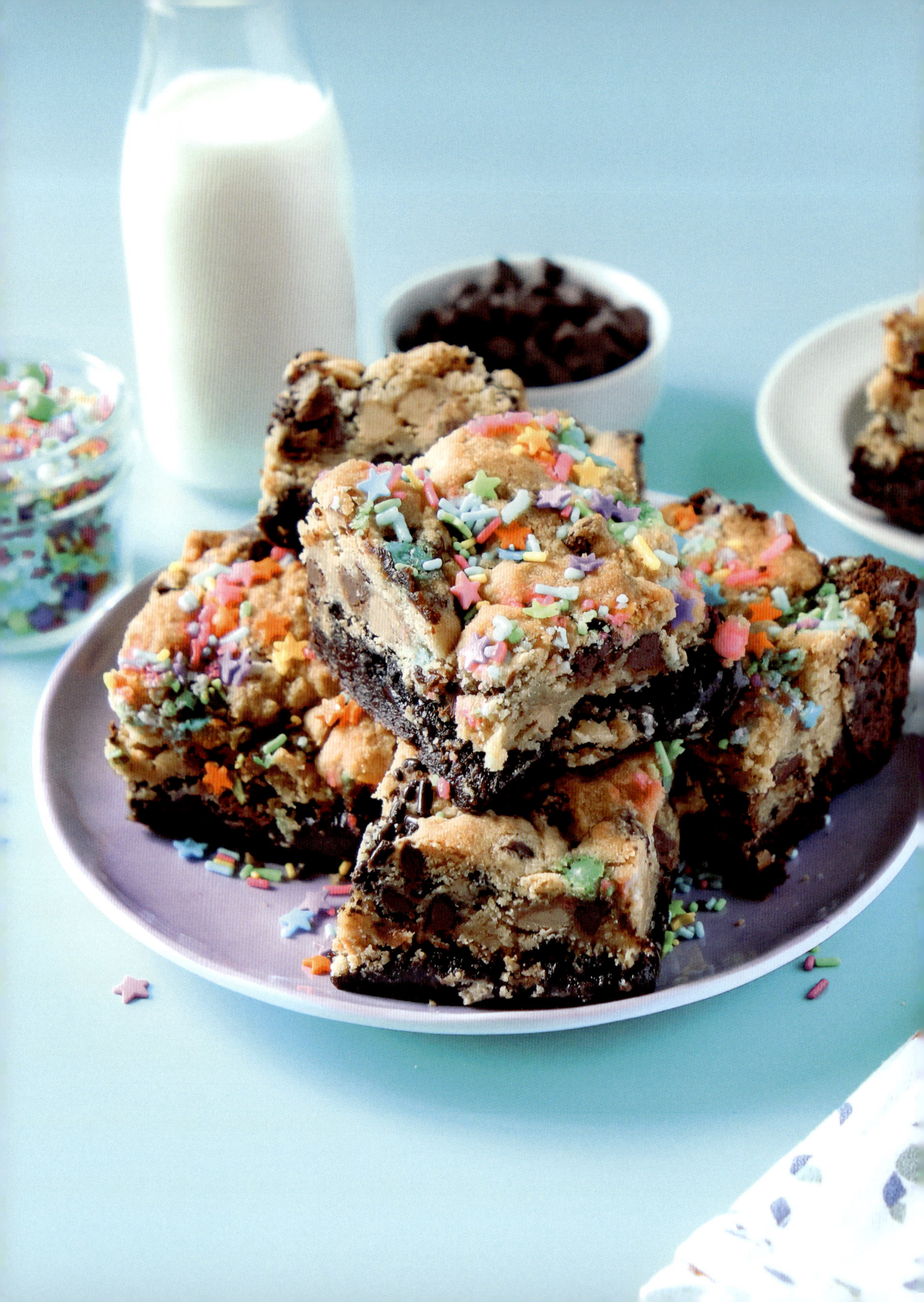

JUMBO BROOKIES

If you've never had a brookie before, it's a genius combination of a brownie and a cookie. These are jumbo brookies, and I assure you they are super easy! All you need are two classic box mixes—chocolate brownies and chocolate chip cookies—and a few other friends in the cookie family. I used chopped Oreos and Nutter Butter® cookies, but if you aren't a fan of any of these, just swap them out! Chips Ahoy!®, flavored Oreo cookies or Keebler® Fudge Stripes™ would all be delicious.

Makes: 9 brookies

1 (18-oz [510-g]) box double chocolate brownie mix*

4 Oreo Dark Chocolate Flavor Creme cookies, crushed**

4 Nutter Butter cookies, crushed**

1 (17.5-oz [496-g]) package Betty Crocker™ Chocolate Chip Cookie Mix*

⅓ cup (55 g) peanut butter chips

Chocolate or colorful sprinkles, for topping

Preheat the oven to 350°F (177°C). Prepare an 8-inch (20-cm) square pan with baking spray. (I love the baking spray that has flour in it, but regular baking spray will also work.) Line the bottom of the pan with two strips of parchment paper in a crisscross pattern with the edges hanging over. This makes it easier to pull the brookies out. Spray again with baking spray after the sheets are in place.

Make the brownie batter according to the directions on the package. Pour the batter into the prepared pan. Spread the crushed cookies on top of the brownie layer, gently pressing them in.

Make the chocolate chip cookie dough according to the package instructions. Fold in the peanut butter chips. Add the dough on top of the crushed cookie layer. I find that the easiest way to do this is to take pinches of the cookie dough, flatten it between my palms and lay it on top of the crushed cookies. Cover the brownie/cookie layer the best you can, but it doesn't have to be perfect. The cookies will spread during the baking process. Add the sprinkles to the top—as many or as little as you'd like!

Bake for 40 to 45 minutes, or just until the top is lightly golden brown. Tent the pan lightly with aluminum foil and bake for 5 to 10 minutes, or until a deeper golden brown. This will give them a crunchy outer layer and fudgy center.

Move the pan to a wire rack, remove the foil and allow the brookies to cool completely in the pan before removing. Slice into squares and serve.

*Plus the ingredients listed on the package.

**The easiest way to crush the cookies is to place them in a plastic bag and break them up using a kitchen mallet, rolling pin or the back of a large spoon.

PEANUT BUTTER FUDGE COOKIE CUPS

We are regulars at the local cookie shop in the mall, and one of our favorites is the classic peanut butter cookie cup with fudge filling. It tastes as good as it sounds! I recreated them with a few simple steps and homemade chocolate fudge frosting. Psst! Be sure to save this chocolate buttercream recipe to use on cakes and cupcakes. I promise you'll want to add this frosting to everything! And per usual, each cookie cup is topped with chocolate sprinkles for an extra sweet crunch.

Preheat the oven to 350°F (177°C). Prepare a mini muffin tin with baking spray. Be sure to generously spray the entire tin and not just the cups. Sometimes the cookies bake taller than the tin cavities, so you want to make sure that they don't stick to the bottom of the pan.

Roll each square of cookie dough into a ball with your hands, and place them into the mini muffin cups. With your knuckle or a teaspoon, lightly press in the center of each ball. You want to make a slight indentation in each cookie. This step will be repeated after they bake. Bake them according to the package instructions, and let them cool completely. I used the baking time for regular cookies, and it worked perfectly!

Meanwhile, in a stand mixer or large mixing bowl with a handheld mixer, beat the butter for 2 minutes, or until smooth. Add 1 cup (120 g) of the powdered sugar and mix. Add the remaining powdered sugar, cocoa powder, Nutella and heavy cream, and mix until fully incorporated.

Fit a disposable piping bag with a 1M tip. Place the piping bag in a cup, making sure to hang the edges of the bag over the sides of the cup. Add the frosting to the bag, remove it from the cup and push all of the frosting towards the bottom by the tip so that you can twist the bag closed. Pipe a swirl of frosting onto each cookie cup and top with chocolate sprinkles. You could also simply add spoonfuls of frosting to each cookie cup.

Makes: 24 cookie cups

1 (16-oz [454-g]) package peanut butter cookie dough (such as Pillsbury™ Reese's Peanut Butter Cookie Dough Eat or Bake)

½ cup (114 g) salted butter

2 cups (240 g) powdered sugar, divided

2 tbsp (11 g) cocoa powder

2 tbsp (37 g) Nutella

2–3 tbsp (30–45 ml) heavy cream

Chocolate sprinkles, for topping

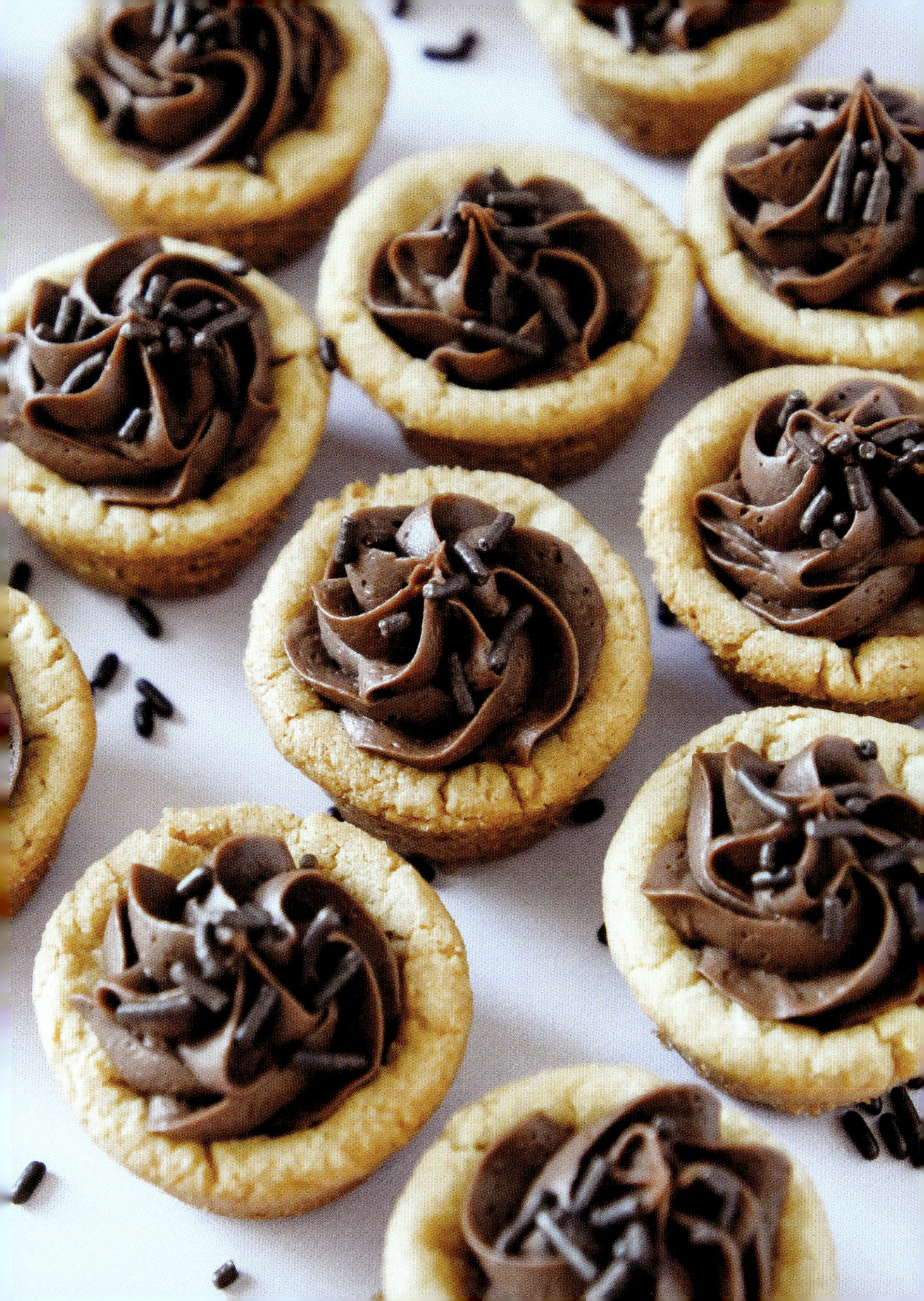

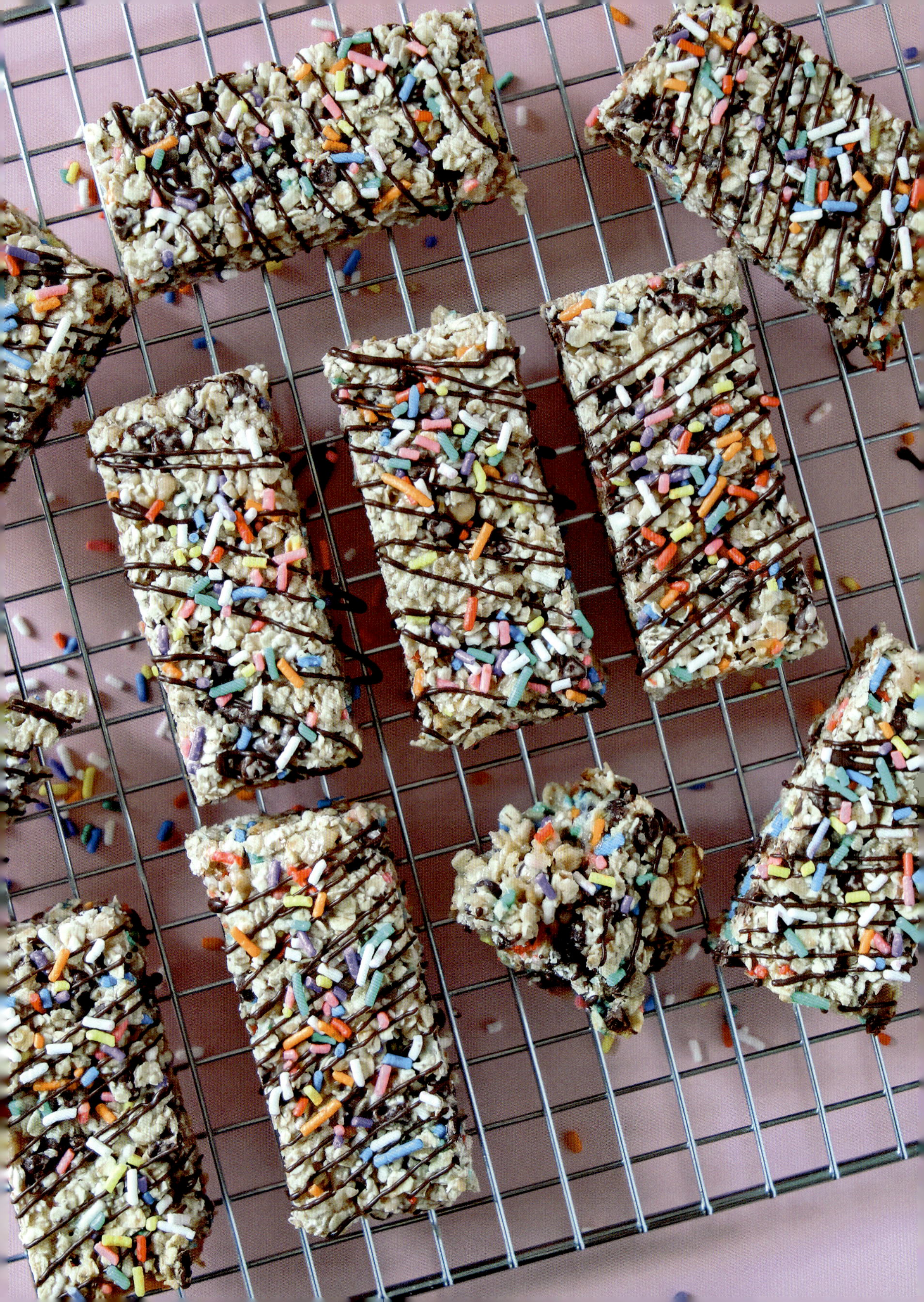

SWEET AND CHEWY GRANOLA BARS

These aren't just granola bars; I truly believe they can also double as the perfect party snack. Filled with toffee, chocolate chips and colorful rainbow sprinkles, these are such a treat! It's a recipe that I adapted from a friend years ago that also happens to be my kryptonite. I can't stop eating them, they are that good. I describe them as a dessert-style granola bar with an extra chewy texture. I've tried so many mix-ins, and they're all super tasty, so get creative and switch them up. Then you'll have an excuse to make them over and over again!

Preheat the oven to 350°F (177°C). Prepare a 9 x 13–inch (23 x 33–cm) pan with baking spray. Line the bottom of the pan with two strips of parchment paper in a crisscross pattern with the edges hanging over. This makes it easier to pull the bars out. Spray again with baking spray after the sheets are in place.

In a large mixing bowl, add the oats, condensed milk, butter, chocolate chips, toffee and sprinkles, and mix until they are all fully combined. Press the mixture into the prepared pan, and flatten the top with a spoon or spatula if needed.

Bake for 20 to 24 minutes, or until lightly browned. Let the granola cool completely in the pan. Then, lift the granola out of the pan and place it on a cutting board. Cut into 20 bars. Drizzle each bar with melted chocolate (if using) and add extra sprinkles. Serve right away or refrigerate until ready to eat.

Makes: 20 bars

3 cups (240 g) quick-cooking oats

1 (14-oz [300-ml]) can sweetened condensed milk

2 tbsp (30 ml) melted butter

1 cup (168 g) mini chocolate chips

1 cup (250 g) toffee bits

½ cup (96 g) rainbow sprinkles, plus extra for topping

Melted chocolate, for topping (optional)

CRUNCHY COOKIE BARK STICKS

What started off as a total experiment turned into one of my favorite desserts ever. It's not quite biscotti but not quite a cookie either; they're more of a crispy biscotti-cookie mashup. I decided to name this recipe Crunchy Cookie Bark Sticks because they have a longer rectangle shape, a perfect crunchy and chewy texture and a thinner cookie base. I used dried cranberries for this recipe, but you can always substitute dried cherries if you prefer. I absolutely love the texture of dried fruit in any sort of cookie or biscotti. For this cookie bark, it's the ultimate contrast to the chocolate chip cookie dough and white chocolate chips.

Makes: 16–18 pieces

1 (16.5-oz [468-g]) tube refrigerated chocolate chip cookie dough, room temperature

½ cup (84 g) white chocolate chips, plus more for topping (optional)

½ cup (61 g) dried cranberries or cherries

Sparkling sugar, for topping (optional)

Preheat the oven to 375°F (191°C). Line a baking sheet with parchment paper.

In a large mixing bowl, combine the cookie dough, chocolate chips and dried cranberries. Place the dough onto the baking sheet, and, using your hands, form it into a 3 x 13–inch (8 x 33–cm) rectangle. It doesn't have to be perfect, but try to make sure it's fairly even throughout. Worst case scenario, you'll have crispier ends, but they happen to be my favorite.

Bake for 15 to 16 minutes, or until lightly golden brown. Remove it from the oven and then, with a spatula or butter knife, gently reshape the dough to smoothen the edges. It should end up being 5 x 14 inches (13 x 36 cm). Let it cool on the pan for 10 to 15 minutes. Cut the rectangle widthwise into strips. Move them apart a little bit on the sheet, and then bake for 5 minutes, or until a warm golden brown.

Remove them from the oven and let them cool completely. As they cool, they'll get crispy like bark. If you'd like, melt some white chocolate to drizzle on top and add some sparkling sugar.

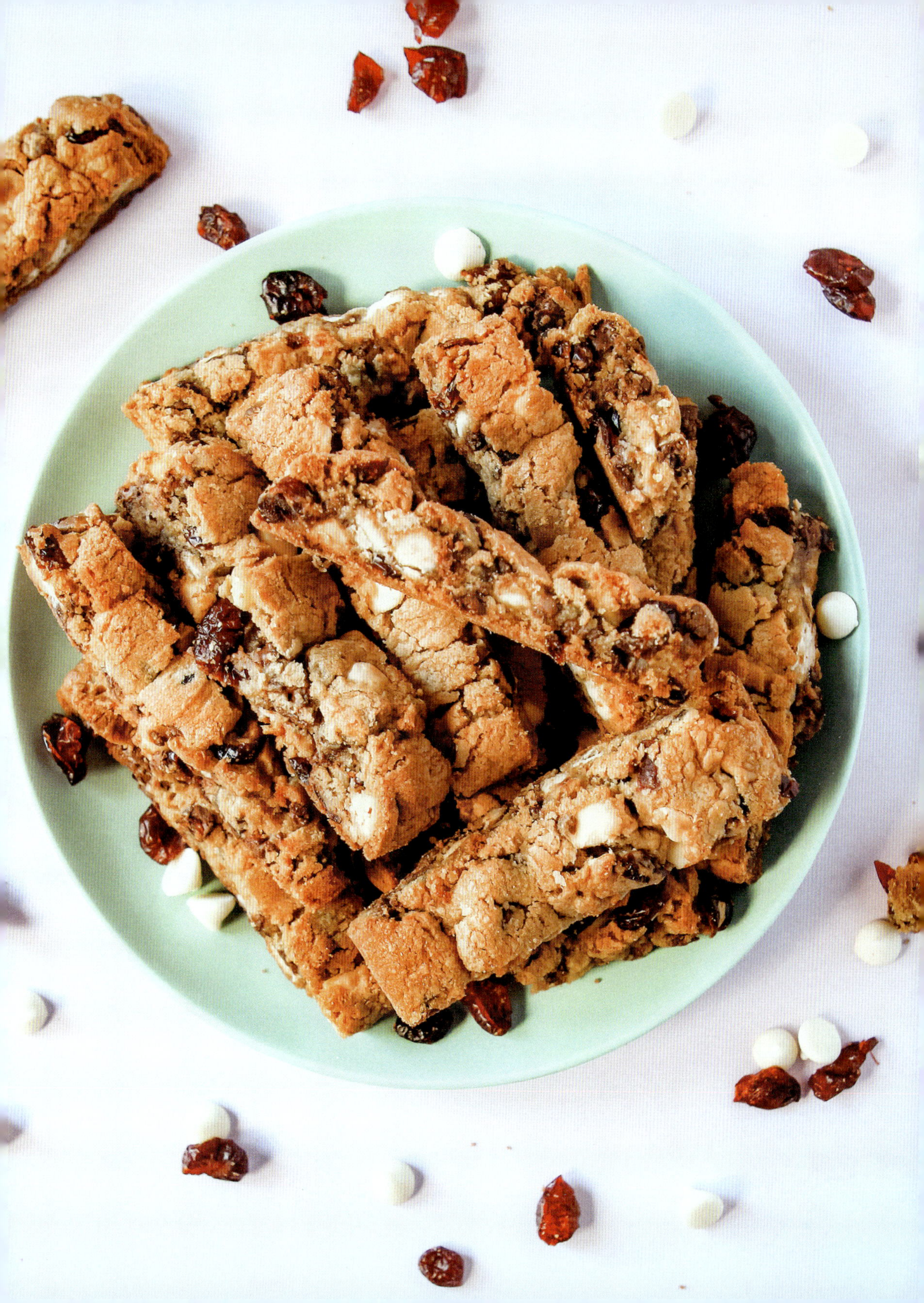

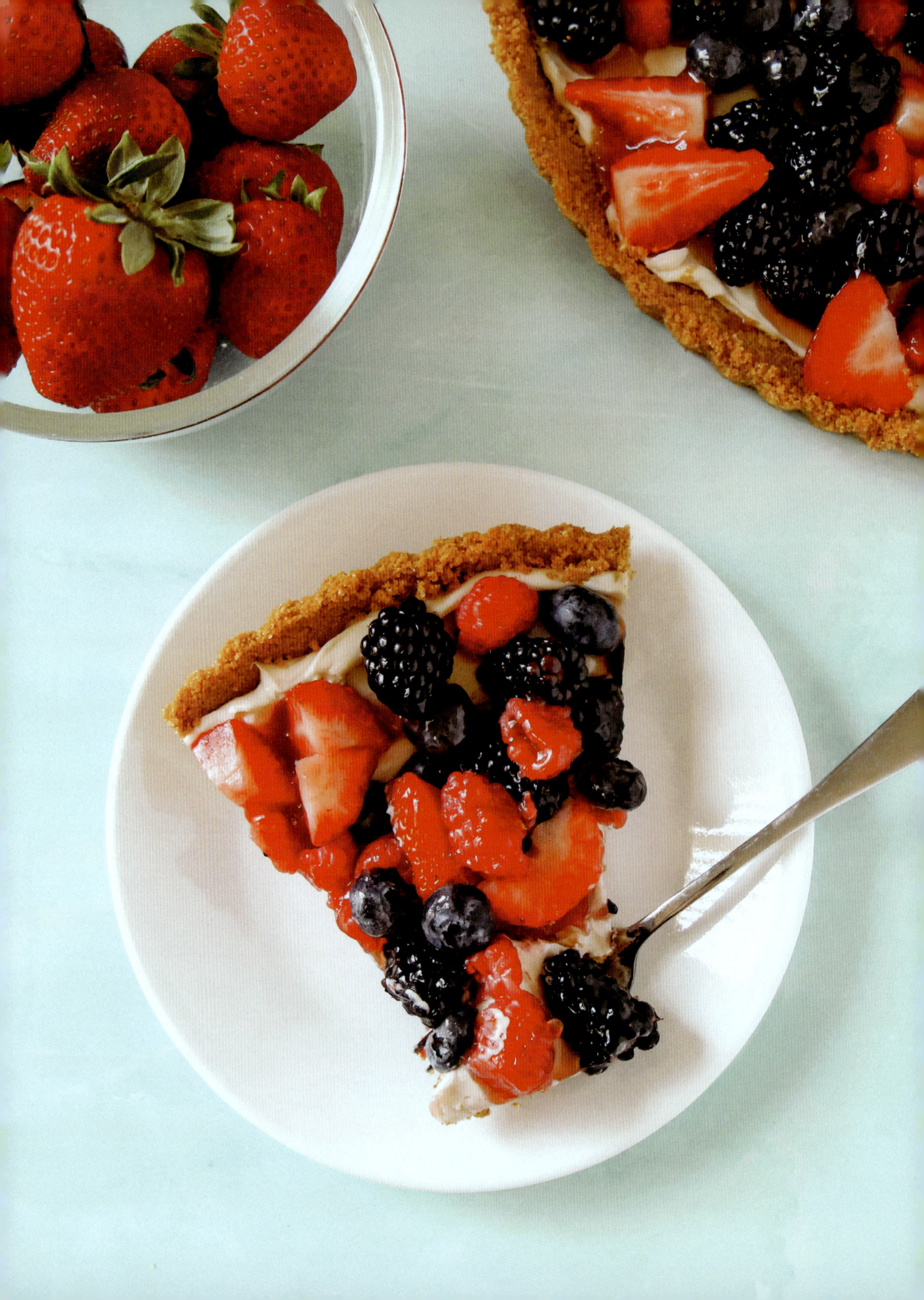

Fruity and Fun Treats

This chapter is all about fruity sweets and treats! I live in Florida, and it is HOT here the majority of the year, so I often crave fruity flavors, especially when paired with richer ingredients. A personal favorite is the Coconut Raspberry Cake Jars (page 109). The coconut and raspberry filling completely balance out the layers of buttercream. I could have written fifty more fruit-centric recipes, because there are so many wonderful dessert combos. I condensed it down to twelve that I think you'll have the fruitiest fun with! I love them all but couldn't stop "taste testing" the Orange Amaretto Sheet Cake (page 106) and the Tropical Cake Bars (page 124). The orange cake is not only great for summer, as it also makes the perfect New Year's dessert with the addition of amaretto and glitter flakes. The tropical cake bars are guaranteed to be a showstopper with their creamy base and pineapple-coconut topping. They are the epitome of summer in dessert form. I hope these recipes make all of your sunshiny days even brighter!

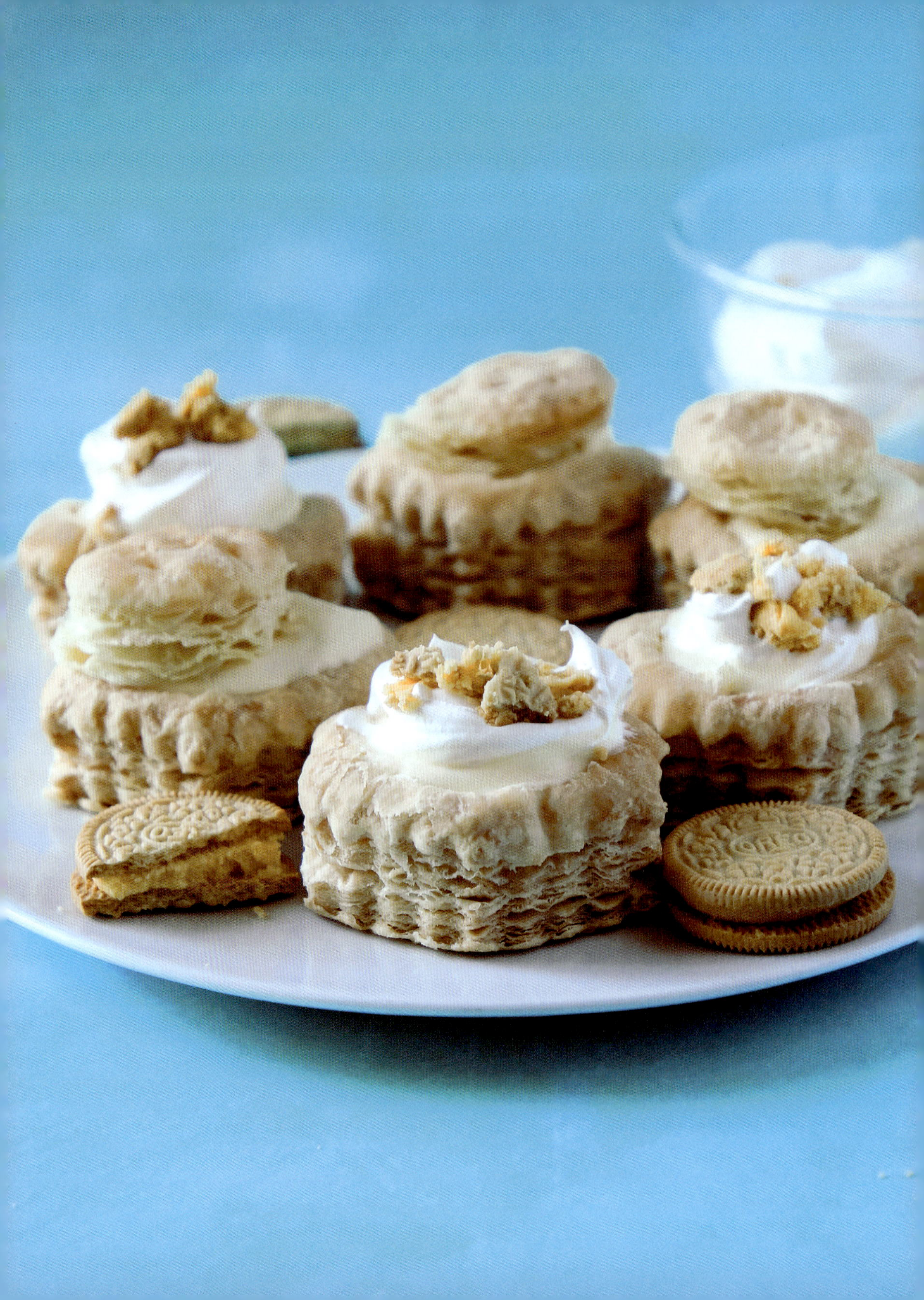
OREO

LEMON CREAM PASTRY CUPS

Every time I make these Lemon Cream Pastry Cups, people think I spent hours measuring and mixing in the kitchen. The pastry shells are actually from the freezer section of the grocery store, and they're super easy to make! They have the buttery flaky texture of classic puff pastry, and I fill them with smooth and sweet lemon pudding. They're topped with whipped cream and crushed lemon cookies, but you can experiment with different fillings or pudding flavors like chocolate fudge or pistachio. As simple as this dessert is, it'll have you looking like a pastry chef!

Makes: 12 pastries

2 (10-oz [283-g]) packages Pepperidge Farm® Puff Pastry Shells*

1 (3.4-oz [96-g]) box instant lemon pudding mix

2 cups (480 ml) cold milk

¾ cup (54 g) whipped topping

2 lemon cookies, crushed

*Each package has 6 shells.

Start by baking the puff pastry shells according to the package instructions. Be sure to keep an eye on them because they do puff up fairly quickly. Let them cool for a few minutes, and then scoop out the insides. Set the inside/tops aside to use later. Let the shells cool completely.

In a medium bowl, mix the lemon pudding mix and milk for 2 minutes, as directed on the package. Let it set for an additional 2 minutes. Refrigerate for at least 1 hour to get the pudding a bit cooler if you didn't use really cold milk.

Fill each puff pastry to the rim with lemon pudding. Top them with 1 tablespoon (9 g) of whipped topping and then a sprinkle of crushed cookies. If desired, return the tops of the puff pastry to slightly cover the whipped cream, or set them aside tilted against the pastry shell.

BANANA OATMEAL CREME PIE TRIFLE

A few years ago, I was making banana pudding, and I wanted to give it a little twist and create a really unique flavor. I couldn't stop thinking about pairing it with Little Debbie® Oatmeal Creme Pies. Turns out, they are a dream flavor combination! The oatmeal pies are perfectly chewy, sweet and spicy against the creamy banana pudding. I am a huge fan of trifles, so my trifle bowl gets used almost monthly. If you don't have one, no problem! Just use a large bowl and add all the delicious layers of chopped Oatmeal Creme Pies, sliced bananas, pudding and whipped topping.

In a medium bowl, combine the banana pudding mix, milk, vanilla and condensed milk. Gently fold in half of the whipped topping. If you can't get it completely smooth, use a whisk and gently mix until it is fully incorporated. Refrigerate the mixture overnight.

When you're ready to assemble and serve the trifle, start by placing the Oatmeal Creme Pies at the base. Cut 6 pies into eight pieces each and place in an even layer. Next, add the banana slices. Pour the banana pudding mixture on top. Spread the remaining whipped topping over the pudding and sprinkle with cinnamon. To decorate, cut the remaining pies in half and place them around the border. Serve immediately or refrigerate until ready to eat.

Makes: 1 large trifle

1 (3.4-oz [96-g]) box instant banana pudding mix

2 cups (480 ml) milk

1 tsp vanilla extract

1 (14-oz [300-ml]) can sweetened condensed milk

1 (8-oz [226-g]) container whipped topping, divided

9–10 Oatmeal Creme Pies, divided

4 bananas, sliced

Cinnamon, for sprinkling

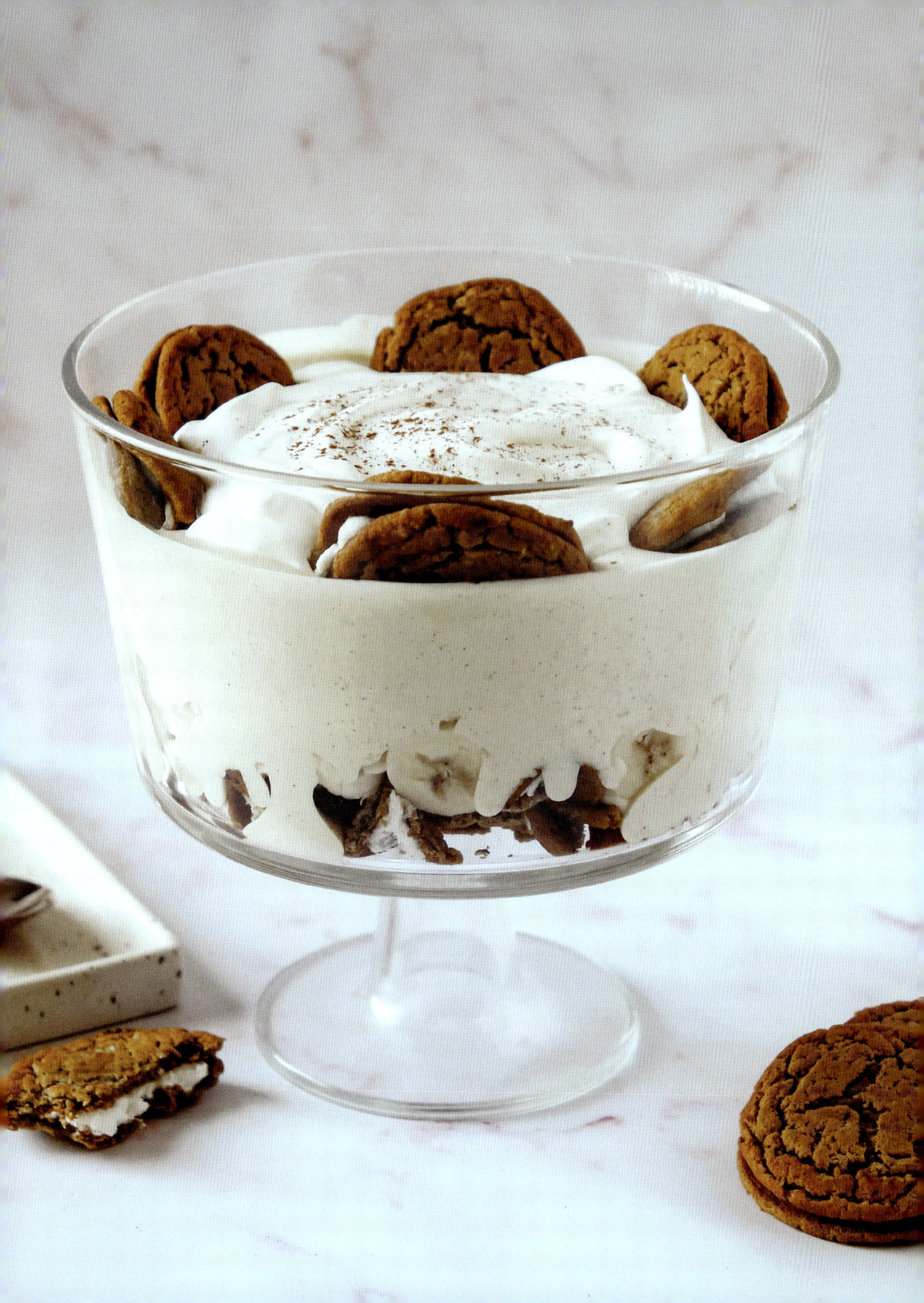

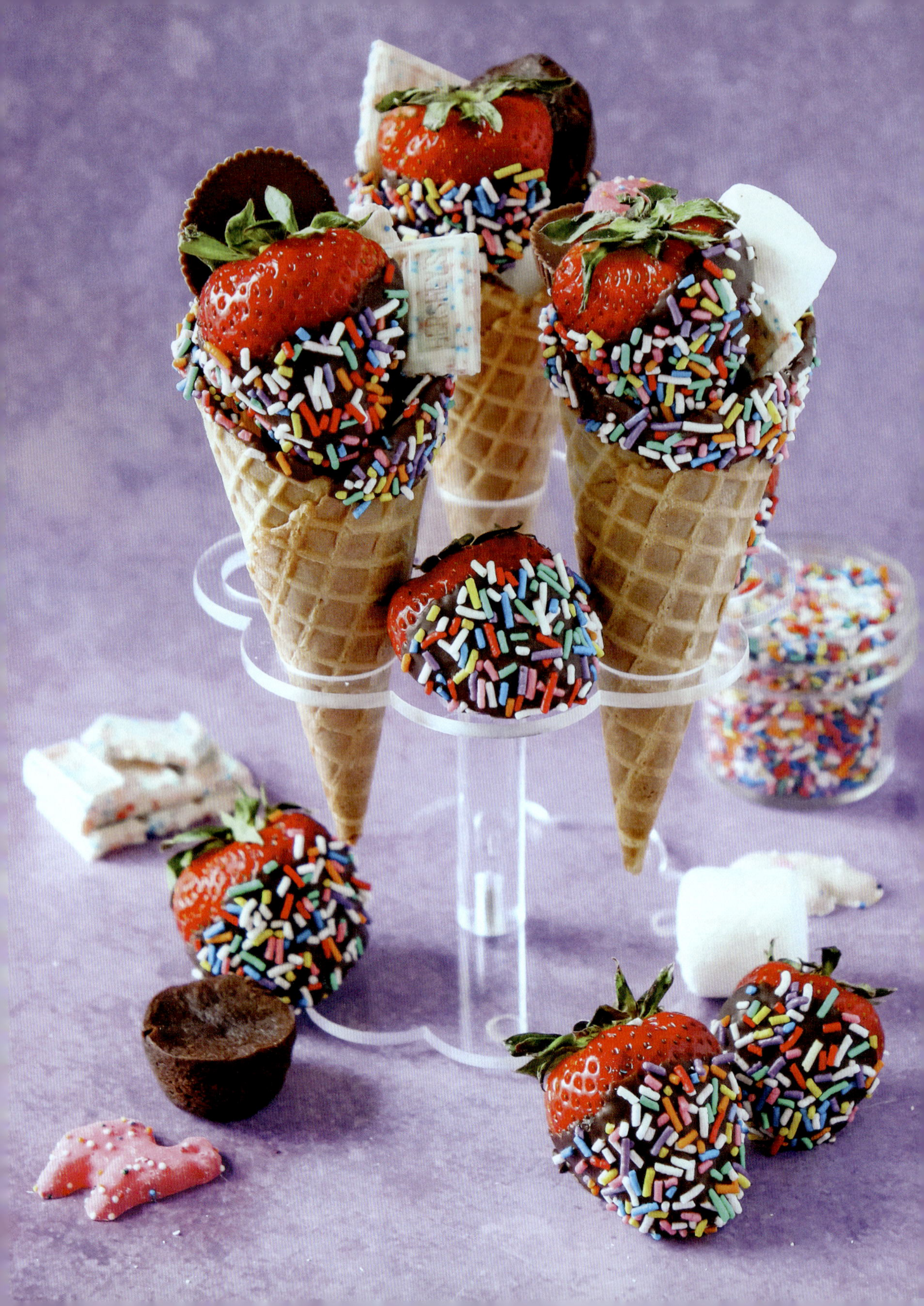

SPRINKLED AND DIPPED FRUIT CONES

There's just something about a sweet and crunchy waffle cone covered in milk chocolate and bright rainbow sprinkles that gets me excited. They can be filled with ice cream or frozen yogurt for sure, but I decided to load these up with chocolate-dipped fruit and a few extras. Get creative and dip the cones in white chocolate, or swap out some of the candy and marshmallows for other dipped fruit, like oranges!

Makes: 4 cones

1 (10-oz [284-g]) bag milk or dark chocolate melting wafers (such as Ghirardelli)

1 (10.5-oz [297-g]) container rainbow sprinkles

4 waffle cones (such as Joy® Waffle Cones)

Fruit of your choice, for dipping

Sweets such as mini marshmallows, peanut butter cups, chocolate bars or mini brownies, as needed

In the microwave, heat the melting wafers in 30-second intervals, stirring after each interval, for 90 seconds, or until fully melted. Let the chocolate cool for 5 minutes, or until it's warm but not burning hot. If it's too hot, it will slide down the cone. Chocolate that has cooled will be thicker and easier to stick.

Make sure that your cone holder (or a tall, narrow glass) is close. Set out the bowl of melted chocolate, a bowl of rainbow sprinkles and an empty bowl. Dip one waffle cone into the chocolate. Be sure to press the cone into the chocolate, so you cover the entire top portion of the cone at least 1 inch (2.5 cm) of the way down. Shake off any excess chocolate. Hold the cone over the empty bowl and gently drop the rainbow sprinkles onto the chocolate. Cover the entire chocolate portion of the cone. You may have to turn the cone a few times to make sure it's totally sprinkled! Place the cone into the cone holder. Repeat with the remaining cones. Let them set at room temperature.

Set out a cookie sheet with parchment paper to place the dipped fruit on. Using the same bowls, repeat the process with the fruit. Use your fingers to hold the fruit, or use a toothpick or skewer if you have them available. Place the dipped fruit onto the prepared cookie sheet. Let them set at room temperature.

To assemble each cone, add some of your sweets to the bottom. Place the fruit in the center, and arrange other candy or treats around the fruit. You will have to play around with the positioning to make sure that your fillings fit.

Note: I highly recommend using an ice cream cone holder when dipping cones. It helps them set faster and stay upright instead of lying flat.

ORANGE AMARETTO SHEET CAKE

Simple syrup is one of the tastiest ways to flavor a cake. It's extremely easy to make, and it adds such a great upgrade without changing the recipe. The cake layers become extra moist and have a boost of sweetness. For this cake, I made an amaretto simple syrup and poured it onto a baked yellow cake. Since the cake has the added syrup, the only topping it needs is a thin layer of buttercream. Orange frosting is the perfect pairing and gives it a light citrus flavor. I added a sprinkle of gold glitter flakes, but they don't have a taste; they're just for decoration.

Note: If you want an alcohol-free option, use regular simple syrup.

To make the simple syrup, in a small pot, combine the amaretto, sugar and water. Bring it to a boil over high heat and then reduce to a simmer. Allow the mixture to simmer for 8 to 10 minutes, or until reduced to a thick maple syrup consistency. Set aside to cool.

Preheat the oven to 350°F (177°C). Prepare a 9 x 13–inch (23 x 33–cm) baking dish with baking spray.

To make the cake, in a medium bowl, combine the cake mix, buttermilk, oil, pudding mix and eggs. Stir for 2 minutes, or until it's completely combined. Pour the batter into the prepared pan, and bake it according to the cake mix package instructions.

Remove the cake from the oven, and poke holes throughout the top using a fork. Slowly pour the simple syrup on top, making sure to coat the cake evenly. Let it soak for at least 4 hours in the refrigerator.

(continued)

Makes: 24 small or 12 large square slices

For the Simple Syrup

⅓ cup (80 ml) amaretto

⅓ cup (66 g) sugar

3 tbsp (45 ml) water

For the Cake

1 (15.25-oz [432-g]) box yellow cake mix

1 cup (240 ml) buttermilk

⅓ cup (80 ml) vegetable oil

1 (3.4-oz [96-g]) box instant vanilla pudding mix

3 eggs

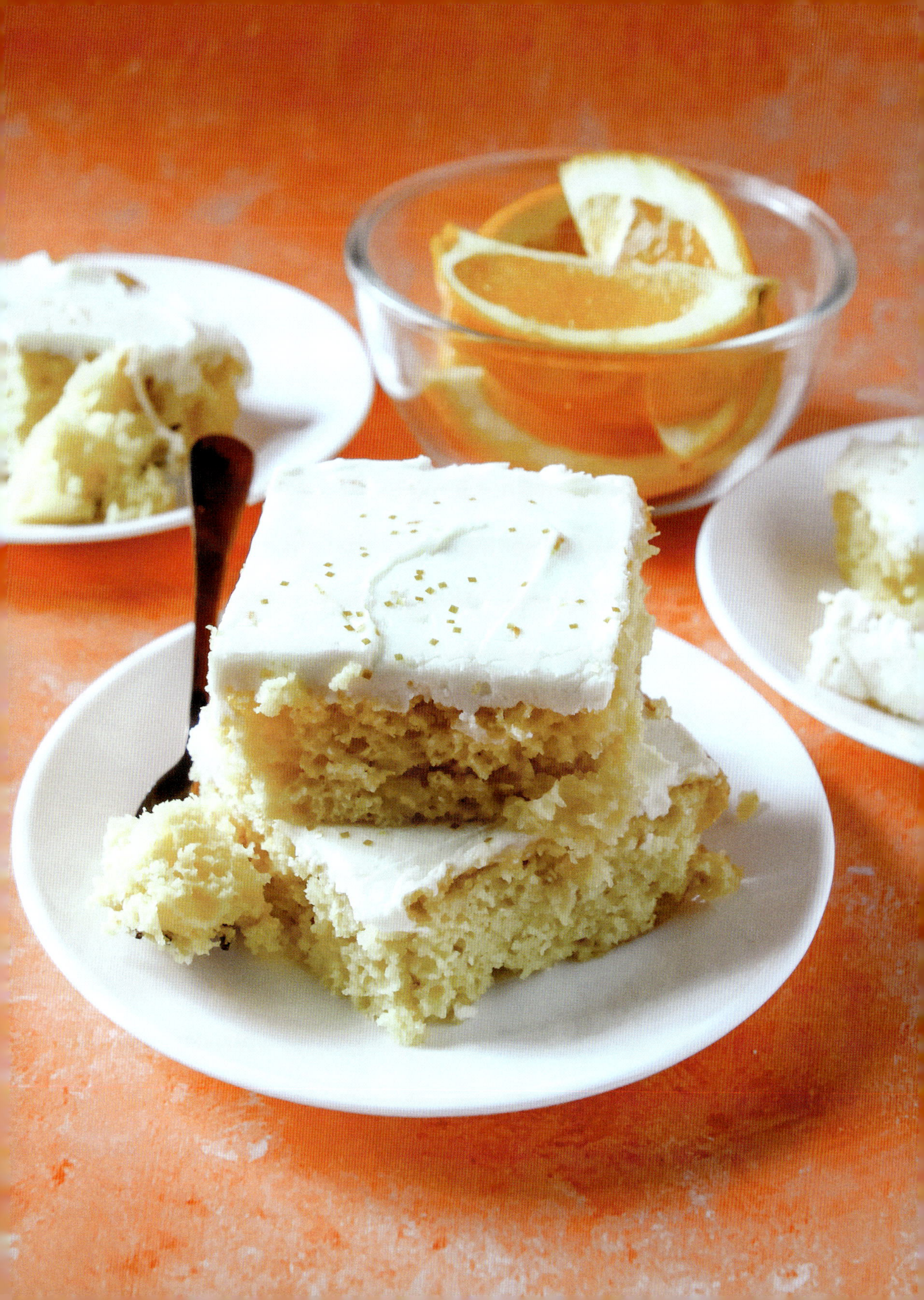

ORANGE AMARETTO SHEET CAKE (CONTINUED)

To make the buttercream, in a mixing bowl, beat the butter until smooth. Add the powdered sugar, orange zest, orange juice and vanilla. Beat until it's smooth and completely incorporated. Using an offset spatula or a knife, spread the frosting onto the cake in a thin, even layer. Sprinkle with glitter flakes, if desired, and serve.

For the Buttercream

½ cup (114 g) salted butter

2 cups (240 g) powdered sugar

1 tsp orange zest

1 tsp fresh orange juice

1 tsp vanilla extract

Edible gold glitter flakes, for sprinkling (optional)

COCONUT RASPBERRY CAKE JARS

Growing up, my dad absolutely loved Hostess® Raspberry Zingers® snack cakes. If you haven't had them, they're a sponge cake with a raspberry-coconut coating. I decided to use that flavor combo as an inspiration for these cake jars. Each Mason jar is layered with coconut cake, sweet vanilla coconut frosting, raspberry preserves and a sprinkle of coconut on top. I love, love, love cake jars because they're easy to eat over time instead of all at once. Eat a few bites, screw the lid back on and save the rest for later!

Makes: 6 large cake jars

Preheat the oven to 350°F (177°C). Prepare a 9 x 13–inch (23 x 33–cm) baking dish with baking spray.

In a medium bowl, combine the cake mix plus the ingredients on the package, and mix for 2 minutes, or until smooth. Pour the cake batter into the prepared pan and bake as directed on the package. Let the cake cool completely.

(continued)

1 (15.25-oz [432-g]) box coconut cake mix*

*Plus the ingredients listed on the package.

Note: Use 16-ounce (454-g) Mason jars with lids for this recipe.

FRUITY AND FUN TREATS · 109

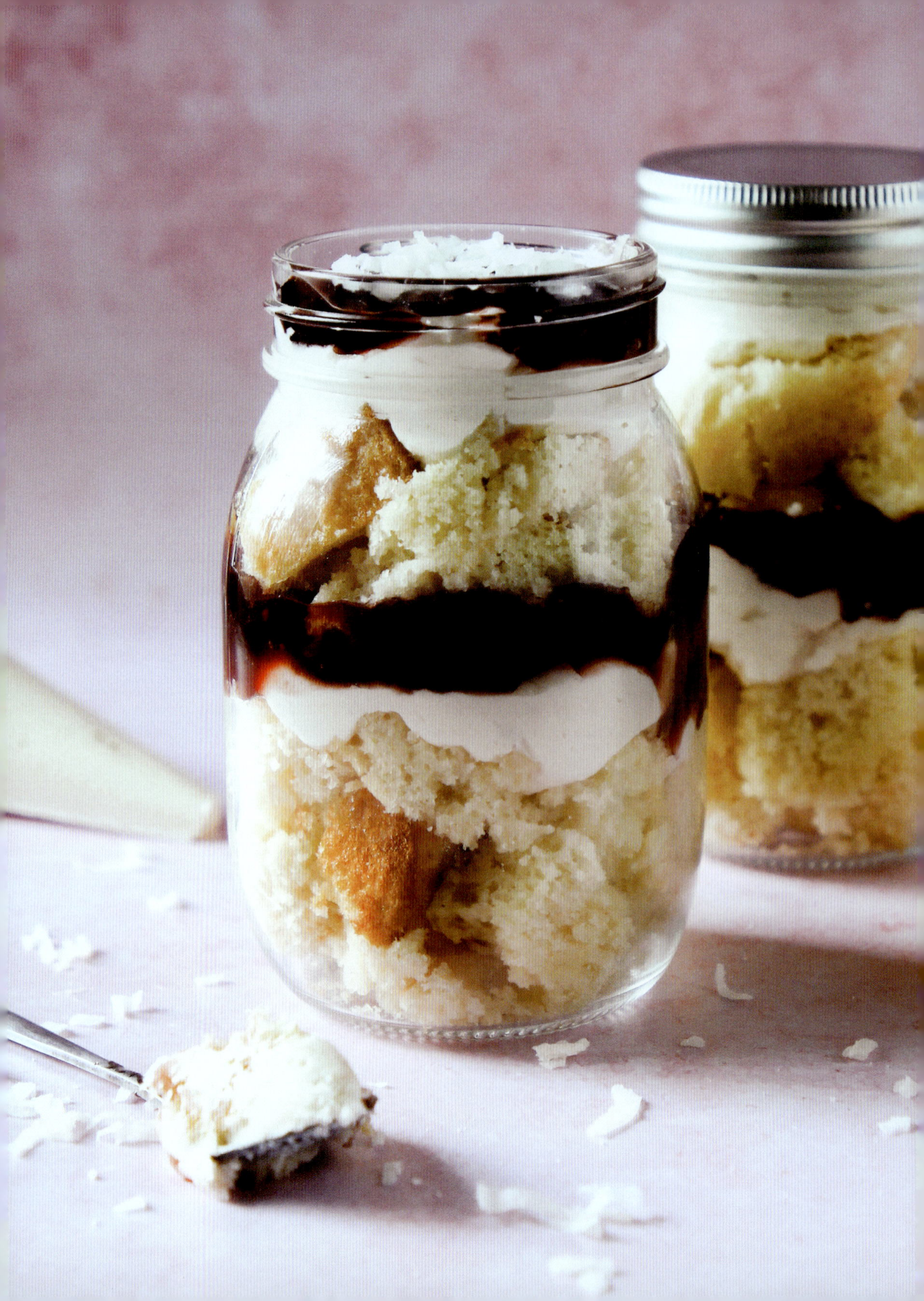

COCONUT RASPBERRY CAKE JARS (CONTINUED)

In a stand mixer or a medium bowl with a hand mixer, beat the butter for 2 to 3 minutes, or until smooth. Add 3 cups (360 g) of the powdered sugar and beat again. Add the remaining powdered sugar, vanilla, coconut and heavy cream. If it's too thick, add a little more heavy cream, and if it's too thin, add a bit more powdered sugar.

Cut the fully cooled coconut cake into 1-inch (2.5-cm) squares. Start by only cutting half of the cake into squares, so that you can decide the cake-to-frosting ratio you'd like in each jar. Unscrew all of the lids of your Mason jars. Place cake cubes at the bottom of each jar. They should fill the jar one-third of the way full. Top with a swirl of coconut buttercream. Either pipe the frosting on top of the cake with a piping bag and open star tip, or simply smooth it out with the back of a spoon. Add 1 to 2 tablespoons (15 to 30 ml) of raspberry preserves. It's best to stir the preserves ahead of time so that it's looser and easy to spread on the frosting. Repeat the layers, and top with a sprinkle of coconut flakes and fresh raspberries, if using. The cake jars should be filled up three-quarters of the way to the top so that they don't overflow and hit the lid—and so you can easily eat the cake with a spoon! Serve right away or refrigerate until using, and then serve at room temperature.

¾ cup (180 g) butter

6 cups (720 g) powdered sugar, plus more if needed

1 tbsp (15 ml) vanilla extract

1 tsp coconut extract

6 tbsp (90 ml) heavy cream, plus more if needed

1 (16-oz [454-g]) jar raspberry preserves, room temperature**

Sweetened coconut flakes, for topping (optional)

Fresh raspberries, for topping (optional)

**Use seedless if preferred, but either works.

BLUEBERRY PIE SNACK MIX

A few years back, I tried marshmallow treats made with Blueberry Chex™ cereal, and I fell head over heels in love. I've never been a huge blueberry person, but after trying this cereal, I had to create a snack mix. For a little twist, I added shortbread cookies, which give it a blueberry pie–like flavor. You can totally serve the snack mix with just the cookie, cereal and chocolate components, but I highly suggest adding white chocolate–covered blueberries. They're similar to yogurt-covered raisins with their wonderful sweet and chewy texture.

Line a baking sheet with parchment paper.

In a large bowl, toss the cereal and chopped cookies. You'll want to start snacking during this part, and I don't blame you!

In the microwave, heat the melting wafers in 30-second intervals, stirring after each interval, for 90 seconds, or until fully melted. Pour it over the cereal mixture and gently stir until it's fully coated. Transfer the mixture to a very large resealable bag and add the powdered sugar. Close the bag and shake until it's completely coated. Return the mixture to the bowl and gently stir in the white chocolate–covered blueberries, if using.

Spread the snack mix onto the baking sheet. Let it cool for 30 minutes, or until the chocolate is set.

Makes: 8 (1-cup [118-g]) servings

1 (12-oz [340-g]) box Blueberry Chex cereal

1 cup (87 g) chopped shortbread cookies

1 (10-oz [284-g]) bag white chocolate melting wafers (such as Ghirardelli)

1 cup (120 g) powdered sugar

1 (4-oz [113-g]) bag white chocolate–covered blueberries (optional)

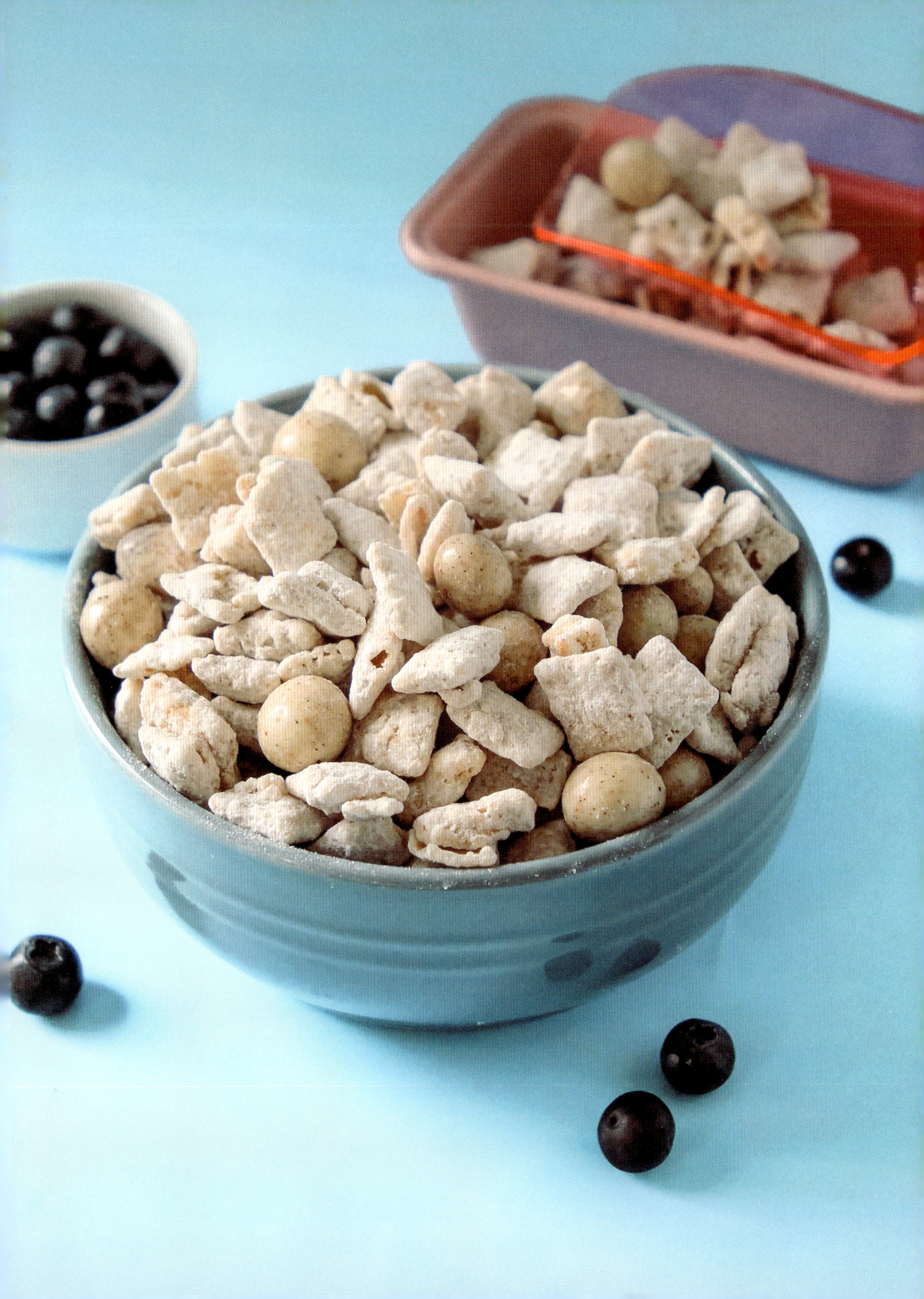

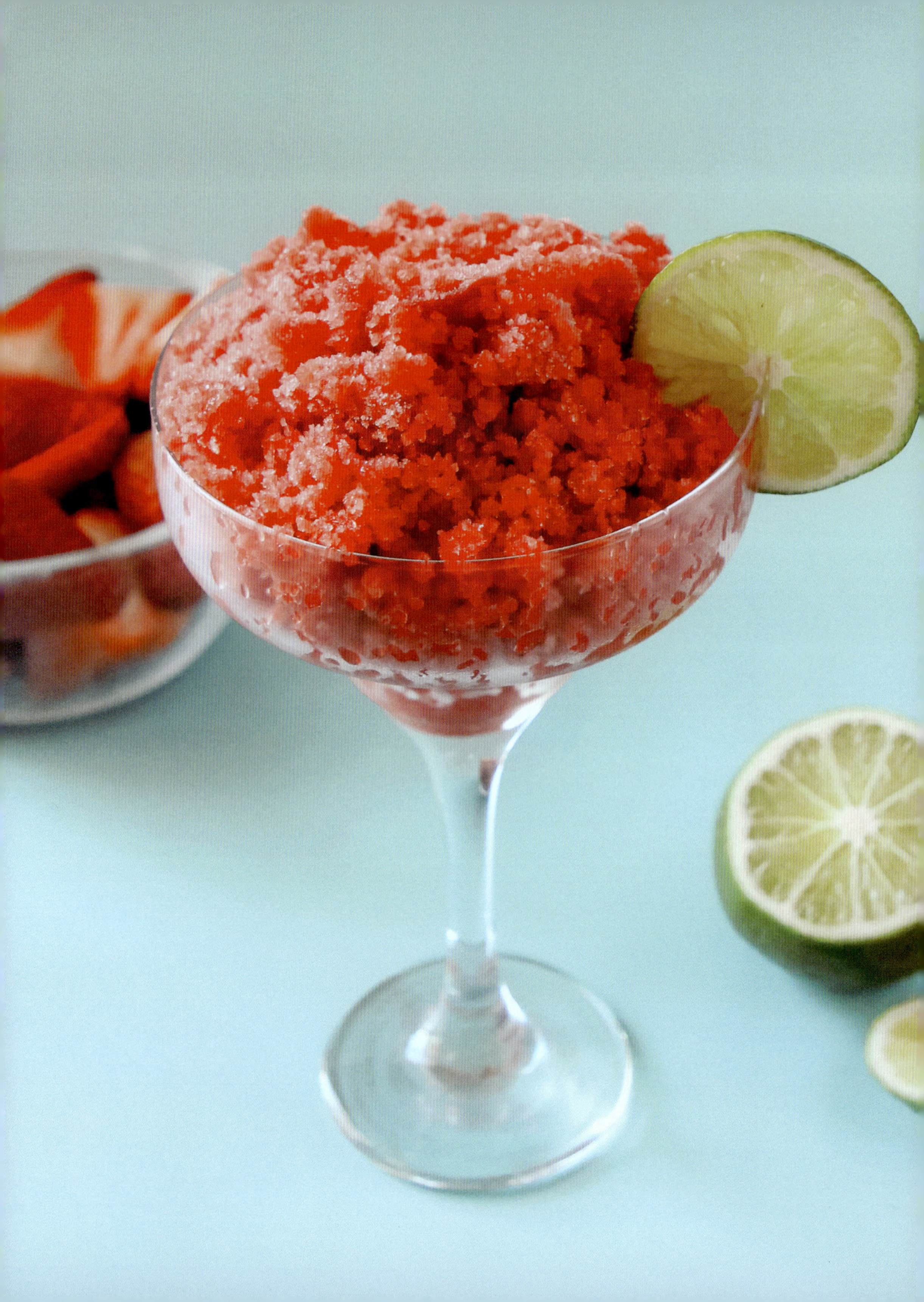

STRAWBERRY LIME POOLSIDE SLUSH

I live in Florida, and for most of the year it is hot, hot, HOT! There's nothing better than lying by the pool, listening to music and enjoying a refreshing frozen sweet treat. My daughter described this recipe as "frozen cotton candy," and I fully agree with her description. Not a strawberry fan? No problem! You can easily adapt this recipe with your favorite frozen berry or tropical fruit. How about cherry lime or maybe even blueberry lemon?

Makes: 3 servings

1 (16-oz [454-g]) bag frozen strawberries, thawed

1½ tbsp (23 ml) lime juice

¼ cup (50 g) granulated sugar

1 cup (240 ml) water

Lime slices and pink sanding sugar, for garnish (optional)

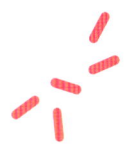

Add the strawberries to a food processor, and blend them into a puree. Place the strawberry puree in a large pot along with the lime juice, sugar and water. Begin to heat the pot over medium-high heat. Bring the mixture to a boil, and then reduce the heat to medium or medium-low, and allow the mixture to simmer for 10 minutes.

Remove it from heat and strain out the strawberry seeds with a mesh strainer into a shallow freezer-safe dish. Place a lid on the dish or cover tightly with plastic wrap, and place it into the freezer overnight.

When ready to serve, remove it from the freezer, and with a sturdy fork, scrape the frozen mixture to create the slush. You will want to work fast as the slush will start to melt. If you notice the mixture thawing too fast, pop it back into the freezer. Repeat until finished and scoop into glasses. Serve poolside right away with lime slices on the side and topped with sanding sugar, if using.

GLAZED FRUIT TART

I totally had my sister in mind while I was creating this tart. She loves fruit desserts, whereas I gravitate to chocolate. We do have one thing in common though: We both LOVE a good crust. The crust-to-filling ratio is extremely important to me. It has to be thick and flavorful! This tart has a homemade buttery graham cracker crust. Although I love a store-bought crust, making it yourself for this dessert really does make a difference. The inside of the tart has a smooth and creamy vanilla filling, and it's topped with an assortment of berries. Feel free to use any jam, but I love the sweetness of raspberry.

Makes: 8–10 slices

Preheat the oven to 350°F (177°C). Prepare the tart pan with baking spray.

To make the crust, in a medium mixing bowl, mix the graham cracker crumbs, butter and sugar until well combined. It should resemble wet sand. Firmly press the mixture into the tart dish, making sure to cover the bottom and sides. Bake for 10 to 12 minutes, or until lightly golden brown, and let it cool completely.

To make the filling, in a large mixing bowl with an electric hand mixer or stand mixer, beat the cream cheese, sugar, vanilla and almond extract (if using) for 2 to 3 minutes, or until smooth and creamy. Spread the mixture onto the cooled crust.

(continued)

For the Crust

1½ cups (180 g) graham cracker crumbs*

½ cup (120 ml) melted unsalted butter

¼ cup (50 g) granulated sugar

For the Filling

2 (8-oz [226-g]) packages cream cheese, softened

1 cup (200 g) granulated sugar

2 tsp (10 ml) vanilla extract

1 tsp almond extract (optional)

*I used the ready-made crumbs, but if making them yourself, it's about 12 graham crackers worth of crumbs.

To make the topping, wash and dry the fruit, and then arrange it onto the tart in your desired pattern, or simply scatter them over the top. Heat the raspberry jam in the microwave for 15 to 30 seconds, or until it's a syrup. Using a pastry brush, add the jam to the tart, making sure to cover all of the fruit so that you have a shiny glaze. Add sparkling sugar, if using. Refrigerate the tart for 2 to 3 hours and serve chilled.

Note: I recommend using a 10-inch (25-cm) round tart dish. If you only have a pie plate, that'll work, but the tart pan is a lot easier to work with! It has a removable bottom so that the pie won't stick.

For the Topping

16 oz (454 g) fresh fruit**

3 tbsp (45 ml) seedless raspberry jam

Sparkling sugar (optional)

**You can usually find a mix of blackberries, raspberries, strawberries and blueberries at the grocery store!

FRUITY AND FUN TREATS • 117

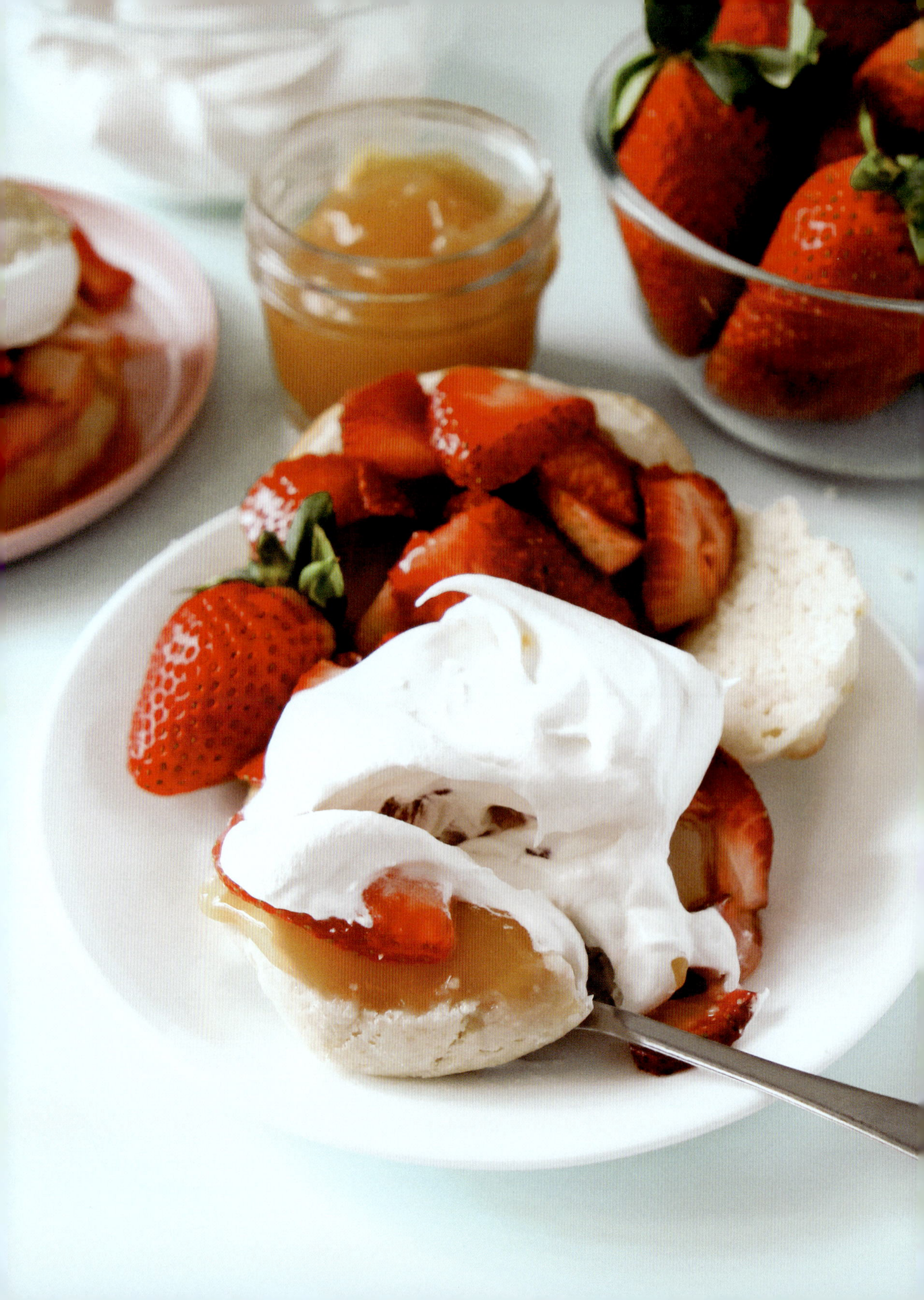

LEMON STRAWBERRY SHORTCAKES

The change from winter to spring is my favorite time of year. Everything starts to feel alive again, and the days are full of sunshine. I love eating dinner outside on the patio, and there's nothing like a fruity dessert to go with the warm and breezy weather. Strawberry shortcake is one of my favorites, and I decided to jazz it up here with a hint of lemon and sweetened strawberries. It has the perfect balance of freshness and comfort. I hope you enjoy it as much as I do, and bonus points if you eat it outside on a patio.

Makes: 6 shortcakes

2 cups (288 g) sliced fresh strawberries*

¼ cup (60 g) granulated sugar, divided, plus more for sprinkling

2 cups (240 g) Bisquick™ Pancake & Baking Mix

⅔ cup (160 ml) milk

3 tbsp (45 ml) melted butter

2 tsp (2 g) lemon zest

6 tbsp (90 ml) lemon curd

¾ cup (54 g) whipped topping

*Slice them into flat pieces, not into quarters.

In a small bowl, combine the strawberries and 2 tablespoons (30 g) of the sugar. Stir to combine, cover the bowl with plastic wrap and move it to the fridge for 1 to 2 hours.

Preheat the oven to 425°F (218°C). Line a cookie sheet with parchment paper.

In a medium bowl, combine the remaining sugar, Bisquick mix, milk, butter and lemon zest. Mix it until a dough forms. Divide the dough into six equal scoops, and place them onto the prepared cookie sheet. Using the back of a spoon or spatula, gently press down and mold the biscuits into a circular disc-like shape. The dough can be quite sticky, so if needed, spray the spoon with baking spray. Sprinkle the top of each biscuit with sugar, and bake for 10 to 11 minutes, or until lightly golden brown on the edges. Remove the cookie sheet from the oven and allow the biscuits to cool completely.

To assemble, slice each biscuit in half horizontally. Take the strawberries out of the fridge (do not discard the juice!). Drizzle a little bit of the juice on the bottom half of each biscuit. Use 1 to 2 teaspoons (5 to 10 ml) of juice on each, but feel free to add more or less depending on your preference. Next, spread 1 tablespoon (15 ml) of lemon curd on top of each. Add 1 tablespoon (9 g) of sliced strawberries on top of the lemon curd, and top that with 2 tablespoons (10 g) of whipped topping. Place the top of the biscuit on the whipped topping and serve.

This is a dessert that's best eaten right away. If you'd like to prepare it a bit ahead of time, just keep all of the components separate and assemble right before serving.

BERRY FLUFF MINI PARFAITS

These parfaits are a little bit fruity and a little bit sweet. They're made with a layer of crushed shortbread cookies, and then topped with the fluffiest berry filling. I love all berries, so I did an assortment, but feel free to sub for all of one kind. Each parfait is garnished with sparkling sugar and an extra shortbread cookie, making them a perfectly portioned special event treat.

In a stand mixer or a bowl with a hand mixer, beat the cream cheese for 2 minutes, or until smooth. Add the powdered sugar, ground freeze-dried strawberries and vanilla and almond extracts. Beat until smooth and fully combined. Fold in the whipped topping. The mixture should be more fluffy than creamy. Refrigerate for 1 hour.

Set the glasses on a flat surface. At the bottom of each glass, crush 1 shortbread cookie. Top each with 2 tablespoons (30 g) of your berry fluff and then a scoop of berries. Add a shortbread square to garnish each cup, and top with a sprinkle of sparkling sugar, if using.

Note: I use 2.7-ounce (76.5-g) glass dishes. If you don't have this specific size, no problem! Use any glasses that you have and just layer them the same way. They'll be a hit no matter what.

Makes: 12 parfaits

1 (8-oz [226-g]) package cream cheese, softened

½ cup (60 g) powdered sugar

2 tbsp (15 g) ground freeze-dried strawberries

1 tsp vanilla extract

½ tsp almond extract

1 (8-oz [226-g]) container whipped topping

24 square shortbread cookies (such as Lorna Doone®) (about 360 g)

2–3 cups (250–375 g) berries*

Sparkling sugar, for topping (optional)

*Use a mixture of strawberries, raspberries, blueberries and blackberries (or whichever you like best)!

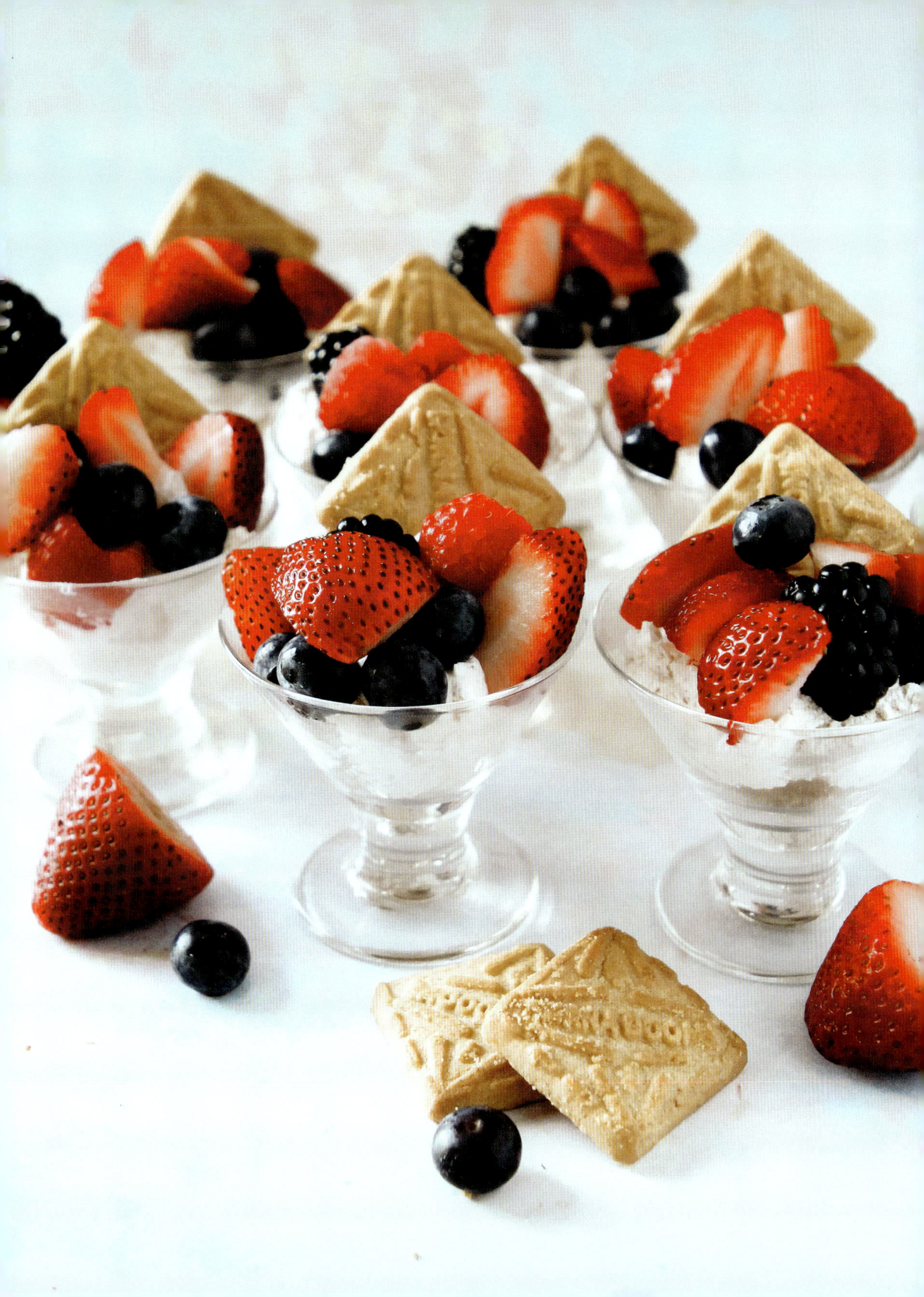

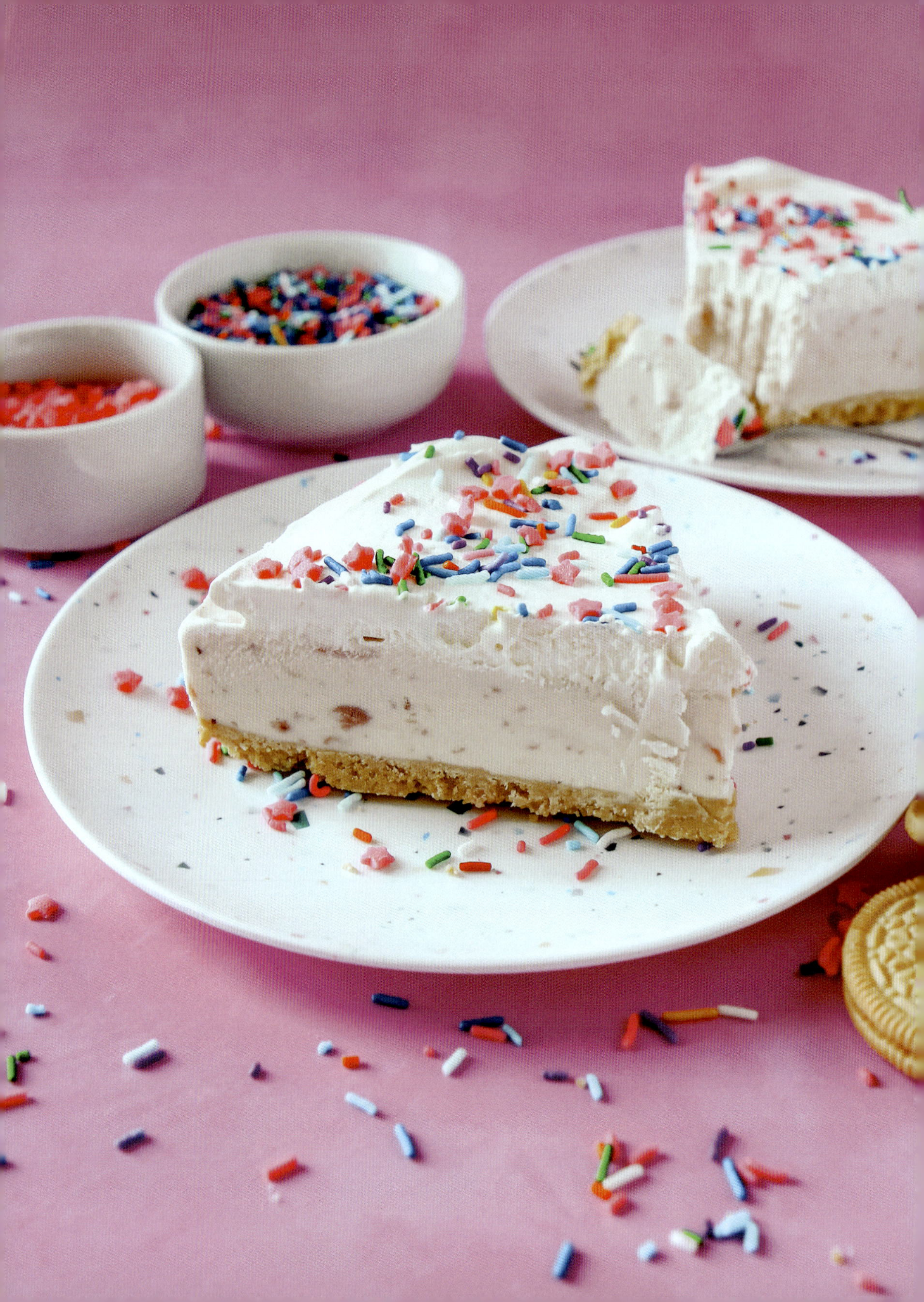

STRAWBERRY ICE CREAM CAKE

There's nothing better than ice cream cake during the summer, and this one is so wonderfully simple and sweet. You can get creative and customize it to make it over and over again throughout the hotter months. The base of this ice cream cake is made with Golden Oreo cookies and filled with fresh strawberry ice cream. Swapping out other sandwich cookies and ice cream flavors can lead to endless combinations. Try out different flavors like Dark Chocolate Flavor Creme Oreo cookies and peanut butter cup ice cream, Lemon Creme Oreo cookies and vanilla ice cream or classic Oreo cookies and cookie dough ice cream! Remember, this cake is only as good as the ice cream. Be sure to get a quality brand or get it from a local ice cream shop.

Preheat the oven to 350°F (177°C). Prepare a 9-inch (23-cm) springform pan with baking spray. Additionally, cut a parchment paper round to fit in the bottom of the pan.

In a small bowl, combine the Oreo crumbs and melted butter. Press the mixture evenly into the bottom of the pan. Bake for 6 to 8 minutes, or until golden brown. Let the crust cool completely.

About 15 minutes before assembling the cake, take the ice cream out of the freezer and set it out on the counter. In a stand mixer or in a large mixing bowl, beat the ice cream until it's smooth and creamy. It should look like soft serve or a milkshake rather than hard-packed ice cream.

Spray the inner perimeter of the pan with a little more baking spray, if needed. Spread the ice cream on top of the cooled crust. Freeze it overnight so that it turns back into hard-packed ice cream.

Remove the ice cream cake from the freezer, add the whipped topping to the top of the cake and spread it evenly. Add the sprinkles, then freeze for at least 1 hour for a harder whipped cream, or serve as is.

Before cutting the cake, let it sit out for 5 minutes. Then, gently release the latch on the pan. If the ice cream sticks to the pan, it's no problem! That's the great thing about ice cream cakes—all you need to do is take a spatula and smooth it out. Using a knife or metal spatula, lift the cake from the base of the pan, and transfer it to a cutting board. Cut into slices and serve.

Makes: 12–18 slices

22 Golden Oreo cookies, crushed into fine crumbs (about 319 g)

¼ cup (60 ml) melted salted butter

1 (½-gal [1.9-L]) container strawberry ice cream

1½ cups (108 g) whipped topping

Pink or decorative sprinkles, for topping

TROPICAL CAKE BARS

These tropical cake bars are a tropical drink in cake form. They have an amazing cake crust base, creamy filling and usually a topping or two. My tropical twist has pineapple, coconut and crunchy macadamia nuts. I added rum extract and tropical sprinkles for an extra splash of vacation fun.

Preheat the oven to 350°F (177°C). Prepare a 9 x 13–inch (23 x 33–cm) pan with baking spray. (I love the baking spray that has flour in it, but regular baking spray will also work.)

To make the cake, in a mixing bowl, stir the cake mix, melted butter and egg with a spoon. Press the mixture into the prepared pan. It's very sticky and might look like it will not fit, but keep pressing it down flat. Set aside.

To make the creamy layer, in another bowl, beat the cream cheese for 1 to 2 minutes, or until smooth. Add the powdered sugar and vanilla and rum extracts, and beat for 1 minute, or until creamy. Spread the cream cheese mixture on top of the yellow cake mixture.

For the topping, add the crushed pineapple to the top of the cream cheese mixture. Make sure that it's evenly spread. Top with the shredded coconut and macadamia nuts. Sprinkle the confetti sprinkles, if using.

Bake for 35 to 37 minutes, or until the edges are golden brown. The cake should be set, but it will still be slightly gooey due to the texture of the cake. It will set more once fully cooled. Allow to cool completely in the pan on a wire rack. You can cut and serve them as is, but I prefer moving them to the refrigerator for 1 to 2 hours. They'll be easier to cut and nicely set. Serve at room temperature.

Makes: 32 bars

For the Cake

1 (15.25-oz [432-g]) yellow cake mix

½ cup (120 ml) melted salted butter

1 egg

For the Creamy Layer

1 (8-oz [226-g]) package cream cheese, softened

2 cups (240 g) powdered sugar

1 tsp vanilla extract

2 tsp (10 ml) rum extract

For the Topping

1 (20-oz [567-g]) can crushed pineapple, well-drained

1 cup (186 g) shredded sweetened coconut

1 (4-oz [113-g]) bag macadamia nuts, chopped

Tropical color confetti sprinkles (optional)

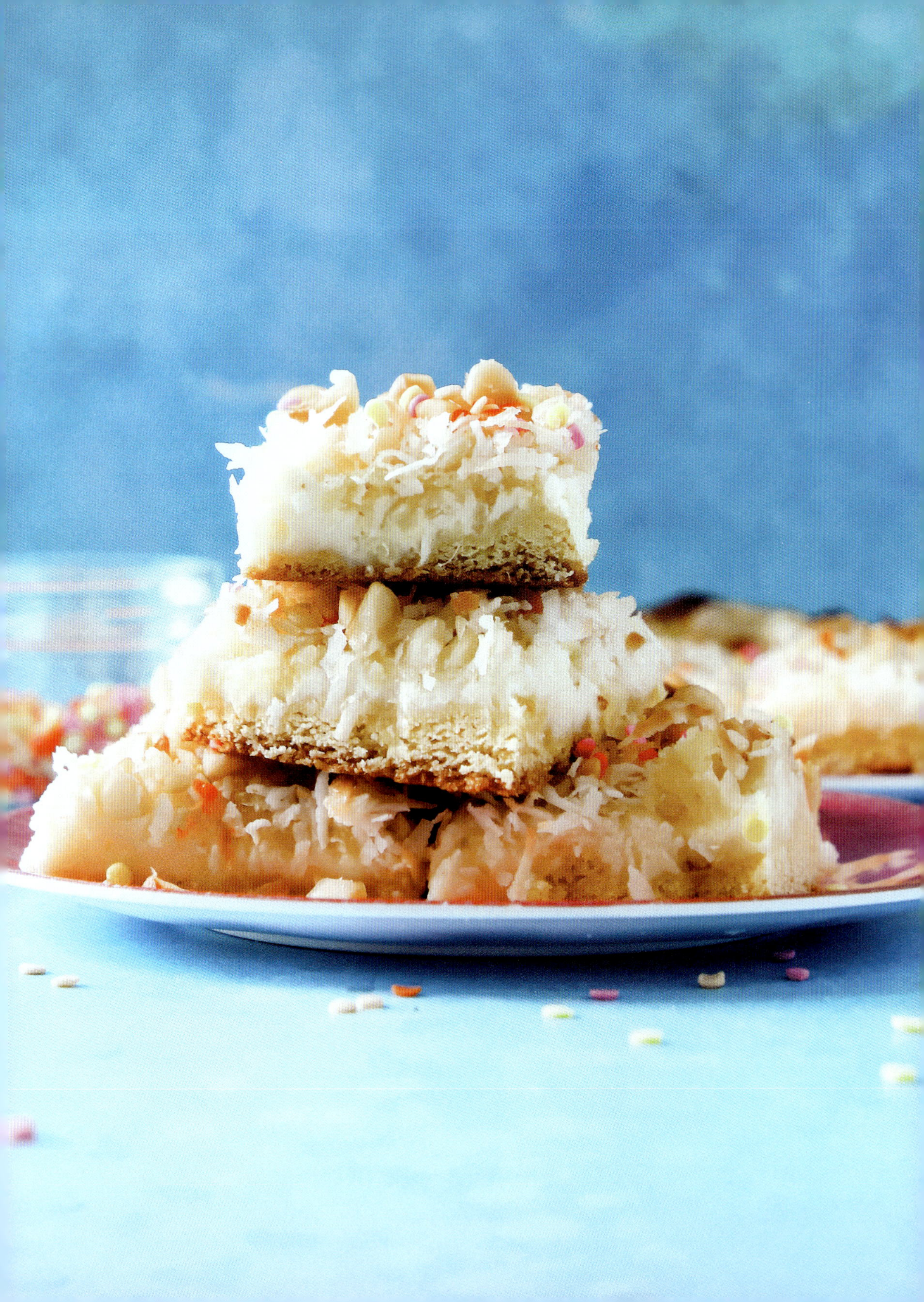

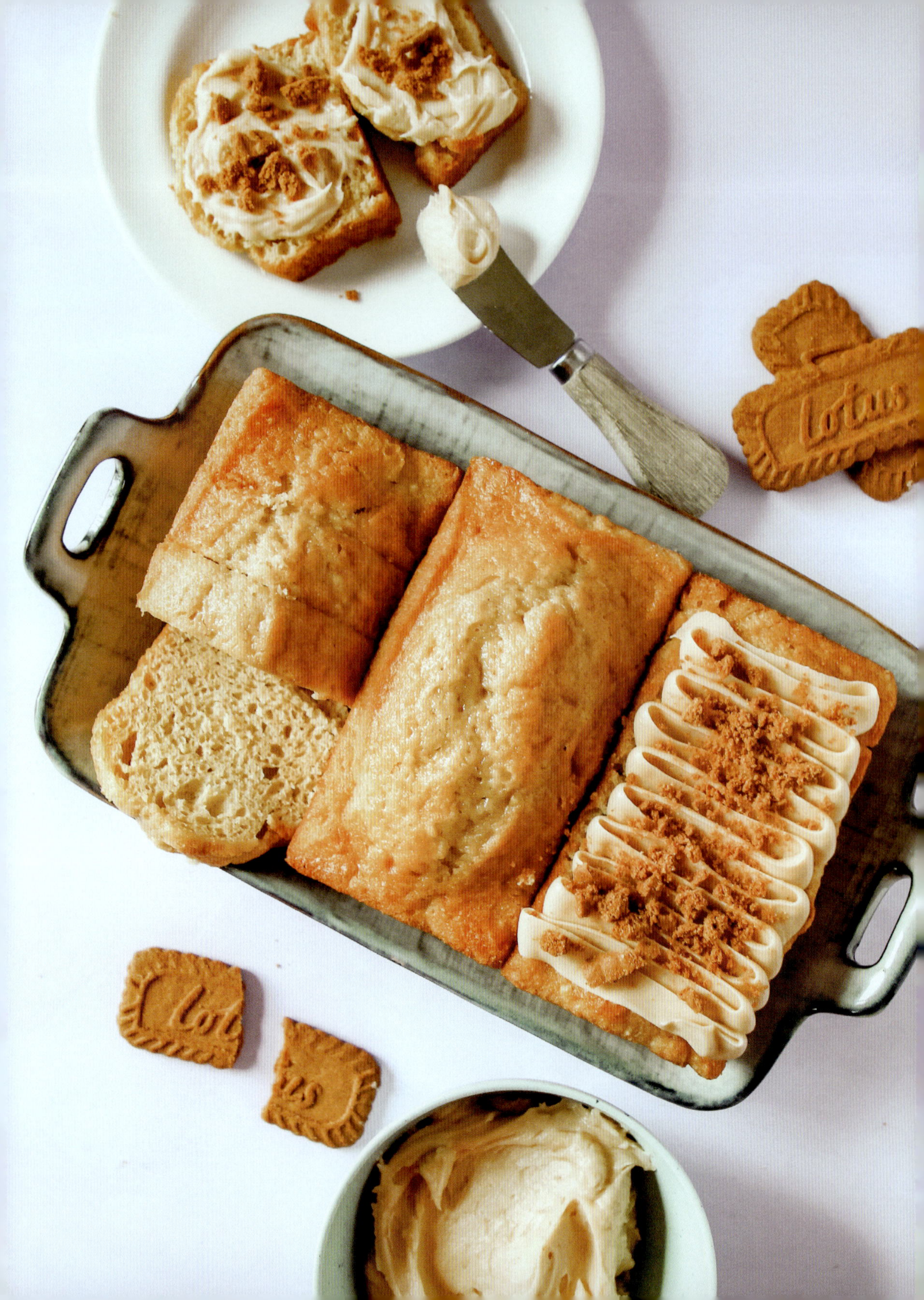
Lotus

COMFORTING AND NOSTALGIC
Sweets

The desserts in this chapter will make your house smell incredible! Filled with spices and rich batters, these recipes are perfect for weekend mornings, cold weather days and dinners chatting with friends. I am a huge fan of cookie butter, and in this cozy section, you'll see two of my favorite recipes: Cookie Butter Apple Pie Biscuits (page 134) and Cookie Butter Mini Loaf Cakes (page 146). If I had the chance, I'd make an entire cookie butter series on my blog because the ideas are endless, and both kids and adults can't get enough of the flavor. Cookie butter is just so perfectly sweet and satisfying. As autumn approaches, I fully embrace the baking and holiday movie mindset. Let me tell you, the Cinnamon Crunch Muffins (page 130) are the epitome of fall. Get your blankets ready and curl up with one of these treats. While you're at it, maybe make the obligatory pumpkin spice latte! ;)

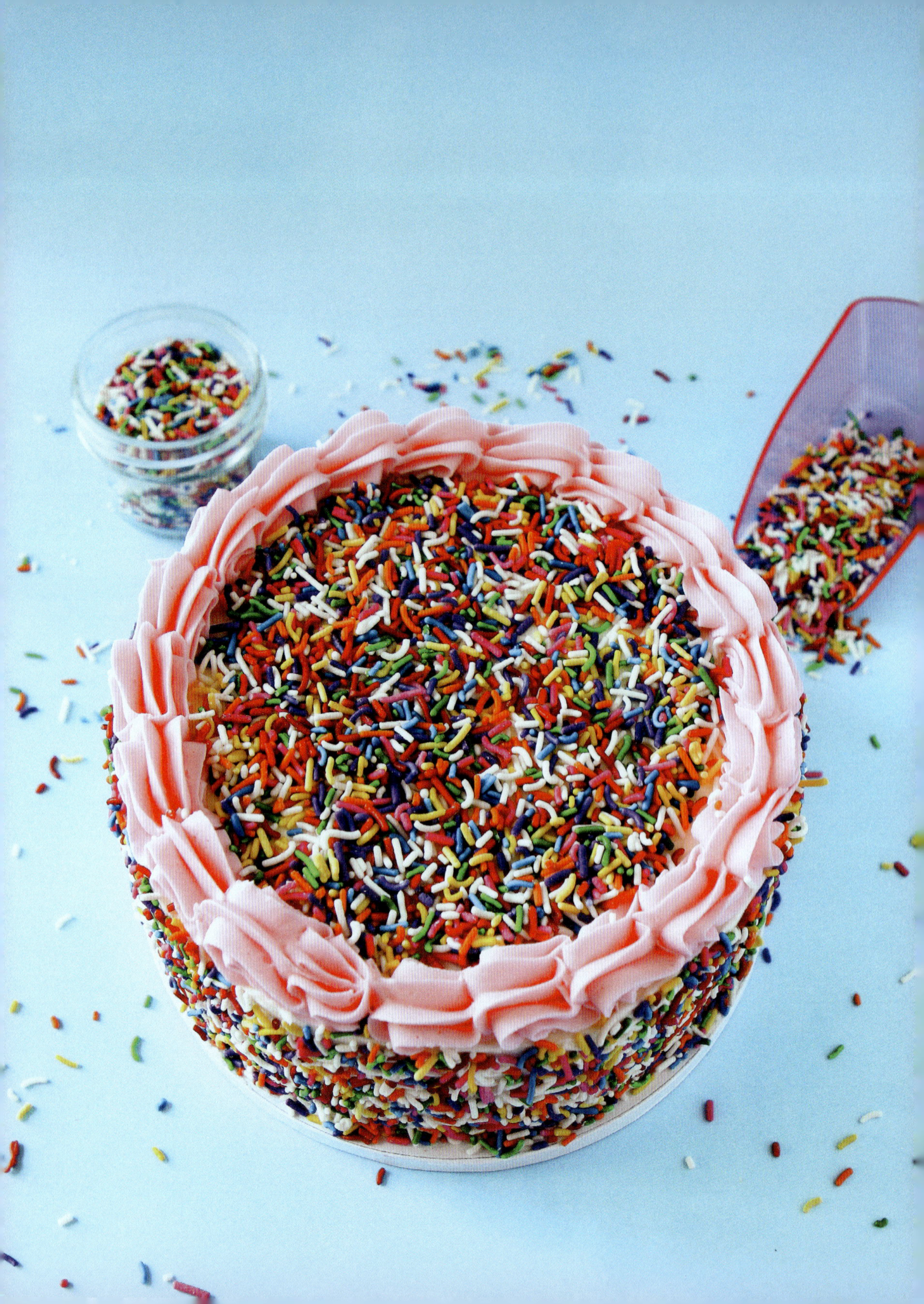

CAKE ON THE COVER

Surprise! The cake on the cover is a special variation of the Sprinkle-tastic Party Cake (page 35). I absolutely love making layer cakes, especially when they're covered in sprinkles. The best part about this cake is that you don't have to worry about perfectly smoothing the frosting—the rainbow sprinkles will hide any imperfections!

Preheat the oven to 350°F (177°C). Spray two 8-inch (20-cm) round pans with baking spray. Alternatively, grease and flour both pans. Combine the cake mix, water, eggs, oil and extracts. Fold in the sprinkles, a.k.a. use a spatula to distribute them throughout the cake batter.

Divide the batter between both pans and bake according to the package instructions. Let them cool in the pans and then move them to baking racks to cool completely. After that, move them to the fridge, covered in plastic wrap, for at least an hour.

Meanwhile, to make the frosting, beat the butter until smooth. Add in half of the powdered sugar, and mix. Add in the rest of the sugar, heavy cream and vanilla, and mix. If the frosting is too thick, add 1 tablespoon (16 ml) of additional heavy cream at a time. Place ½ cup (110 g) of the frosting in a small bowl. This will be for the border, so add the pink food coloring, stir it in completely and set the bowl aside.

Place the first cake layer onto a flat plate or cake drum. Spread 1 cup of frosting on top of that layer, making sure to reach the edges of the cake. Flip the second cake layer over and put it on top of the frosting. The bottom of that cake layer will be the top of the cake. Using an offset spatula, spread the vanilla frosting over the entire cake. Place it in the fridge for about 30 minutes.

Remove the cake from the fridge and add another layer of frosting. Smooth it out with the spatula. Place the cake onto a rimmed baking sheet. Using your hand, press sprinkles on the outside of the cake, making sure to cover it completely (not the top yet.)

Place the pink buttercream into a piping bag fit with a 1M tip. Pipe a swirl around the top of the cake. Fill in the center with more rainbow sprinkles. Slice and serve at room temperature.

Makes: 10-12 slices

For the Cake

1 (15.25-oz [432-g]) box white cake mix

1 cup (240 ml) water

4 eggs

½ cup + 1 tbsp (195 ml) vegetable oil

1 tsp vanilla extract

1 tsp almond extract

⅓ cup (64 g) rainbow sprinkles

For the Frosting

3 sticks (1½ cups / 341 g) butter, softened (2 salted, 1 unsalted)

6 cups (720 g) powdered sugar, divided

5-6 tbsp (75-90 ml) heavy cream

2 tsp (10 ml) vanilla extract

Pink food coloring

For Decorating

2 cups (320 g) rainbow sprinkles

CINNAMON CRUNCH MUFFINS

These muffins are full of the classic, comforting flavors of apple and cinnamon. When they start to bake, they bring an immediate scent of cozy spices into the kitchen. The base is an easy muffin mix, and I highly recommend the one listed. I tried quite a few, but this one is extra special. If you can't find it, I assure you the other mixes were delicious as well. Each muffin has a hint of apple, and they're finished with a crunchy buttery cinnamon topping that is out of this world. They are best enjoyed fresh out of the oven with a smear of apple butter, salted butter or cream cheese.

Preheat the oven to 350°F (177°C). Line a muffin pan or cupcake pan with 16 liners. These are regular-sized muffins, not jumbo. For muffins, I always love to use parchment liners. They are super easy to peel away and don't stick to the muffins.

In a mixing bowl, combine the muffin mix with the ingredients listed on the package and mix for 2 minutes, or until smooth and fully combined. Add half of the cinnamon packet from the muffin mix package and the apple pie spice, and mix for 30 seconds, or until combined. Gently fold in the apples and walnuts.

Divide the batter into the prepared muffin pan. Drizzle the melted butter on the top of each muffin and gently spread it around with the back of a spoon. Sprinkle the remaining cinnamon mixture from the package on top of each muffin.

Bake for 22 to 25 minutes, or until golden brown. Let them cool in the muffin tins before removing to wire racks to fully cool.

Makes: 16 muffins

1 (21-oz [595-g]) box Krusteaz® Cinnamon Swirl Crumb Cake & Muffin Mix*

1 tsp apple pie spice

½ cup (63 g) finely chopped apples

⅓ cup (66 g) finely chopped walnuts

2 tbsp (30 ml) melted butter

*Plus the ingredients listed on the package.

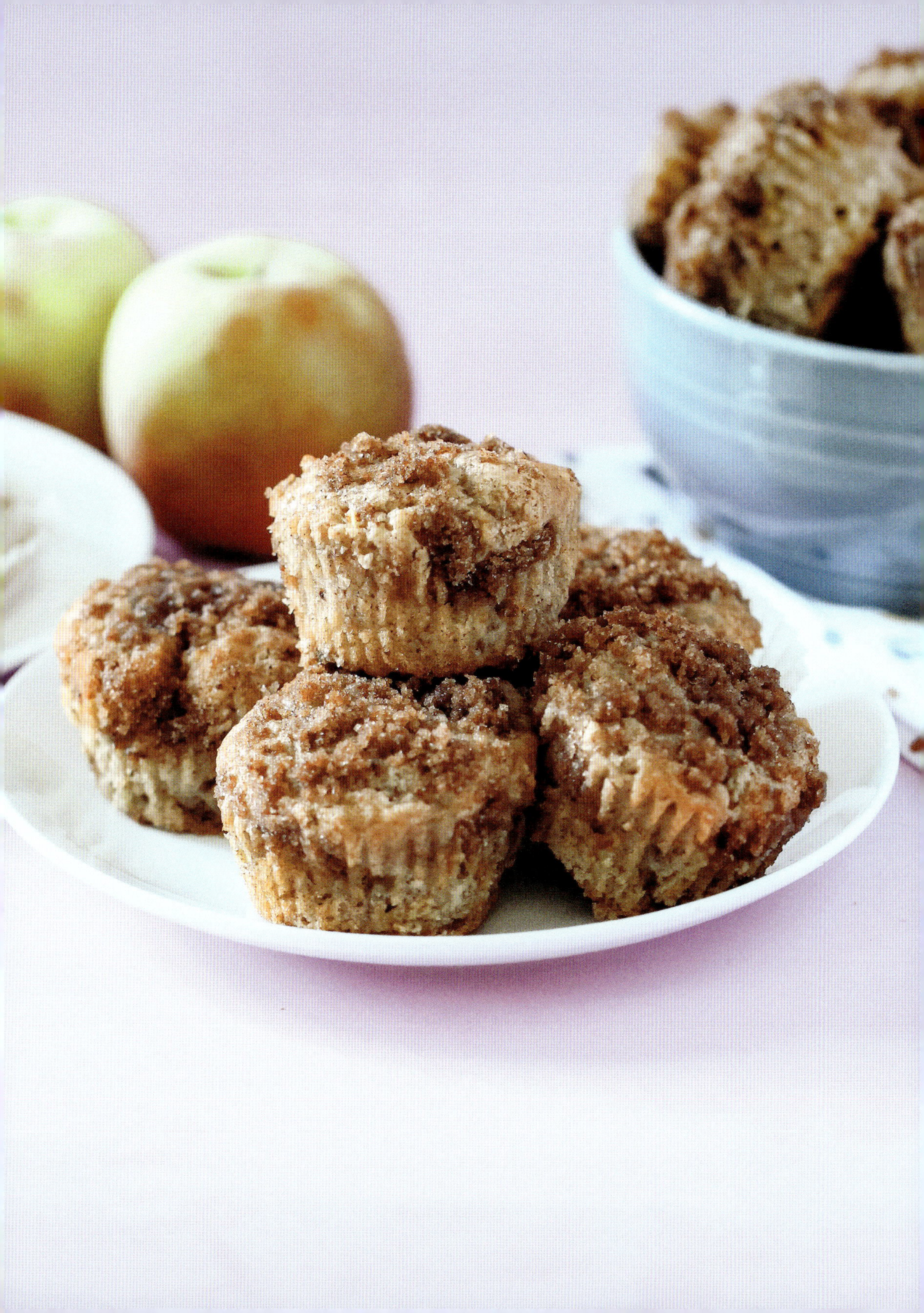

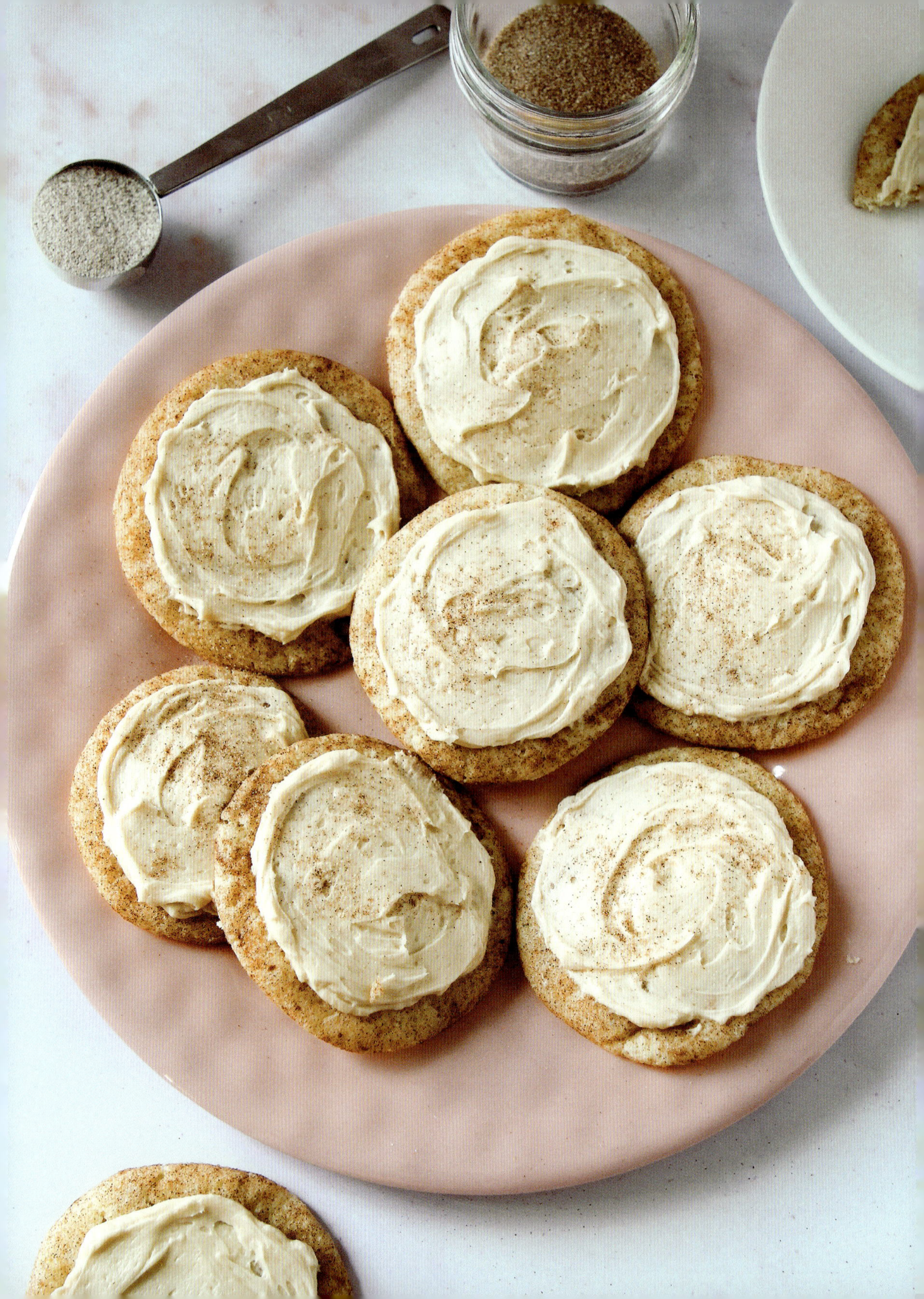

SNICKERDOODLE LATTE FROSTED COOKIES

Before I discovered piping bags, I was the master of spreading frosting with a knife. I still love the simplicity of it, and sometimes, all you need is a light layer of frosting. These cookies are inspired by a coffee shop and includes the nostalgic taste of cinnamon and sugar. I used a packaged snickerdoodle cookie mix, but feel free to use homemade or store-bought, if desired. The cookies are topped with a rich vanilla latte frosting and a sprinkle of cinnamon. Sidenote: This frosting pairs wonderfully with gingerbread, so during the winter you can switch out snickerdoodle for gingerbread cutouts!

Prepare the cookie mix according to the instructions on the package, and place it in the fridge for 30 minutes. This will help the cookies hold their shape when baking.

Preheat the oven to 350°F (177°C), and line two cookie sheets with parchment paper.

Using a small cookie scoop, place the dough scoops 2 inches (5 cm) apart on the prepared cookie sheets. Bake them according to package instructions and let them cool completely.

In a stand mixer or large mixing bowl with a handheld electric mixer, beat the butter on high for 2 to 3 minutes, or until light and fluffy. In a small bowl, combine the whipping cream and instant coffee, and stir together until mostly dissolved. Add 1 cup (120 g) of the powdered sugar to the butter and mix. Add the remaining powdered sugar, vanilla and cream mixture and beat for 5 minutes, or until smooth. Using a knife, spread 1 tablespoon (15 g) of frosting onto each cookie. Add a sprinkle of cinnamon.

Makes: 22–24 cookies

1 (17.9-oz [508-g]) package snickerdoodle cookie mix*

½ cup (114 g) salted butter

2 tbsp (30 ml) heavy whipping cream

½ tbsp Maxwell House® International French Vanilla Café-Style Beverage Mix instant coffee

2 cups (240 g) powdered sugar, divided

1 tsp vanilla extract

Cinnamon, for sprinkling

*Plus the ingredients listed on the package.

COOKIE BUTTER APPLE PIE BISCUITS

Truth be told, I am not an apple pie person. In fact, any apple-inspired dessert has to be truly spectacular for me to eat it. With all that said, I could have eaten the entire pan of these! The special ingredient that sets these over the top is cookie butter. It adds a sweet and rich taste to each biscuit. And I've gotta say, apple pie filling and cookie butter make a mind-blowing combo. These are most definitely perfect for fall, but I can promise you, they're a hit all year round.

Preheat the oven to 350°F (177°C). Spray an 8-inch (20-cm) round pan with baking spray. (I love the baking spray that has flour in it, but regular baking spray will also work.)

In a small mixing bowl, mix the cinnamon and sugar, and set aside.

Place the biscuits on a flat surface, such as a cutting board. Flatten each biscuit with your hands until they are 5 inches (13 cm) in diameter. It'll take a little bit to press them out, but the larger diameter makes them much easier to fill. Spread 1 tablespoon (30 g) of cookie butter in the middle of each biscuit, leaving a ½-inch (1.3-cm) border around the edge. Top that with 1 tablespoon (15 ml) of the apple filling. Pull the edges of each biscuit together to form a ball, pinching the ends together into a tight seal.

Roll each biscuit in the melted butter and then in the cinnamon sugar. Place each biscuit into the pan, seam side down. There will be one in the center and seven around it. Pour any remaining butter on top of the biscuits, and sprinkle them with a little bit of any extra cinnamon sugar.

Bake for 30 to 35 minutes, or until lightly golden brown. What do you do if a few come apart? They'll taste just as good, I assure you—simply transfer them to a bowl and add a scoop of ice cream! Serve warm and add an extra sprinkle of cinnamon sugar or caramel drizzle, if desired.

Makes: 8 biscuits

½ tsp cinnamon

¼ cup (50 g) granulated sugar

1 (16.3-oz [462-g]) can Pillsbury Grands!™ Flaky Layers biscuits*

½ cup (240 g) creamy cookie butter (such as Biscoff® Cookie Butter)

⅔ cup (160 ml) chopped canned apple pie filling

2 tbsp (30 ml) melted butter

Caramel, for drizzling (optional)

*There are 8 biscuits per can.

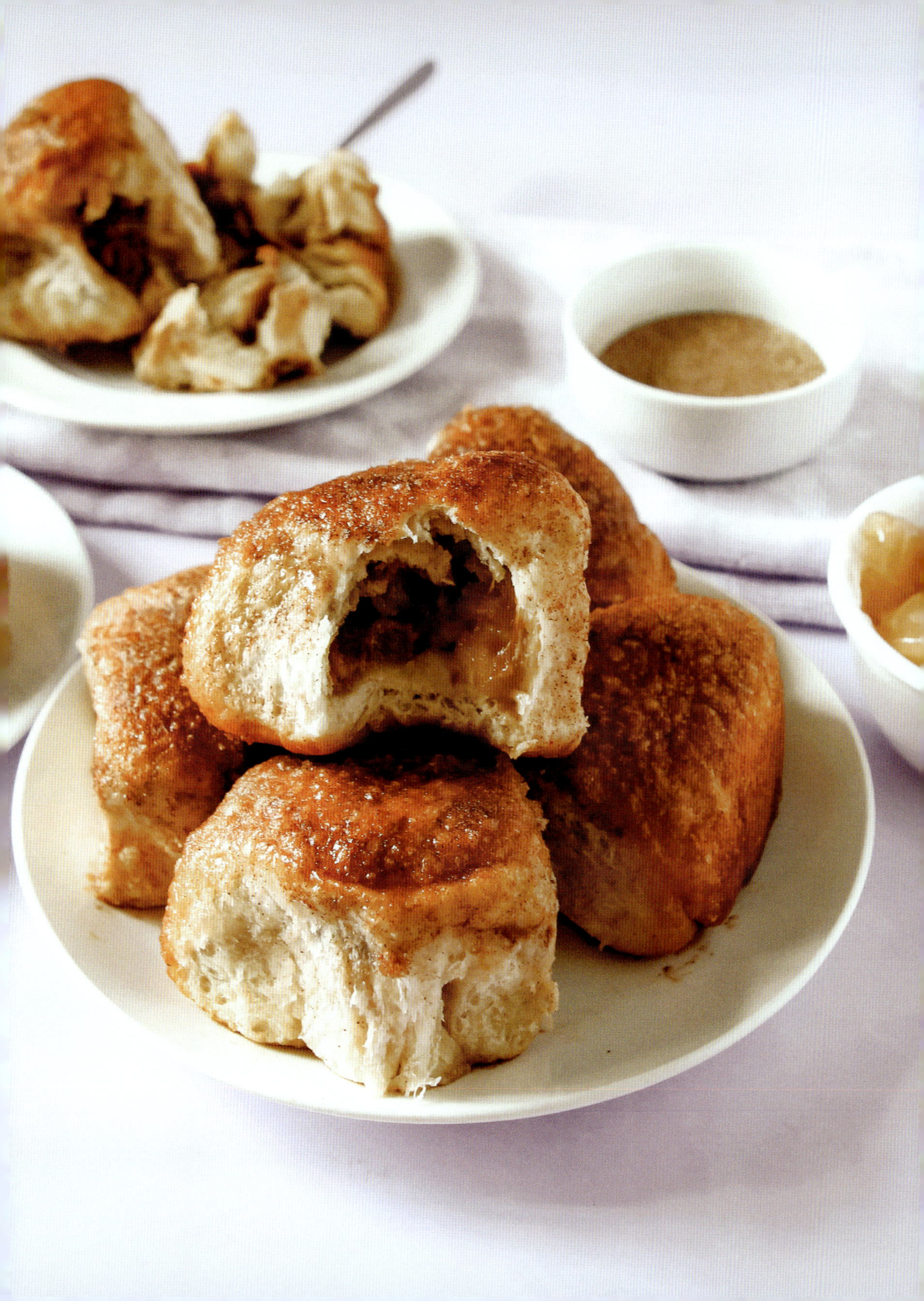

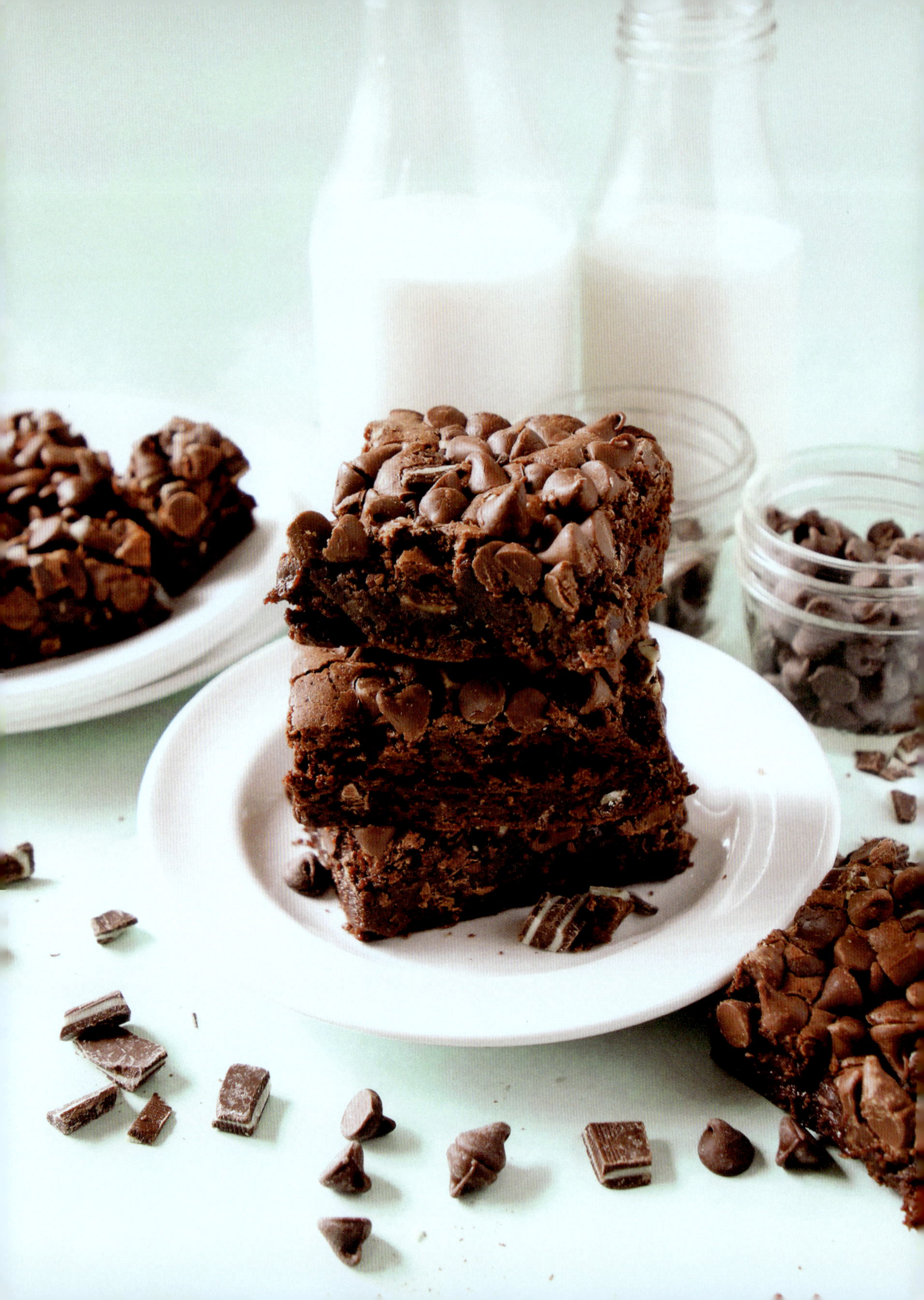

MINT CHOCOLATE CHIP BROWNIES

This is my favorite brownie recipe, hands down. These brownies are perfectly fudgy and have a generous layer of chocolate chips on top. I made these with mint chips, which are delicious year-round. If you'd like to give them an extra holiday touch, use peppermint bark or peppermint chips instead. Not a mint fan? Leave them out and just add extra milk chocolate chips in place of them. One of my go-to desserts is a brownie sundae. Top these with a few scoops of mint chocolate chip ice cream, and you've made it a summer hit too!

Makes: 9 brownies

1⅓ cups (166 g) all-purpose flour

1 cup (88 g) cocoa powder

1 tsp salt

1 tsp baking powder

¾ cup (180 ml) vegetable oil

2 cups (400 g) granulated sugar

2 tsp (10 ml) vanilla extract

4 eggs

1⅓ cups (224 g) milk chocolate chips, divided

½ cup + 2 tbsp (140 g) chopped Andes® Crème de Menthe Thins, divided*

*These should be chopped into small pieces about the same size as the chocolate chips.

Preheat the oven to 350°F (177°C). Prepare a 9-inch (23-cm) square dish with baking spray. Line the bottom of the pan with two strips of parchment paper in a crisscross pattern with the edges hanging over. This makes it easier to pull the cake out. Spray again with baking spray after the sheets are in place.

In a medium bowl, whisk together the flour, cocoa powder, salt and baking powder. In another medium bowl, beat the oil and sugar with a hand mixer for 1 to 2 minutes, or until well blended. If you have a stand mixer, you can use that instead. Add the vanilla to the wet ingredients and mix again. Add 1 egg at a time, beating well after each addition. Slowly add the flour mixture and mix until just combined. Fold in ⅓ cup (56 g) of the milk chocolate chips and ½ cup (112 g) of the chopped Andes Thins.

Spread the batter into the prepared pan. Sprinkle the remaining Andes Thins on top. They won't cover the whole thing; they're just there to add a little pop of extra mint here and there. Add the remaining milk chocolate chips on top of that.

Bake for 40 to 45 minutes, or until a toothpick comes out mostly clean. Let it cool completely in the pan. Cover the pan with foil and move it to the refrigerator for at least 1 hour. Refrigerating the brownies will give them a fudgy texture. Remove it from the fridge, let them get back to room temperature, slice and serve.

BANANA NUT CINNAMON ROLLS

I am a creature of habit and pretty much eat the same breakfast every day, except on holidays and vacations. On those days, I love to venture outside my comfort zone and try a sweet treat. One of my top picks is cinnamon rolls. They're delicious plain, but I always go for the ones with extras . . . like this version. These cinnamon rolls have a fruit and nut topping that makes them the ultimate breakfast treat. I start with a simple can of store-bought cinnamon rolls and top them with a sweet banana mixture and chopped pecans. Of course, they aren't complete without a generous drizzle of icing, making them a perfect ooey gooey morning treat.

Preheat the oven to 400°F (204°C). Spray an 8-inch (20-cm) round cake pan with baking spray and set it aside. (I love the baking spray that has flour in it, but regular baking spray will also work.)

In a medium bowl, combine the mashed bananas, brown sugar and cinnamon. Fold in the chopped pecans. Open the cinnamon roll can, and place the rolls into the pan. Top them with the banana mixture, spreading it over the tops. If some drips off into the pan, it's totally fine!

Bake for 22 to 25 minutes, or until lightly golden brown and fully baked through. Let them cool for 15 minutes. If you add the icing too soon, it will melt against the banana topping. Heat the icing in the microwave for 10 seconds, and then drizzle it over the rolls.

Makes: 8 cinnamon rolls

2 ripe bananas, mashed

¼ cup (55 g) brown sugar

1 tsp cinnamon

⅓ cup (36 g) chopped pecans

1 (12.4-oz [351-g]) can cinnamon rolls*

*Includes 8 rolls with icing.

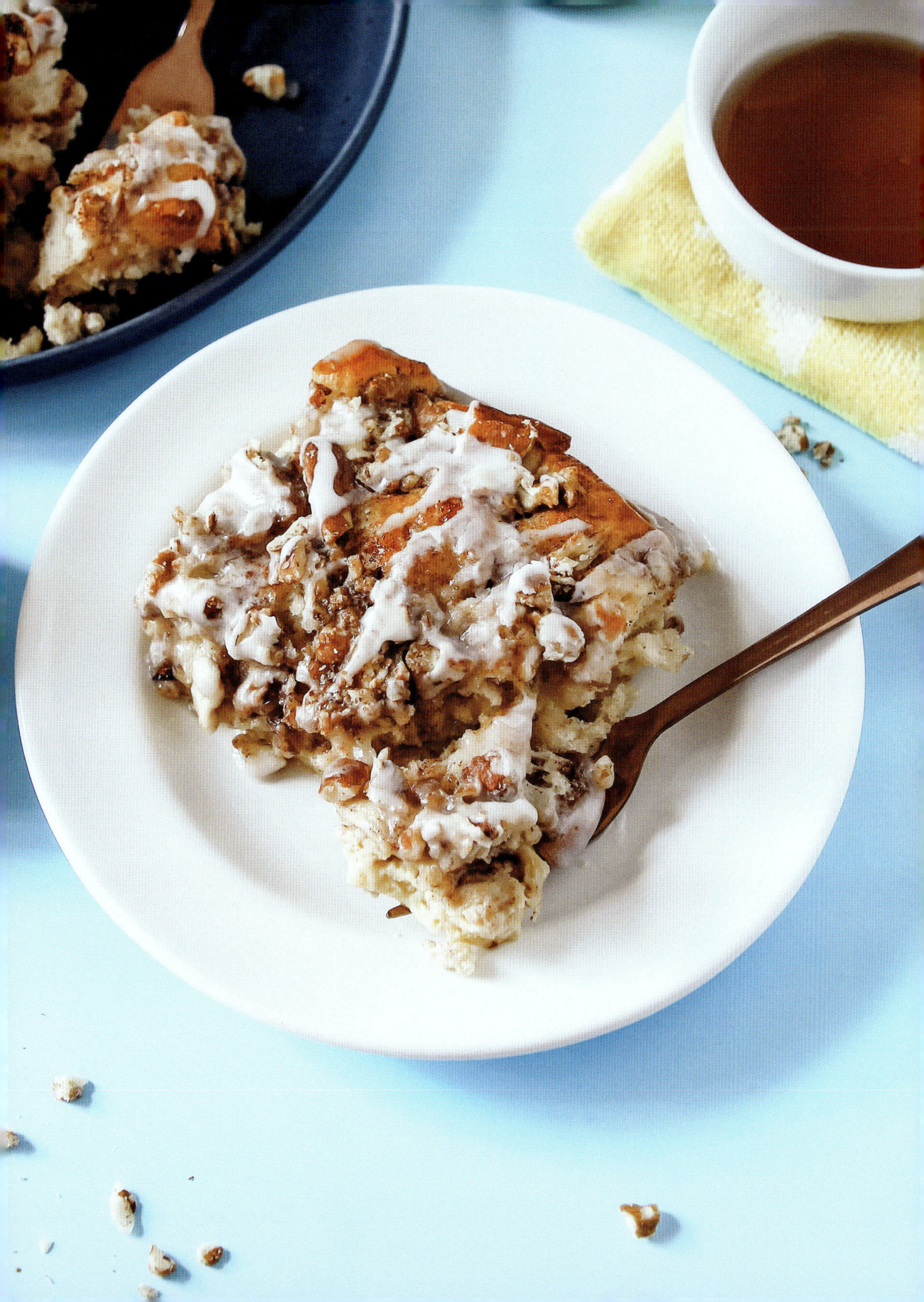

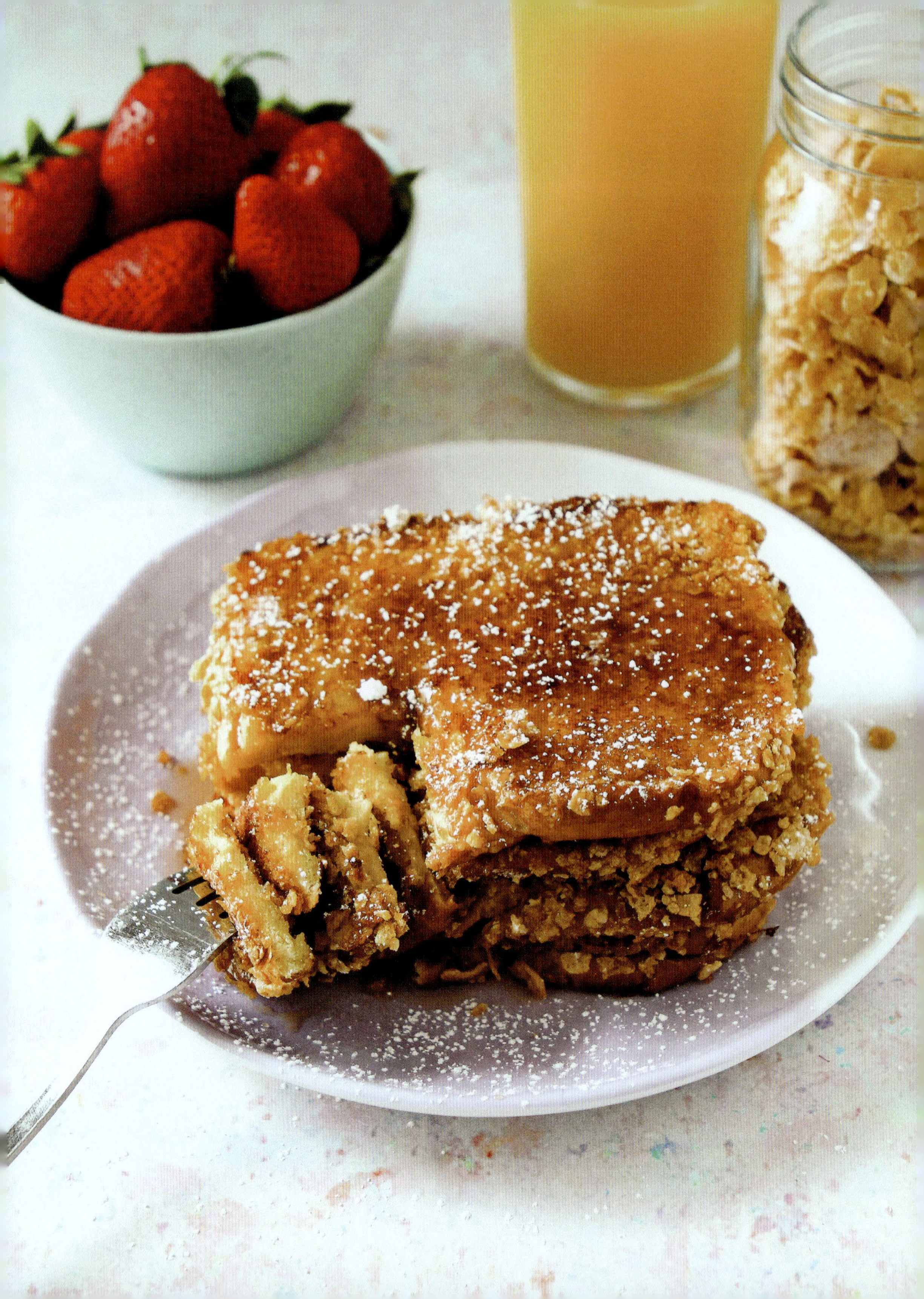

FROSTED FLAKES FRENCH TOAST

I am all about the crunch, so I definitely like my French toast to have a crispy outside. What better way to give breakfast a sweet (and crunchy) touch than by adding Frosted Flakes cereal. They add so much nostalgia for me because that was our "special" cereal of choice growing up. This is the cereal we got for Saturday morning cartoon-watching days. In this recipe, I started with brioche bread, but you can sub any thicker bread, such as Texas toast. It's dipped in a classic French toast mixture, and then coated in Frosted Flakes. Sprinkle some powdered sugar and drizzle a bit of maple syrup, and it's a breakfast dream. And don't forget to turn on the cartoons.

Place the cereal crumbs in a wide, shallow dish. In another shallow dish, whisk together the eggs, milk, granulated sugar, vanilla and salt until well combined. Dip each slice of bread in the egg mixture, coating it on both sides. Allow any excess mixture to drip off. Immediately, dip the bread into the Frosted Flakes crumbs.

Heat a nonstick skillet or grill pan over medium heat. Add the butter to the bottom of the skillet. Place the coated bread slices onto the skillet in a single layer. Make sure there's space between them. Depending on the size of your skillet or pan, you might need to do this in more than one batch. Cook for 2 to 3 minutes on each side, or until golden brown and cooked through.

If you need to cook a second batch, wipe the skillet clean of any Frosted Flakes and coat it again with butter. Once they're all cooked, serve warm with a drizzle of maple syrup and sprinkle of powdered sugar.

Makes: 6 slices

3 cups (114 g) finely crushed Frosted Flakes

2 eggs

¼ cup (60 ml) milk

1 tbsp (15 g) granulated sugar

1 tsp vanilla extract

Pinch of salt

6 slices brioche bread

½ tbsp (7 g) butter, or more as needed

Maple syrup and powdered sugar, for topping

VANILLA CINNAMON SPICE CUPCAKES

Who can resist the scents of autumn baking? I assure you these cupcakes will have your house smelling incredible. They have a spiced cake base made from a cake mix with a few extra touches and a sweet vanilla-cinnamon frosting. I love using cake mix as a starting point in most of my recipes. It's easy enough to put together quickly, while still giving it your own special touch. To finish these cupcakes with a little bit of crunch, I added a sprinkling of chopped honey roasted almonds. Any sweetened or glazed almonds will work, and you can even switch them out for peanuts or pecans!

Preheat the oven to 350°F (177°C), and line a cupcake pan with cupcake liners.

In a medium mixing bowl, combine the spice cake mix, vanilla pudding mix, water, eggs and oil. Whisk for 2 minutes, or until there are no more streaks of dry cake mix. Divide the batter among the cupcake liners, filling them two-thirds of the way full. Bake according to the spice cake mix directions and let them cool completely.

In a mixing bowl with an electric hand mixer or a stand mixer, beat the butter until smooth. Add 2 cups (240 g) of the powdered sugar and mix. Add the remaining powdered sugar, vanilla, heavy cream and cinnamon, and mix until combined and smooth. Place the frosting into a piping bag fitted with a round tip. Alternatively, spread the frosting onto the cupcakes with a knife. If you're using a piping bag, add a swirl of frosting onto each cupcake. Sprinkle the tops with the almonds and serve!

Makes: 24 cupcakes

1 (15.25-oz [432-g]) box spice cake mix

1 (3.4-oz [96-g]) box instant vanilla pudding mix

1 cup (240 ml) water

4 large eggs

½ cup + 1 tbsp (135 ml) vegetable oil

1 cup (227 g) butter, softened

4 cups (480 g) powdered sugar, divided

2 tsp (10 ml) vanilla bean paste or vanilla extract

4–5 tbsp (60–75 ml) heavy cream

1 tsp cinnamon

½ cup (72 g) chopped honey roasted almonds, for sprinkling

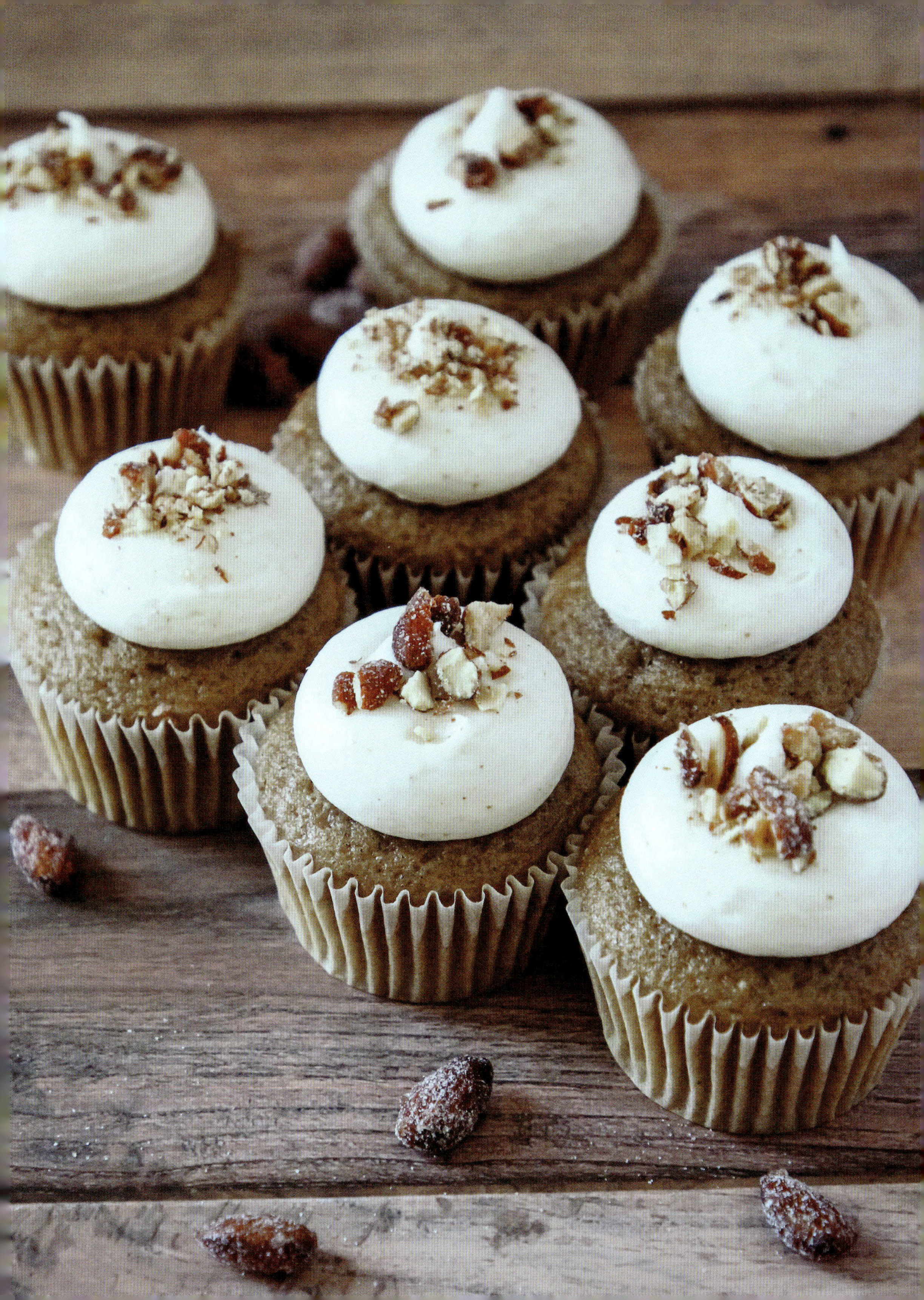

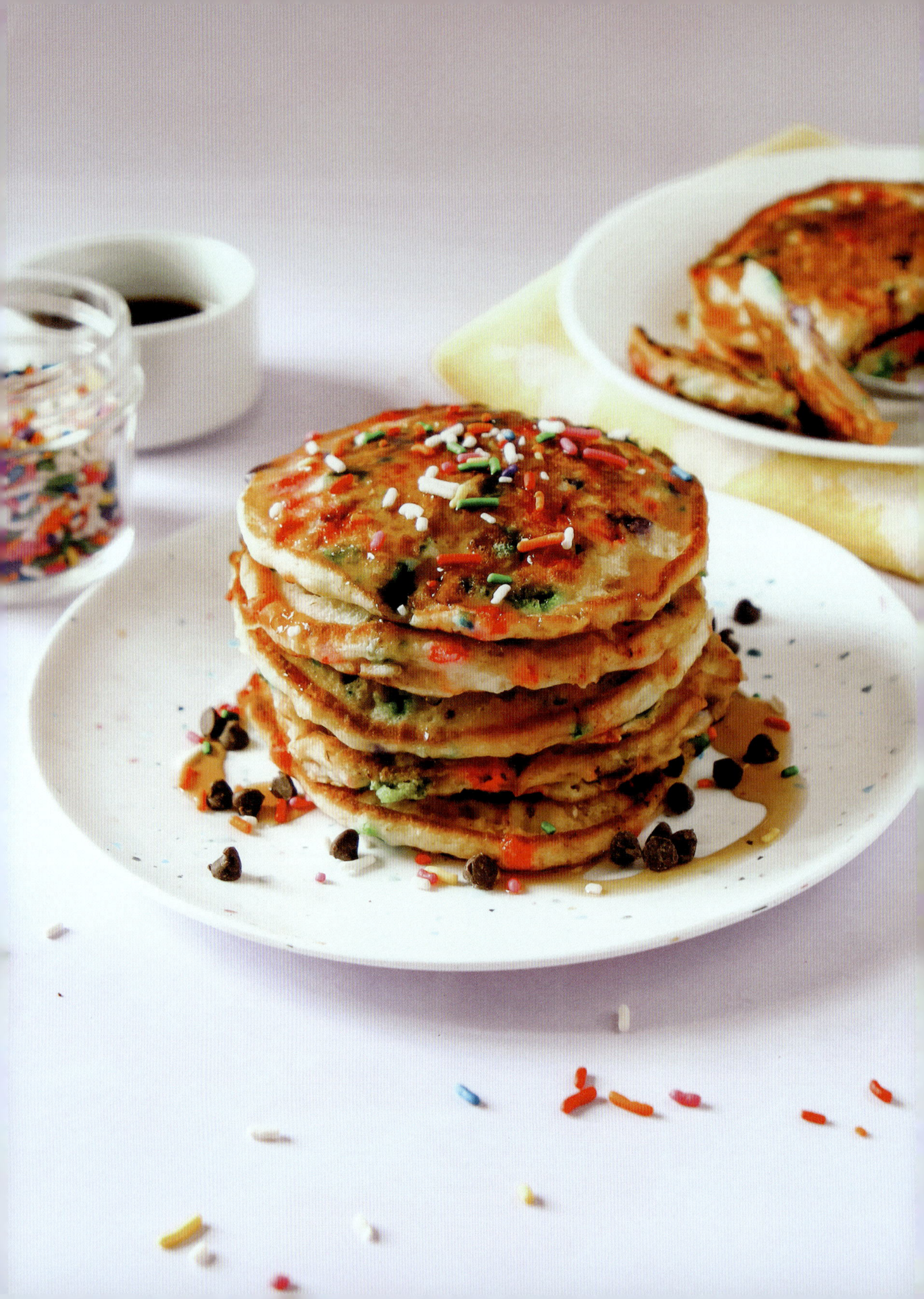

CELEBRATION CHOCOLATE CHIP PANCAKES

Chocolate chip pancakes hold a special place in my heart. Every year, my daughter requests them for birthday breakfast. I hope that I'm lucky enough to make them for years and years to come. They have a classic buttermilk pancake base with a few extra touches and TONS of mini chocolate chips. I can safely bet that's her favorite part. If you have the time, be sure to make a double or even a triple batch, and freeze the leftover pancakes for a quick special breakfast treat any day of the week.

In a large mixing bowl, combine the flour, sugar, baking powder, baking soda and salt. In a separate bowl, mix the vanilla, buttermilk, milk and egg for 1 minute, or until fully combined. Stir in the melted butter. Pour the wet ingredients into the dry ingredients and stir for 2 minutes, or until mixed through. Fold in the mini chocolate chips and sprinkles.

Heat a griddle or frying pan over medium heat and add 1 tablespoon (14 g) of butter to melt.

Pour or scoop the batter by ¼-cup (60 g) scoops onto the preheated pan. Cook for 1 to 2 minutes, or until bubbles appear on the surface. Flip the pancakes with a spatula and cook until golden brown on the other side, another 1 to 2 minutes. Repeat with the remaining batter, and be sure to add more butter each time so that the pancakes don't stick to the pan. Top with maple syrup or any extra fun "party" toppings!

Makes: 14 pancakes

1½ cups (188 g) all-purpose flour

2 tbsp (30 g) granulated sugar

1½ tsp (7 g) baking powder

¾ tsp baking soda

¼ tsp salt

1 tsp vanilla extract

1½ cups (360 ml) buttermilk

¼ cup (60 ml) milk

1 egg

3 tbsp (45 ml) melted butter, plus more unmelted for cooking

½ cup (42 g) mini chocolate chips

⅓ cup (64 g) rainbow sprinkles

Maple syrup, for topping (optional)

COOKIE BUTTER MINI LOAF CAKES

These mini loaf cakes were created for my dad, so I was completely delighted when they were met with such great reviews. They can be made with either yellow or butter pecan cake mix. The butter pecan flavor is sometimes trickier to find, but it's my dad's all-time favorite. I topped each loaf cake with an incredibly delicious cookie butter frosting and an extra sprinkling of Biscoff cookies.

Preheat the oven to 350°F (177°C). Prepare four 3 x 5¾–inch (8 x 15–cm) mini loaf pans with baking spray.

In a medium bowl, combine the cake mix with the ingredients listed on the box, pudding mix, extra egg and extra vegetable oil. Divide the batter evenly among the mini loaf pans.

Bake for 25 to 28 minutes, or until the cakes spring back when touched. Let the cakes cool in the pans for 1 hour, and then remove them from the pans and let cool on baking racks.

In a mixing bowl, beat the cream cheese for 2 minutes, or until smooth with no lumps. Add the butter and beat until fully incorporated and smooth. Mix in half of the powdered sugar. Mix in the rest of the sugar, vanilla and cookie butter. Beat until smooth.

There are a few fun ways to eat these cakes. If you'd like to frost them like a regular cake or cupcake, trim the cake with a knife so you have a flat top. Don't toss out the extra cake! I like to either save it for snacking (*wink, wink*) or to test frosting flavors. Then, use a piping bag with a piping tip (I love to use the Wilton 137 tip) and pipe a swirl back and forth from top to bottom. Sprinkle with the crushed Biscoff cookies.

My preferred way to serve the loaves is to set them out like the way you'd get bread served at a restaurant. Place a mini loaf of bread on a cutting board with a knife and a small ramekin full of frosting. Friends, family or guests can add the frosting amount of their choice, just like butter!

Note: If you'd like the frosting to be thicker, set it in the fridge for 1 to 2 hours.

Makes: 4 mini loaves

1 (15.25-oz [432-g]) box yellow cake mix or butter pecan cake mix*

1 (3.4-oz [96-g]) box instant vanilla pudding mix

1 egg

1 tbsp (15 ml) vegetable oil

4 oz (113 g) cream cheese**

½ cup (114 g) salted butter

2 cups (240 g) powdered sugar, divided

1 tsp vanilla extract

¼ cup (60 g) creamy cookie butter

2 Biscoff cookies, crushed, for sprinkling

*Plus the ingredients listed on the package.

**Be sure to take it out of the fridge 10 to 15 minutes before using.

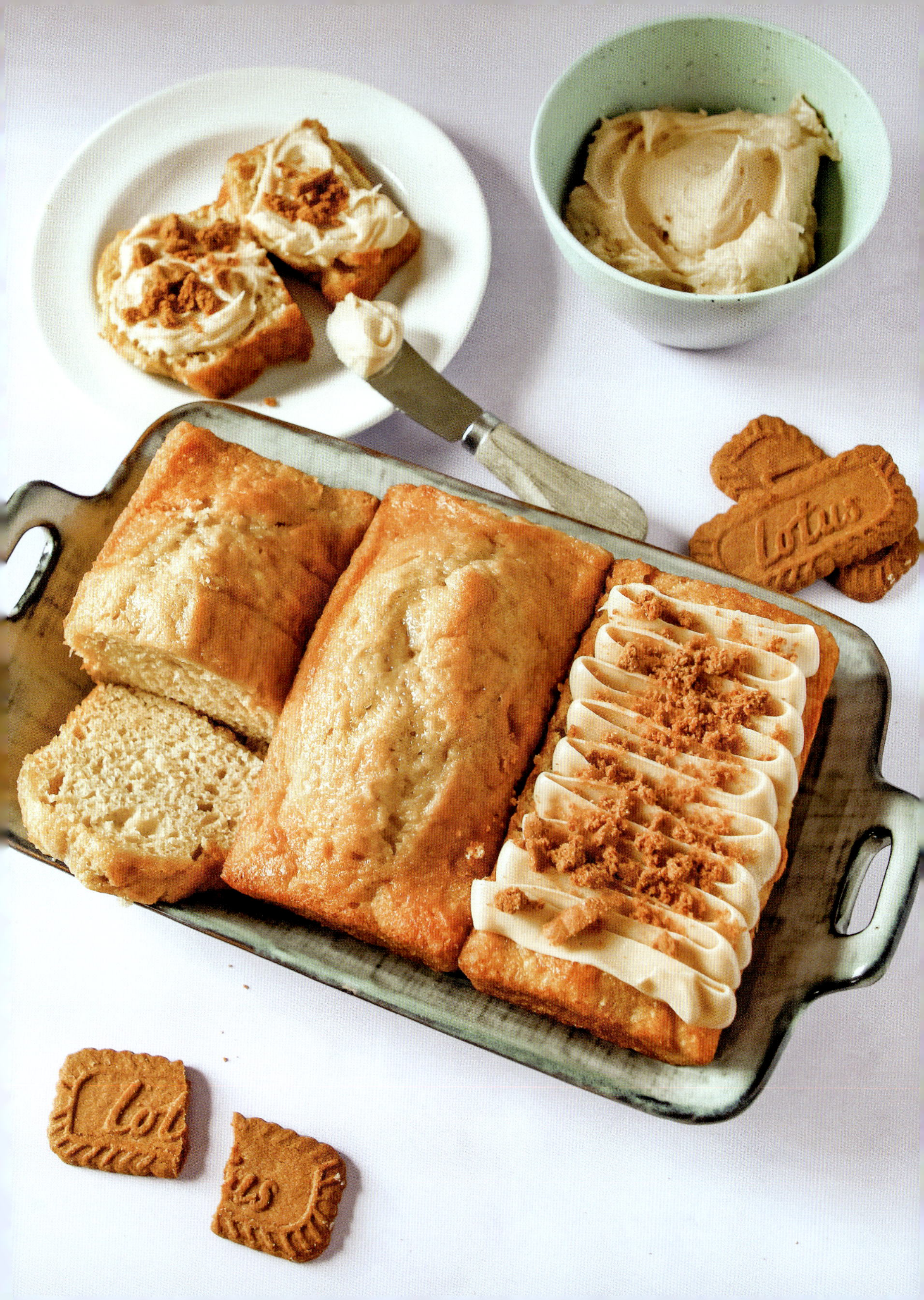
Lotus

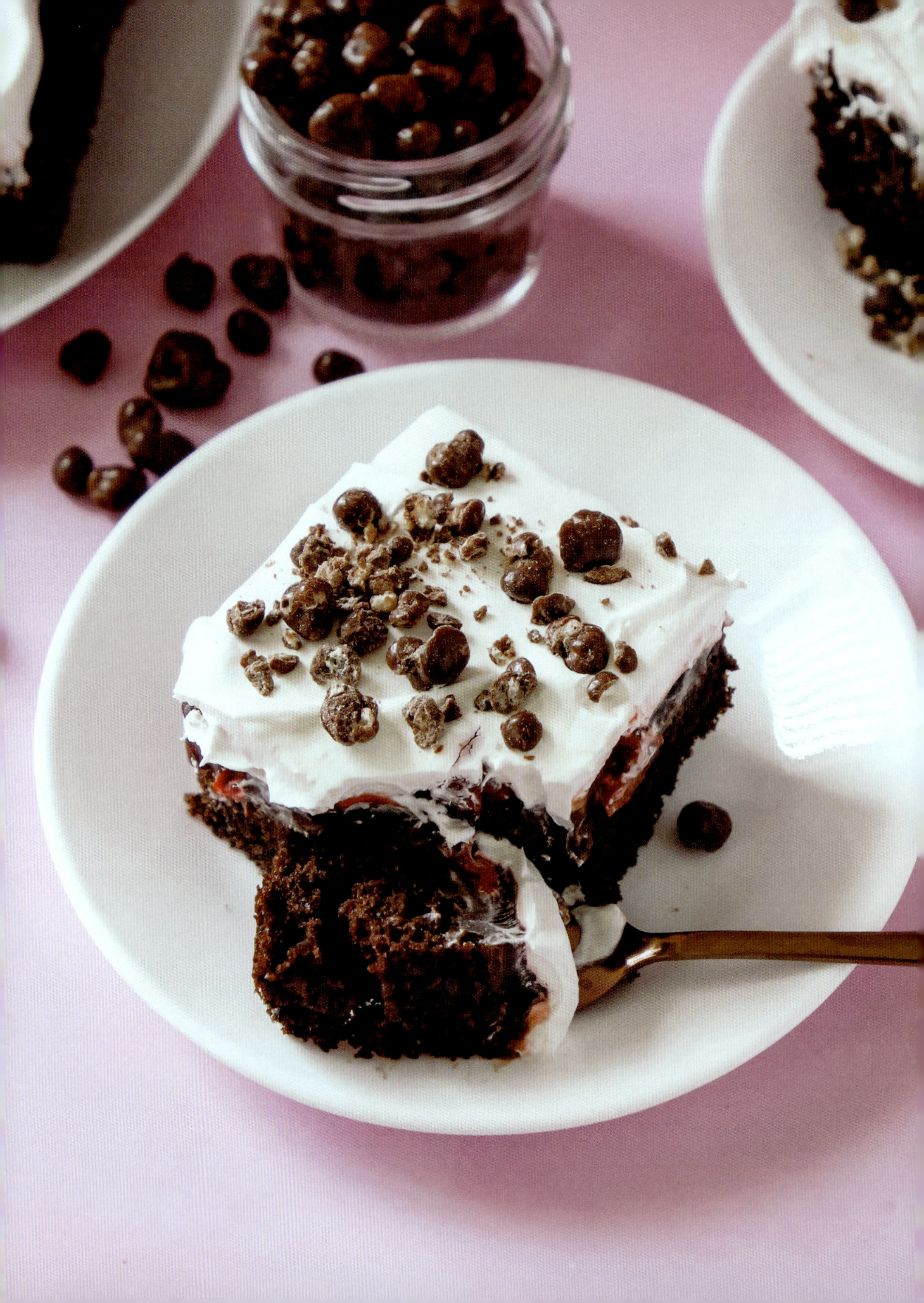

CHOCOLATE CHERRY POKE CAKE

Poke cakes are one of the easiest and most versatile cakes to make. They can be filled with pudding, chocolate sauce, caramel or sweetened condensed milk, to name a few. We have some cherry lovers in my family, so this easy Chocolate Cherry Poke Cake gets made for birthdays on repeat! It starts with a simple chocolate cake base, and it's topped with canned cherry pie filling and whipped cream. The cake is delicious as is, but to level up, I added a little chocolate candy crunch on top. I used Nestlé Buncha Crunch, but feel free to substitute with chocolate syrup, nuts, chocolate curls, crushed cookies or chocolate sprinkles!

Preheat the oven to 350°F (177°C), and spray a 9 x 13–inch (23 x 33–cm) baking dish with baking spray.

Prepare the fudge cake according to the box directions. Pour the batter into the prepared pan and bake according to the box directions.

While the cake is baking, prepare the pudding by combining the pudding mix and milk, and mixing vigorously for 2 to 3 minutes, or until smooth. Set it aside, but not in the fridge.

When the cake is ready, remove it from the oven and immediately poke holes all over it with a wide straw or the end of a small wooden spoon. Pour the pudding mixture over the cake, making sure to fill in all of the holes. Let it cool for 30 minutes, and then move it to the fridge for 1 to 2 hours to cool and set completely.

Pour the cherries onto a cutting board, leaving as much of the cherry gel in the can as possible. Roughly chop the cherries, and then return them to the can. This makes them easier to spread on the cake. Pour the entire can of cherries onto the cake. Spread it out evenly with a spoon or offset spatula.

Remove the lid from the whipped topping and add the almond extract to the topping. Stir for 1 minute, or until fully combined. Spread the whipped topping on top of the cherry filling. Sprinkle the Nestlé Buncha Crunch on top of the whipped topping. If you'd like it cold, refrigerate it for at least 1 hour, or serve at room temperature.

Makes: 18–24 slices

1 (15.25-oz [432-g]) box chocolate fudge cake mix*

1 (3.4-oz [96-g]) box instant chocolate pudding mix

1½ cups (360 ml) milk

1 (21-oz [595-g]) can cherry pie filling

1 (8-oz [226-g]) container whipped topping

1 tsp almond extract

Nestlé Buncha Crunch or Crunch King Size Bar, lightly crushed

*Plus the ingredients listed on the package.

COMFORTING AND NOSTALGIC SWEETS

MAPLE CINNAMON ROLL CASSEROLE

I have been making this dish for years and years, and it is always a hit no matter the crowd. It has a warm and gooey cinnamon roll base, and it's topped with rich maple syrup and chopped nuts. Each time I make this casserole, I try to change something, even if it's something small. For this version instead of using regular pecans, I added honey-roasted pecans and it was such a fun extra flavor addition. Not only will this cinnamon bun casserole taste amazing, but it might even become a holiday breakfast tradition!

Preheat the oven to 350°F (177°C). Spray a 9 x 13–inch (23 x 33–cm) baking dish with baking spray.

Open the cans of cinnamon rolls, cut each roll into six pieces and each piece evenly in the dish. Set the icing aside.

In a medium bowl, beat the eggs until frothy. Add the butter, buttermilk, cinnamon sugar and vanilla. Mix until completely combined. Pour the mixture over the cinnamon rolls. Drizzle the maple syrup over the submerged rolls, and sprinkle the chopped pecans on top.

Bake for 25 to 30 minutes, or until golden brown and it doesn't jiggle in the center. Let it cool for 5 minutes (so it's not burning hot), and then drizzle with the icing package. Melt the icing in the microwave for 5 to 10 seconds if it's too thick, but remember that it will melt when it touches the rolls. Slice into squares or rectangles. Sprinkle with extra nuts and maple syrup, if desired.

Makes: 12 slices

2 (12.4-oz [351-g]) cans cinnamon rolls*

6 eggs

2 tbsp (30 ml) melted butter, cooled slightly

½ cup (120 ml) buttermilk

2 tsp (12 g) cinnamon sugar**

1 tsp vanilla extract

½ cup (120 ml) maple syrup, plus more if desired

1 cup (109 g) chopped honey-roasted or regular pecans, plus more if desired

*Each includes 8 rolls with icing.

**You can make your own by mixing 1½ teaspoon (7 g) sugar and ½ teaspoon cinnamon.

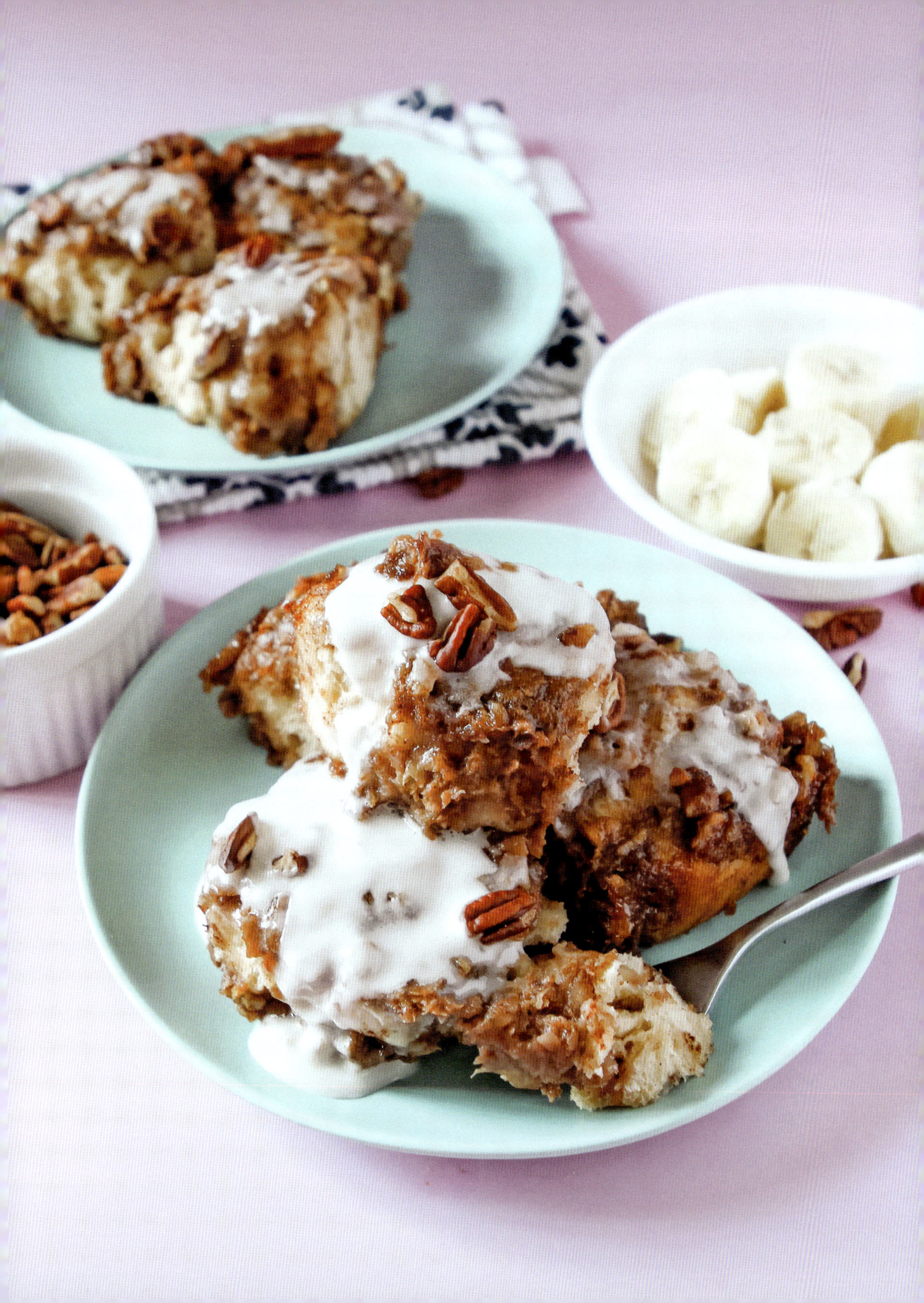

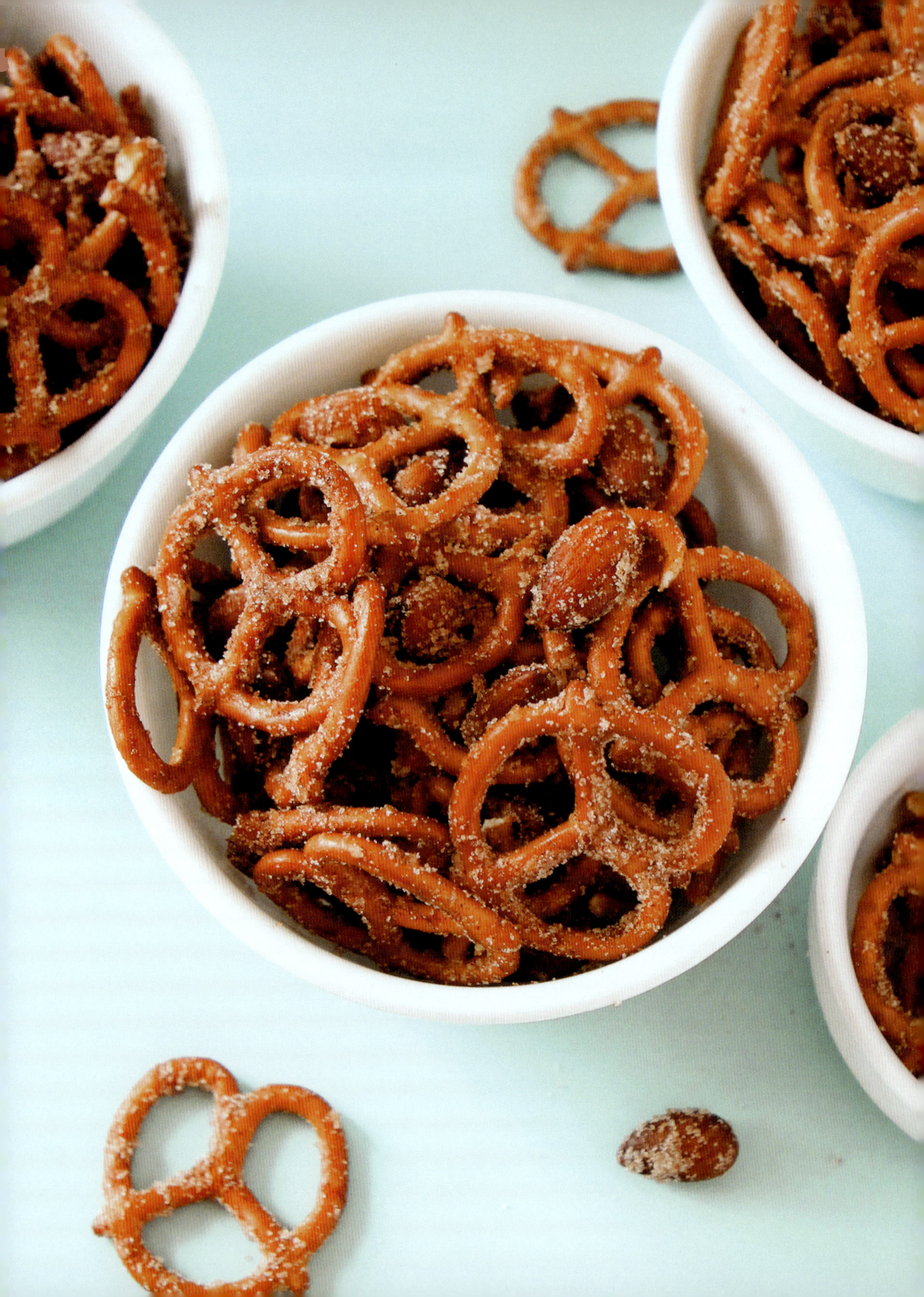

DOUBLE-COATED CINNAMON SUGAR PRETZELS

As a kid, my dad and I always loved getting those cinnamon-sugar roasted almonds and pecans at movie theaters and craft fairs. I decided to incorporate this nostalgic snack into a mix that's a little less sweet and a bit saltier. The result is a super simple recipe made up of pretzels and almonds both coated in butter, and then tossed in a cinnamon sugar mixture. Once they are baked, you toss them in the cinnamon sugar again for a truly irresistible salty sweet snack. They'd be absolutely wonderful for a party or holiday event, so be sure to double or even triple the recipe to feed a crowd.

Preheat the oven to 250°F (121°C). Line a large rimmed baking sheet with parchment paper.

In a small bowl, mix together the sugar and cinnamon. Set the bowl aside.

In a large mixing bowl, combine the pretzels, almonds and butter. Using a spatula or spoon, stir it all together until everything is evenly coated in the butter. Transfer the pretzel mixture to a large resealable bag. Pour half of the cinnamon sugar mixture in the bag, seal it and gently shake the bag until the mixture is fully coated in cinnamon sugar. Pour it onto the prepared pan, spread evenly and bake for 8 minutes. Do not discard the bag.

Remove the pan from the oven and let the pretzel almond mixture cool enough to handle. Place the mixture back into the bag, and add the rest of the cinnamon sugar. Gently toss it all again, then return the mixture to the baking sheet. Bake for 8 minutes, let the snack mix cool completely and serve.

Makes: 8 servings

¼ cup (60 g) granulated sugar

1 tbsp (8 g) cinnamon

8 oz (226 g) thin twist pretzels

½ cup (72 g) salted almonds

½ cup (120 ml) melted salted butter

BONUS RECIPE: HOMEMADE SPRINKLES

If the name Life & Sprinkles doesn't give it away, I'm clearly a sprinkle girl. The colors, the crunch, the creativity—I love it all. My pantry is rarely without tons of varieties of sprinkles, but should there ever be an occasion where my sprinkle supply is insufficient, no sweat! I simply make my own. Homemade sprinkles are far easier than you'd think to make. Here's my go-to recipe for the perfect sprinkle you can custom-make to match your special occasion sweet treat. Want a flavor burst? Swap out the vanilla extract for a different one like lemon, cotton candy or coconut. The sky is the sprinkle limit!

Makes: 1 cup (350 g)

1½ cups (180 g) powdered sugar

¼ tsp salt

1 tbsp (15 ml) light corn syrup

½ tsp vanilla extract

1½–2 tbsp water (22–30 ml), room temperature

Assorted gel food coloring

Line two large cookie sheets with parchment paper.

In a large mixing bowl, combine the powdered sugar, salt, corn syrup, vanilla and 1½ tablespoons (22 ml) of water. Mix with a spatula until a thick-but-workable consistency is achieved. If needed, add the remaining water to achieve a stiff-but-moldable consistency. Divide the icing into batches depending on how many colors you want. Mix the food coloring into each batch of icing until well incorporated and no streaks remain.

Pipe the icing onto the prepared cookie sheets using a disposable piping bag and a small round tip, such as a number 3, 4 or 5. You can pipe into shapes like hearts, circles, dots and/or long straight lines. You can also use a resealable bag and cut the tip of one corner instead of a piping bag. Set the trays aside, and allow the icing to dry for at least 12 hours.

Once the icing is dry, they are ready to go! Remove them from the parchment paper, and store in a clean airtight container until ready to use. If you piped a long line, cut or break the sprinkles apart to the desired size.

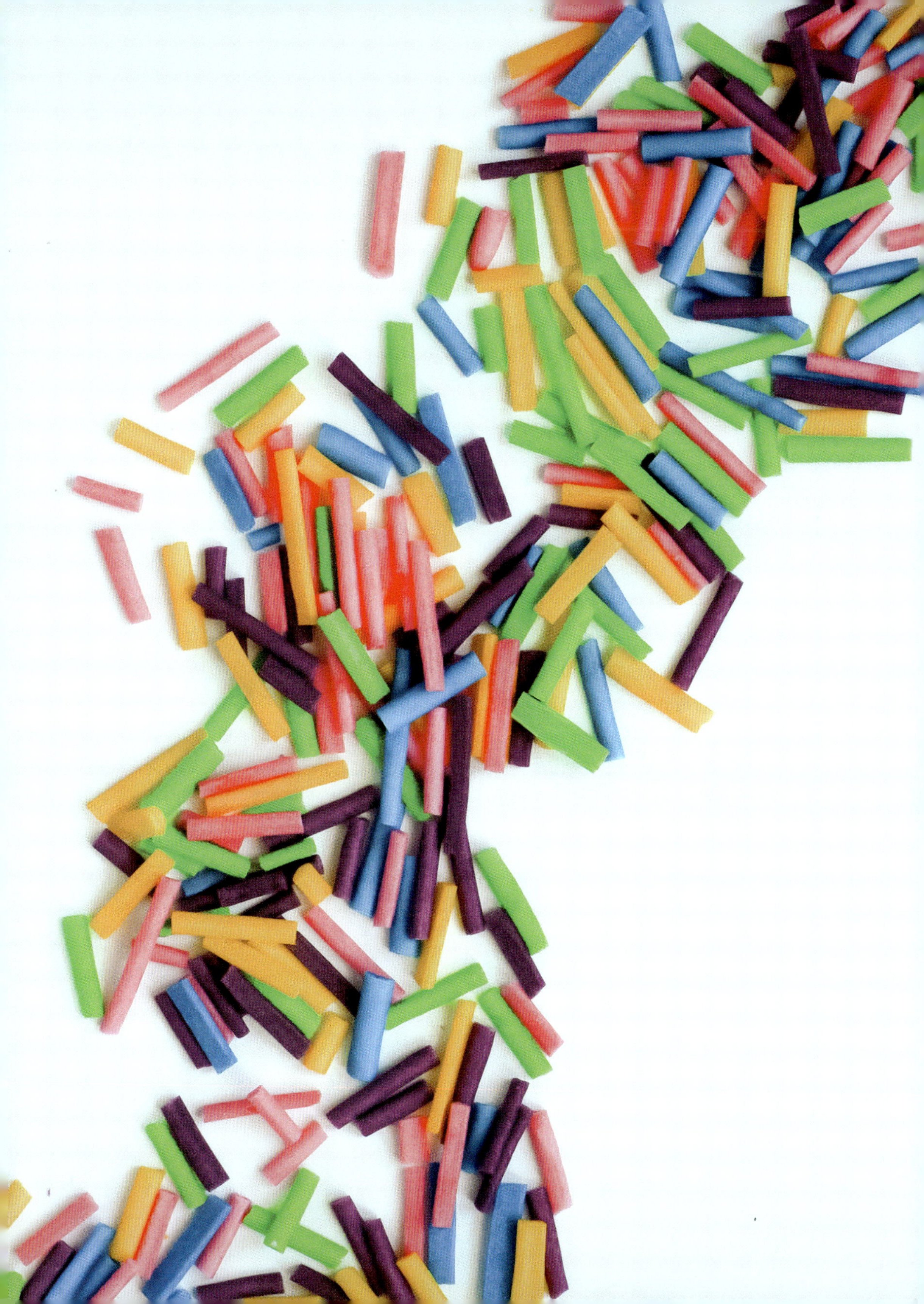

Acknowledgments

There are a few special people that have made this book come to life. First, Katie Stymiest has helped me write and rewrite every single recipe. She's had to fix measurements and taste-test countless recipes. Without her, this book wouldn't be nearly as organized—I can promise you that! I met Katie on Instagram, which shows that social media does have a bright side. She has brought light and positivity to every step of this process. To say that I owe her big time is an understatement.

My sister, Kelly, has also been crucial to creating this cookbook. Kelly has absolutely no baking experience, and her focus has always been on sports, while I've loved to be creative in the kitchen. That being said, she tested each of these recipes and gave me so much insight from a beginner's standpoint. I would have never, ever thought to add most of the tips and extra little explanations without her spending the time to try them out. She also kept most of my social media pages going while I was completing this book, which was an enormous help! Also, a special shout-out to Kelly's son Brayden, who gave every recipe a 10 out of 10.

And of course, my amazing daughter, Hayley. She has a sweet tooth just like her mother and is always willing to brainstorm with me. Hayley is the sweetest girl in the world and never fails to give positive feedback. I affectionately call her "Little Sprinkles," but truth be told, she's far better than me. She's going to light up this world, and I can't wait to read her book one day.

Last but not least, thank you to the team at Page Street Publishing. I have always loved recipe development more than the writing process, so they really stepped in and taught me things about the cookbook world that were immensely helpful. I have taken the tips they gave me and implemented them into my blog and posts, which shows how much I have learned. Krystle and Marissa have taken the time to brainstorm ideas with me to make this book even better than when it started. The design team put together colors and layouts that created such a fun book. It's been such a huge learning experience for me!

About the Author

Taryn Camp is a content creator, marketing guru and full-time mom with a passion for all things fun. When she is not whipping up seasonal recipes or filming tons and tons of videos, you'll find her working on her blog, Life & Sprinkles. It's her own corner of the internet filled with bright and colorful recipe ideas, e-magazines and all the behind-the-scenes magic that makes up her world. She is all about embracing new experiences and taste-testing fun food. Every day needs a sprinkle of joy, and she is thrilled to share each sweet moment with you!

She calls Oviedo, Florida home, and it's the perfect playground for her and her daughter, Hayley. Together they spend their days having the best adventures. They love to go to the movies, draw and craft stories, indulge in shopping sprees and—their favorite—explore Orlando's theme parks!

You can find Taryn's recipes on lifeandsprinkles.com, or follow along on social media to get inspired by her fun and unique desserts.

Index

A

almonds
- Double-Coated Cinnamon Sugar Pretzels, 153
- Triple-Layer Chocolate Bars, 87–88
- Vanilla Cinnamon Spice Cupcakes, 142

Amaretto Sheet Cake, Orange, 106–108
Animal Cookie Blondies, Frosted, 82
apples
- Cinnamon Crunch Muffins, 130
- Cookie Butter Apple Pie Biscuits, 134

B

bananas
- Banana Nut Cinnamon Rolls, 138
- Banana Oatmeal Creme Pie Trifle, 102
- Banana Split Cupcakes, 33–34
- Brownie Sundae Dessert Pizza, 16
- Chocolate Cookie Banana Bread, 81

bark
- Crunchy Cookie Bark Sticks, 96
- Dark Chocolate Cashew Pretzel Toffee, 26
- Easy Candy Bark, 75
- Movie Night Caramel Popcorn Bark, 65

bars
- See also brownies
- Cinnamon Sugar Marshmallow Treats, 25
- Frosted Animal Cookie Blondies, 82
- Jumbo Brookies, 91
- Raspberry Cheesecake Cookie Bars, 13–15
- Sweet and Chewy Granola Bars, 95
- Triple-Layer Chocolate Bars, 87–88
- Tropical Cake Bars, 124

Biscoff cookies
- Cookie Butter Mini Loaf Cakes, 146
- Irresistible Cookie Butter Pie, 43

Biscuits, Cookie Butter Apple Pie, 134
blackberries: Glazed Fruit Tart, 116–117
Blondies, Frosted Animal Cookie, 82
blueberries
- Berry Fluff Mini Parfaits, 120
- Blueberry Pie Snack Mix, 112
- Glazed Fruit Tart, 116–117

Boston Cream Brownies Cups, 19–20
Bread, Chocolate Cookie Banana, 81
brownies
- See also bars
- Boston Cream Brownie Cups, 19–20
- Brownie Blast Soft Serve, 57
- Brownie Sundae Dessert Pizza, 16
- Jumbo Brookies, 91
- Mint Chocolate Chip Brownies, 137
- Mint Chocolate Chip Mini Trifles, 21–22

Bundt Cake, Party Time, 78
Butterfinger Cookie Sandwiches, Chocolate Peanut-, 11–12
butterscotch: Drizzled Pretzels, 75

C

cakes
- Cake on the Cover, 129
- Chocolate Cherry Poke Cake, 149
- Chocolate Chunk Sea Salt Cookie Cake, 39
- Coconut Raspberry Cake Jars, 109–111
- Cookie Butter Mini Loaf Cakes, 146
- Ice Cream Sandwich Cake, 44
- Orange Amaretto Sheet Cake, 106–108
- Party Time Bundt Cake, 78
- Sprinkle-Tastic Party Cake, 35–36
- Strawberry Ice Cream Cake, 123
- Tropical Cake Bars, 124

Caramel Popcorn Bark, Movie Night, 65
Cashew Pretzel Toffee, Dark Chocolate, 26
Cheesecake Cookie Bars, Raspberry, 13–15

cherries
- Chocolate Cherry Poke Cake, 149
- Crunchy Cookie Bark Sticks, 96
- Pistachio Marshmallow Milkshake, 47

chocolate
- See also white chocolate
- Banana Split Cupcakes, 33–34
- Boston Cream Brownie Cups, 19–20
- Brownie Blast Soft Serve, 57
- Brownie Sundae Dessert Pizza, 16
- Celebration Chocolate Chip Pancakes, 145
- Chocolate Cherry Poke Cake, 149
- Chocolate Chunk Sea Salt Cookie Cake, 39
- Chocolate Cookie Banana Bread, 81
- Chocolate-Dipped Cookie Stacks, 62
- Chocolate Peanut-Butterfinger Cookie Sandwiches, 11–12
- Chocolatey Chip Pudding Cups, 54
- Cookie Truffles, Two Ways, 51–53
- Crunchy Cookie Bark Sticks, 96
- Dark Chocolate Cashew Pretzel Toffee, 26
- Decadent Hot Fudge Sundae, 61
- Giant Cookie Skillet, 71
- Graham Cracker Sandwiches, 48–50
- Ice Cream Sandwich Cake, 44
- Jumbo Brookies, 91
- Loaded Edible Cookie Dough, 58
- M&M's Chocolate Chunk Cookies, 85–86
- Mint Chocolate Chip Brownies, 137
- Mint Chocolate Chip Mini Trifles, 21–22
- Movie Night Caramel Popcorn Bark, 65
- No-Churn Cookie Mashup Ice Cream, 66
- Peanut Butter Fudge Cookie Cups, 92

158 · JUST ADD SPRINKLES

Raspberry Cheesecake Cookie Bars, 13–15
Sprinkled and Dipped Fruit Cones, 105
Sweet and Chewy Granola Bars, 95
TGIF Dessert Board, 72–75
Triple-Layer Chocolate Bars, 87–88

cinnamon
Banana Nut Cinnamon Rolls, 138
Banana Oatmeal Creme Pie Trifle, 102
Cinnamon Crunch Muffins, 130
Cinnamon Sugar Marshmallow Treats, 25
Double-Coated Cinnamon Sugar Pretzels, 153
Maple Cinnamon Roll Casserole, 150
Snickerdoodle Latte Frosted Cookies, 133
Vanilla Cinnamon Spice Cupcakes, 142

coconut
Coconut Raspberry Cake Jars, 109–111
TGIF Dessert Board, 72–75
Triple-Layer Chocolate Bars, 87–88
Tropical Cake Bars, 124

Cones, Sprinkled and Dipped Fruit, 105

cookie butter
Cookie Butter Apple Pie Biscuits, 134
Cookie Butter Mini Loaf Cakes, 146
Graham Cracker Sandwiches, 48–50
Irresistible Cookie Butter Pie, 43

cookie dough
Cookie Truffles, Two Ways, 51–53
Crunchy Cookie Bark Sticks, 96
Giant Cookie Skillet, 71
Jumbo Brookies, 91
Loaded Edible Cookie Dough, 58
No-Churn Cookie Mashup Ice Cream, 66
Peanut Butter Fudge Cookie Cups, 92
Raspberry Cheesecake Cookie Bars, 13–15

cookies
Chocolate Chunk Sea Salt Cookie Cake, 39
Chocolate-Dipped Cookie Stacks, 62
Chocolate Peanut-Butterfinger Cookie Sandwiches, 11–12

Chocolatey Chip Pudding Cups, 54
Cookies 'N' Cream Cupcakes, 77
Cookie Truffles, Two Ways, 51–53
Crunchy Cookie Bark Sticks, 96
Giant Cookie Skillet, 71
Jumbo Brookies, 91
M&M's Chocolate Chunk Cookies, 85–86
No-Churn Cookie Mashup Ice Cream, 66
Peanut Butter Fudge Cookie Cups, 92
Red Velvet Cream Cheese Cookies, 29
Snickerdoodle Latte Frosted Cookies, 133

cranberries: Crunchy Cookie Bark Sticks, 96

cupcakes
Banana Split Cupcakes, 33–34
Cookies 'N' Cream Cupcakes, 77
Vanilla Cinnamon Spice Cupcakes, 142

F
French Toast, Frosted Flakes, 141
frosting
Buttercream, 108
Cake on the Cover, 129
Cookies 'N' Cream, 77
Peanut-Butterfinger, 12
Triple-Layer Chocolate, 88
vanilla, 36
vanilla bean, 34

fruit
See also specific fruits
Berry Fluff Mini Parfaits, 120
Brownie Sundae Dessert Pizza, 16
Crunchy Cookie Bark Sticks, 96
Glazed Fruit Tart, 116–117
Sprinkled and Dipped Fruit Cones, 105

Fudge, Marshmallow Peanut Butter, 30

G
Graham Cracker Sandwiches, 48–50
Granola Bars, Sweet and Chewy, 95

I
ice cream
Brownie Blast Soft Serve, 57
Decadent Hot Fudge Sundae, 61
Giant Cookie Skillet, 71
Ice Cream Sandwich Cake, 44
No-Churn Cookie Mashup Ice Cream, 66

Pistachio Marshmallow Milkshake, 47
Strawberry Ice Cream Cake, 123

L
lemon
Lemon Cream Pastry Cups, 101
Lemon Strawberry Shortcakes, 119
Lime Poolside Slush, Strawberry, 115

M
M&M's
Giant Cookie Skillet, 71
M&M's Chocolate Chunk Cookies, 85–86

macadamia nuts: Tropical Cake Bars, 124

marshmallow
Brownie Sundae Dessert Pizza, 16
Cinnamon Sugar Marshmallow Treats, 25
Dipped Marshmallows, 72
Graham Cracker Sandwiches, 48–50
Ice Cream Sandwich Cake, 44
Marshmallow Peanut Butter Fudge, 30
Mint Chocolate Chip Mini Trifles, 21–22
Pistachio Marshmallow Milkshake, 47
TGIF Dessert Board, 72–75

Milkshake, Pistachio Marshmallow, 47

mint
Mint Chocolate Chip Brownies, 137
Mint Chocolate Chip Mini Trifles, 21–22

Muffins, Cinnamon Crunch, 130

N
Nutella
Chocolate Oreo Truffles, 53
Graham Cracker Sandwiches, 48–50
Peanut Butter Fudge Cookie Cups, 92

nuts. See specific types

O
Oatmeal Creme Pie Trifle, Banana, 102
oats: Sweet and Chewy Granola Bars, 95
Orange Amaretto Sheet Cake, 106–108
Oreos
Chocolate Cookie Banana Bread, 81
Chocolate-Dipped Cookie Stacks, 62

Cookies 'N' Cream Cupcakes, 77
Cookie Truffles, Two Ways, 51–53
Jumbo Brookies, 91
No-Churn Cookie Mashup Ice Cream, 66
Party Time Bundt Cake, 78
Strawberry Ice Cream Cake, 123

P

Pancakes, Celebration Chocolate Chip, 145
Parfaits, Berry Fluff Mini, 120
peanut butter
    Chocolate Peanut-Butterfinger Cookie Sandwiches, 11–12
    Graham Cracker Sandwiches, 48–50
    Jumbo Brookies, 91
    Marshmallow Peanut Butter Fudge, 30
    Peanut Butter Fudge Cookie Cups, 92
pecans
    Banana Nut Cinnamon Rolls, 138
    Maple Cinnamon Roll Casserole, 150
Pie, Irresistible Cookie Butter, 43
pineapples: Tropical Cake Bars, 124
Pistachio Marshmallow Milkshake, 47
Pizza, Brownie Sundae Dessert, 16
Popcorn Bark, Movie Night Caramel, 65
pretzels
    Dark Chocolate Cashew Pretzel Toffee, 26
    Double-Coated Cinnamon Sugar Pretzels, 153
    Drizzled Pretzels, 75
    Loaded Edible Cookie Dough, 58
    TGIF Dessert Board, 72–75
pudding
    Banana Oatmeal Creme Pie Trifle, 102
    Boston Cream Brownie Cups, 19–20
    Chocolatey Chip Pudding Cups, 54
    Lemon Cream Pastry Cups, 101
puff pastry: Lemon Cream Pastry Cups, 101

R

rainbow sprinkles. See sprinkles
raspberries
    Coconut Raspberry Cake Jars, 109–111
    Glazed Fruit Tart, 116–117
    Raspberry Cheesecake Cookie Bars, 13–15
Red Velvet Cream Cheese Cookies, 29
Reese's
    Chocolate-Dipped Cookie Stacks, 62
    Movie Night Caramel Popcorn Bark, 65
Rice Krispies, Cinnamon Sugar Marshmallow Treats, 25
rolls
    Banana Nut Cinnamon Rolls, 138
    Maple Cinnamon Roll Casserole, 150
rum: Tropical Cake Bars, 124

S

sandwiches
    Chocolate Peanut-Butterfinger Cookie Sandwiches, 11–12
    Graham Cracker Sandwiches, 48–50
    Ice Cream Sandwich Cake, 44
shortbread cookies
    Berry Fluff Mini Parfaits, 120
    Blueberry Pie Snack Mix, 112
Shortcakes, Lemon Strawberry, 119
Slush, Strawberry Lime Poolside, 115
Snickerdoodle Latte Frosted Cookies, 133
sprinkles
    Banana Split Cupcakes, 33–34
    Brownie Blast Soft Serve, 57
    Brownie Sundae Dessert Pizza, 16
    Cake on the Cover, 129
    Celebration Chocolate Chip Pancakes, 145
    Chocolate Cookie Banana Bread, 81
    Chocolate-Dipped Cookie Stacks, 62
    Decadent Hot Fudge Sundae, 61
    Dipped Marshmallows, 72
    Giant Cookie Skillet, 71
    Graham Cracker Sandwiches, 48–50
    Homemade Sprinkles, 154
    Sprinkled and Dipped Fruit Cones, 105
    Sprinkle-Tastic Party Cake, 35–36
    Sweet and Chewy Granola Bars, 95
strawberries
    Berry Fluff Mini Parfaits, 120
    Brownie Sundae Dessert Pizza, 16
    Glazed Fruit Tart, 116–117
    Lemon Strawberry Shortcakes, 119
    Strawberry Ice Cream Cake, 123
    Strawberry Lime Poolside Slush, 115
    Strawberry Shortcake Truffles, 51

T

Tart, Glazed Fruit, 116–117
toffee
    Dark Chocolate Cashew Pretzel Toffee, 26
    Loaded Edible Cookie Dough, 58
    Sweet and Chewy Granola Bars, 95
    TGIF Dessert Board, 72–75
trifles
    Banana Oatmeal Creme Pie Trifle, 102
    Mint Chocolate Chip Mini Trifles, 21–22
Truffles Two Ways, Cookie, 51–53

W

walnuts: Cinnamon Crunch Muffins, 130
white chocolate
    Blueberry Pie Snack Mix, 112
    Crunchy Cookie Bark Sticks, 96
    Easy Candy Bark, 75
    Frosted Animal Cookie Blondies, 82
    Marshmallow Peanut Butter Fudge, 30
    Red Velvet Cream Cheese Cookies, 29
    Strawberry Shortcake Truffles, 51